INTEгNATIONAL MIGRATION, REMITTANCES, AND THE BRAIN DRAIN

INTERNATIONAL MIGRATION, REMITTANCES, AND THE BRAIN DRAIN

Çağlar Özden and Maurice Schiff
Editors

A copublication of the World Bank and Palgrave Macmillan

1 2 3 4 09 08 07 06

A copublication of The World Bank and Palgrave Macmillan.

Palgrave Macmillan
Houndmills, Basingstoke, Hampshire RG21 6XS and
175 Fifth Avenue, New York, N. Y. 10010
Companies and representatives throughout the world

Palgrave Macmillan is the global academic imprint of the Palgrave Macmillan division of St. Martin's Press, LLC and of Palgrave Macmillan Ltd.

ISBN-10: 0-8213-6372-7
ISBN-13: 978-0-8213-6372-0
eISBN-10: 0-8213-6374-3
eISBN-13: 978-0-8213-6374-4
DOI: 10.1596/978-0-8213-6372-0

Library of Congress Cataloging-in-Publications Data has been applied for.

CONTENTS

Figures

Tables

FOREWORD

It is difficult to imagine global economic integration without migration as an integral part of it. Unlike what was observed in the 19th century, the big surge in international flows of goods and capital has not been matched by an equivalent flow of migrants in the post-World War II era. Will the tide turn around in the 21st century? There are some reasons to think so. Diverging demographic trends between the developing and developed countries and the rapid decline in transportation and telecommunications costs are making it increasingly difficult for governments' current policies to restrain international migration. As a result, international migration and its related issues are likely to occupy an increasingly prominent place on the global agenda for the foreseeable future.

Yet our knowledge of the economic effects of migration, especially its impact on economic development, is rather limited. Although considerable effort has been made by economists and sociologists in developed countries to analyze the effects of migration in destination countries, comparatively little research has been conducted on the effects of migration on countries of origin and on development in general. In order to expand our knowledge on migration and to identify policies and reforms that will lead to superior development outcomes and to "win-win-win" results for both sets of countries and for the migrants, the Development Economics Research Group of the World Bank initiated the **International Migration and Development Research Program**. This volume presents the results of a first set of studies carried out within this program.

Economic research indicates that there are significant potential gains from the liberalization of immigration policies, and that these would accrue to all three sets of actors. On the other hand, international migration will likely entail various costs for these actors. For origin countries, these costs include the loss of skilled migrants' positive impact on society and the resources used to educate them. Migrants are likely to suffer from the separation from family, friends, and culture, and from the lack of effective legal protection. Costs for destination countries include the perceived threat to cultural identity and the effect of migrants' competition for the same jobs as natives.

Given the complexity of the issues, great care must be taken before making judgments and policy decisions in this area, and it is essential that any actions be preceded by extensive data collection and rigorous analysis. This book provides both data and analysis, and it tackles two sets of issues. Part I analyzes the determinants and impacts of migration and remittances on different measures of development and welfare, such as poverty, education, health, housing, entrepreneurship, school attendance, and child labor. Part II focuses on questions regarding the so-called "brain drain." It provides the largest dataset to date on the brain drain and examines the issues of brain gain, brain waste, and migrants' contribution to technological progress in destination countries.

Migration is a complex and dynamic process that changes the migrants' home and destination countries and, of course, the migrants themselves. It is a global phenomenon, and dialogue between destination and source countries, migrant communities, and international organizations is critical for finding successful solutions to the myriad of problems we face in this area. There are many questions waiting to be answered about the migration and remittance issues; I hope this volume will stimulate additional research, whether by utilizing the new datasets or building on the research presented here.

François Bourguignon
Senior Vice President & Chief Economist, The World Bank

ACKNOWLEDGMENTS

It takes a village to raise a child and the same can be said about a book. Many people were involved in the creation of this volume. François Bourguignon and L. Alan Winters have been strong advocates of research on migration and development issues at the World Bank. They provided the necessary impetus and environment for undertaking the International Migration and Development Research Program and moving it forward. We are especially grateful to Alan for his detailed comments on the volume and his support during the publication process.

This volume would not have been possible were it not for Maria Lourdes Kasilag and Ileana Cristina Neagu's patience, organizational skills, and efficiency. Other members of the migration "team," Richard Adams and Coralie Gevers, also helped us at every stage of the process.

We would like to thank the authors of the volume for the contributions they have made to our understanding of fundamental migration issues and for ensuring that various revisions of their chapters were done in a timely manner. We are fortunate to have worked with them.

We thank Bernard Hoekman, David Tarr, Dominique Van Der Mensbrugghe, Gershon Feder, Hillel Rapoport, Irena Omelaniuk, Johan Mistiaen, John McHale, Maurice Kugler, Mohammad Amin, Pierre Pestieau, Robert E.B. Lucas, Uri Dadush, Vlad Manole, Will Martin, William Shaw, and Yoko Niimi, for their comments on parts of the volume.

We would also like to thank Ines Garcia-Thoumi and Ivar Cederholm for helping us with a myriad of administrative issues. We are grateful to Santiago Pombo-Bejarano, Susan Graham, and Stephenie DeKouadio from the World Bank's Office of the Publisher for handling the expedited production schedule with great efficiency and for making an early publication possible. Chris Neal and Kavita Watsa from the communications office did everything to make sure that the volume's messages were heard.

Finally, we are grateful to Vivian Budnik and Wedad Elmaghraby for their support and understanding while we were working on this volume.

CONTRIBUTORS

Richard H. Adams, Jr.   International Trade Unit, Development Research Group, World Bank

Gnanaraj Chellaraj   World Bank

Frédéric Docquier   National Fund for Scientific Research (IRES), Catholic University of Louvain, Belgium; Institute for the Study of Labor (IZA), Germany; and Institut wallon de l'Evaluation, de la Prospective et de la Statistique (IWEPS), regional government of Wallonia, Belgium

Abdeslam Marfouk   Free University of Brussels, and Institut wallon de l'Evaluation, de la Prospective et de la Statistique (IWEPS), regional government of Wallonia, Belgium

Claudia A. Martínez   Department of Economics, University of Michigan, Ann Arbor

Keith E. Maskus   Department of Economics, University of Colorado, Boulder

Aaditya Mattoo   International Trade Unit, Development Research Group, World Bank

David J. McKenzie   Growth and Investment Unit, Development Research Group, World Bank

Jorge Mora   Center for Economic Studies, El Colegio de Mexico, Mexico City

Çağlar Özden   International Trade Unit, Development Research Group,
World Bank

Maurice Schiff   International Trade Unit, Development Research Group,
World Bank; and Institute for the Study of Labor (IZA),
Germany

J. Edward Taylor   Department of Agricultural and Resource Economics,
University of California, Davis; and member of the
Giannini Foundation of Agricultural Economics

Dean Yang   Gerald R. Ford School of Public Policy and Department
of Economics, University of Michigan, Ann Arbor

OVERVIEW

Çağlar Özden and Maurice Schiff

Introduction

International migration, the movement of people across international boundaries, has enormous economic, social, and cultural implications in both origin and destination countries. It is estimated that some 180 million people (3 percent of the world's population) are living in countries in which they were not born (United Nations 2002). Among these are millions of highly educated people who moved to developed countries from developing countries that already suffer from low levels of human capital and skilled workers.[1] Furthermore, the flow of formal remittances from migrants to their relatives in their country of birth has exhibited a rapid and accelerating rate of growth. The remittance flow has doubled in the last decade, reaching $216 billion in 2004, with $150 billion going to developing countries (Ratha 2005). It surpasses foreign aid and is the largest source of foreign capital for dozens of countries.[2] As a result of these trends, migration issues have increasingly become the focus of attention, both among governments of origin and destination countries, and within the development community.

There has been extensive analysis of the impact of migration on the receiving countries' economies, especially on markets for unskilled labor (see LaLonde and Topel 1997). However, the links between migration and development issues in the sending countries have been somewhat neglected, particularly as far as empirical research is concerned (Borjas 1999). This oversight is partly due to the relatively minor role played by migration in promoting the integration of developing countries into the world economy in the post–World War II era. In contrast to policies regulating trade and capital flows, immigration policies of destination countries continue to be highly protectionist and explain, in part, the absence of large migration flows, especially when compared with the second half of the nineteenth century. A second reason for this oversight has been the absence of systematic and reliable data on international migration patterns and migrant characteristics at either the aggregate or the household level. Fortunately, such data are finally becoming available. For instance, chapter 5 by Frédéric Docquier and Abdeslam Marfouk introduces the most comprehensive data set on the brain drain to date.

The current demographic trends in both developed and developing countries are pointing toward significant potential economic gains from migration. The labor forces in many developed countries are expected to peak around 2010 and decline by around 5 percent in the following two decades, accompanied by a rapid increase in dependency ratios. Conversely, the labor forces in many developing countries are expanding rapidly, resulting in declines in dependency ratios. This imbalance is likely to create strong demand for workers in developed countries' labor markets, especially for numerous service sectors that can only be supplied locally. There are large north-south wage gaps, however, especially for unskilled and semiskilled labor. The presence of such gaps indicates that liberalization of immigration policies can generate significant welfare gains. For instance, it has been estimated that an increase in the number of migrants equal to 3 percent of the labor force of the Organisation for Economic Co-operation and Development (OECD) countries would result in global welfare gains that surpass those obtained from the removal of all trade barriers, with significant gains for all parties involved (Walmsley and Winters forthcoming; World Bank forthcoming).

Given the size of the potential welfare gains from migration, policies need to be devised to ensure that these gains are not wasted and that their distribution satisfies the sending and receiving countries. Successful design of such policies requires detailed information and should be preceded by a systematic and careful analysis of migration patterns based on solid theory and empirical methodology, as well as lessons from past experiences.

To expand our knowledge on the effects of migration and identify migration policies, regulations, and institutional reforms that will lead to superior development outcomes, the World Bank launched the International Migration and Development Research Program, which is being conducted in the Development Economics Research Group. The Research Program is divided into a number of focus areas. The main ones include (a) the impact of migration and remittances on development indicators, including poverty and inequality, investment (in both human and physical capital), entrepreneurship, and entry into capital-intensive activities; (b) the brain drain; (c) temporary migration, including under Mode IV of the General Agreement on Trade in Services (GATS); and (d) the links between migration, trade, and foreign direct investment (FDI).[3]

Some of the questions the research program aims to answer are as follows: How does migration affect poverty and growth, especially in the sending countries? Who are the main beneficiaries of migration and main recipients of remittances—the poor who have the most to gain or the middle classes who are more likely to have the resources needed to migrate? What are the effects of migration and remittances on investment in both physical and human capital? What are the determinants of the migration of the highly skilled workers and the effects on destination and source countries?

The eight chapters in this volume present the results of studies conducted in the first stage of the research program. These chapters are divided into two parts. Those in Part 1, *Migration and Remittances*, examine the determinants of migration, and the impact of migration and remittances on various development indicators and measures of welfare. Among these are poverty and inequality; investments in education, health, housing and other productive activities; entrepreneurship; and child labor and education. The chapters focus on different source countries, use data collected via different methodologies, and employ different econometric tools. Their results, however, are surprisingly consistent.

The chapters in Part 2, *Brain Drain, Brain Gain, Brain Waste*, focus on issues related to the migration of skilled workers, that is, the brain drain. Despite an extensive body of theoretical literature on the effects of the brain drain, little empirical analysis has been conducted on the topic. In chapter 5, Docquier and Marfouk present the most extensive database on bilateral skilled migration to date. The other chapters examine a number of issues associated with the brain drain that have not been emphasized in the literature so far, uncover a number of interesting and unexpected patterns, and provide answers to some of the debates.

In the next section of this overview, we review each of the eight chapters in this volume by emphasizing their contribution to the migration and development literature and highlighting the answers they provide to ongoing debates. We also call attention to other debates and questions that are likely to occupy the research agenda in the coming years, some of which will be covered in forthcoming volumes.

This volume deals essentially with economically motivated south-north migration. Before turning to the description of the chapters, it should be emphasized that other migration flows—including those by refugees and asylum seekers—are important as well. These flows are typically caused by military conflicts, civil wars, political turmoil, and ethnic and religious repression. Although refugees and asylum seekers constitute a significant share of international migration flows, the topic is not examined here. One reason is that the World Bank has no comparative advantage in these areas, which are best dealt with by other specialized institutions—including the United Nations High Commissioner for Refugees (UNHCR), the United Nations Educational, Scientific and Cultural Organization (UNESCO), and the International Organization for Migration (IOM).

Although part of south-south migration flows consist of refugees and asylum seekers, much of it is motivated by economic factors, such as migration from Southern African countries to South Africa. Tentative figures suggest that economically motivated south-south migration flows are large, even though data are scarce and quite unreliable. Although economically motivated south-south migration is not examined here, we believe that analyses and approaches presented in this volume may be fruitfully applied to south-south migration.

Overview of the Chapters

In this section, we provide an overview of the main findings presented in the chapters in this volume. Rather than presenting the findings of each chapter individually, we examine some of the most important questions in the academic and policy debate on international migration and provide answers based on the findings in the chapters and in the literature.

What Forces Determine Migration Patterns?

Like most other economic flows, migration operates as an equilibrating mechanism. In the presence of wage inequalities, migration permits greater wage and income equality between sending and receiving regions. International labor mobility is subject to restrictive policies and high migration costs when compared with internal mobility. As a result, income levels exhibit much lower variation domestically than internationally.

The principal cause of south-north migration is, in most cases, the difference in (the present value of) expected real wages, adjusted for migration costs. These costs increase with the distance between source and destination countries, and decline with social networks in the destination country. Literature has identified the importance of networks that provide support and information to migrants who are dealing with difficulties ranging from financing the move to other struggles associated with social and cultural differences, such as language and social norms. Migration flows and remittances would be expected to rise with the difference in expected real wages and decline with migration costs. Based on a sample of 71 countries, Adams and Page (forthcoming) find that migration and remittances decline with the distance between source and destination countries.

The main sources of migrants for the European Union (EU) are the Maghreb, Middle Eastern countries, and the remaining portions of Europe to the east, while the dominant sources for the United States are Mexico, Central America, and the Caribbean. This is indicative of the importance of distance in migration decisions, and this applies particularly to unskilled migrants who face financial constraints that permit migration only to nearby countries. Furthermore, most migrants have extensive economic and social links with their home countries, which are more difficult to maintain with more distant countries. The presence of a social network in the destination country is a significant catalyst in easing the costs of moving, especially in the transition stage. Various networks, based on family, community, ethnicity, or even nationality, are likely to help with legal barriers, lower search costs regarding jobs and housing, provide additional insurance in case of unanticipated events, and help with cultural alienation.

Chapter 1 by Jorge Mora and J. Edward Taylor contributes to the existing literature in two important dimensions by incorporating alternative destinations (internal or international) and sectors of employment (farm or nonfarm) for migrants from rural Mexico, and by including new community variables as determinants of migration. Using the 2003 National Rural Household Survey of Mexico, Mora and Taylor include individual, family, and community variables in their estimation. These variables have a distinct impact on migration decisions, depending on the destination and sector of employment. For example, schooling has a significant positive effect on internal migration to nonfarm jobs but has no effect on international migration that is predominantly to the United States.

These patterns are due to the fact that most migrants to the United States are employed in unskilled jobs—such as in agriculture, hospitality sectors, and home services—and investment in education (within the range of education levels in rural areas) has no impact on the type of jobs obtained. In other words, schooling in Mexico is more valued—that is, has a higher rate of return—in the domestic labor market than in the United States, a fact also observed in a different context by Çağlar Özden in chapter 7. Conversely, the wage gain is higher for less educated Mexicans who migrate to the United States rather than internally. Mora and Taylor's results parallel those of Ibarraran and Lubotsky (2005) who use the 2000 Mexican Census, and conclude that migrants are less educated than nonmigrants. Finally, migrant networks, work experience, and household wealth have significant positive effects on international migration to both farm and nonfarm sectors.

In chapter 4, David J. McKenzie finds that migrant networks raise the probability that other community members migrate internationally. Using the 1997 National Survey of Demographic Dynamics for Mexico, McKenzie finds that the effect of networks varies across the wealth distribution. If few members of the community have previously migrated, the cost of migration stays high and only relatively wealthy people manage to migrate and benefit from the network. As a larger share of the community migrates, migration costs fall and relatively poorer members migrate and benefit from the larger network as well.

Another contribution of Mora and Taylor's chapter is the analysis of the relationship between internal and international migration, on the one hand, and local economic integration through trade on the other. The analysis of the relationship between international migration and international trade has a long history, while that between local integration through trade and migration does not.[4] The authors find that local economic integration has a significantly positive impact on internal migration to the nonfarm sector but no impact on internal migration to the farm sector or international migration to either sector.

What Are the Effects of Migration and Remittances On Income, Poverty, and Inequality?

The most important development effect of migration is its direct impact on income and poverty levels in the source countries. By allowing workers to move to areas where they are more productive and valued, migration leads to a direct increase in global output and income. It has recently been estimated that increasing immigration to OECD countries by the equivalent of just 3 percent of their labor forces would generate gains that are larger than those obtained from global trade liberalization (Walmsley and Winters forthcoming; World Bank forthcoming). The gains arise mainly from the mobility of less-skilled workers, rather than from more-skilled workers, and accrue to (a) the migrants themselves, (b) to consumers and complementary factors of production (capital, land, and labor, other than the mobile type) in the recipient countries, and (c) to remittance recipients and labor in the sending country.

Remittances generally reduce poverty and alter income distribution, but the extent and direction of these effects depend on who receives them. The existing evidence on this from a variety of countries (the Philippines, the Arab Republic of Egypt, Pakistan, Mexico, India) is somewhat mixed. Among the more reliable and convincing studies are those based on household surveys. For example, the 2003 Mexico National Rural Household Survey suggests that (a) both internal and international remittances have an equalizing effect on incomes in high-migration areas but not in low-migration ones, (b) international remittances reduce rural poverty by more than internal remittances, and (c) the larger the share of households with migrants in a region, the more favorable the effect of increases in remittances on rural poverty (Mora and Taylor 2004). These results are confirmed by López Córdova (2005) who finds, for a sample of 2,400 observations comprising all municipalities in Mexico, that areas with a larger share of households receiving remittances have lower levels of poverty.

Poverty studies typically use several measures. The standard one is the level of poverty or poverty headcount, that is, the share of the population below a certain poverty level. The depth of poverty measures the average value of the gap between the poverty line and the income of those below that line. The severity of poverty measures the average of the squared gaps, thereby giving more weight to the poorer households. For example, Gustafsson and Makonnen (1993) find that if remittances to Lesotho were completely removed, an additional 11 to 14 percent of households would be classified as poor, with an increase in the associated depth and severity of poverty as well.

Using the 2000 National Household Survey (conducted by the Instituto Nacional de Estadística) in Guatemala, Richard H. Adams Jr. finds in chapter 2 that both internal and international remittances typically reduce the level, depth, and severity of poverty. The greatest impact is on the severity of poverty, because the households in the lowest decile group receive between 50 and 60 percent of their total income from remittances.

Chapter 3 by Dean Yang and Claudia A. Martínez exploits an exogenous event, namely the exchange rate shocks that occurred during Asia's currency crisis in the late 1990s, to examine the impact on poverty in the Philippines. They find that an appreciation of the currency in destination countries relative to the Filipino peso leads to an increase in remittance received by the related households and to a reduction in their poverty. They also find spillover effects to other households, including to those without migrant members, whose poverty falls as well.

In addition to McKenzie's results on the importance of larger migrant networks in raising the probability of other community members migrating, the dynamic patterns he identifies also have important implications for poverty and inequality concerns. For example, inequality tends to increase when migrant networks are small and migration costs are high, because only the better-off community members can afford to migrate. As migration spreads, the increasing network size and associated decline in migration costs enable more of the poorer members to migrate. This tends to reduce poverty and inequality. The evidence suggests that there might be an inverse-U-shaped relationship between migration and inequality.

What is the Impact of Migration and Remittances On Household Human capital (Education, health) and Physical Capital Accumulation, Other Productive Investments, Child Labor and Education, and Entrepreneurship?

After we establish that the remittances increase income levels considerably, especially for the poor, the next question naturally becomes how this income is spent. Remittance recipients typically say that they invest the money received. Because money is fungible, they may simultaneously reduce their investment from other sources of income, so that total investment may increase by less than the investment from remittances or may not increase at all. Glytsos (2002) finds that investment increases with remittances in six of the seven Mediterranean countries he analyzes. Similar results are shown by Leon-Ledesma and Piracha (2004) for Eastern European countries during the 1990s, by Woodruff and Zenteno (2001) for microenterprises in urban Mexico, and by McCormick and Wahba (2003) for small enterprises in Egypt. There is also substantial evidence of increased housing construction because of increased remittances.

In his seminal paper, Lucas (1987) shows that, in the case of migration to South Africa from neighboring countries' agricultural sector, recipients of remittances worked fewer hours in agriculture but substituted their labor with other inputs, including hired labor, which resulted in an increase in productivity levels. Similarly, Rozelle, Taylor, and de Brauw (1999) look at the joint impact of migration and increased remittances in rural productivity in China. They find that migration has a negative effect caused by reduced family labor but this is again compensated by access to capital through increased remittances.

In addition to increased investment in physical capital because of remittances, investment in human capital (especially via increased education and health/nutrition expenditure) may also increase. The latter is likely to be more important for long-term growth prospects of developing countries. Cox-Edwards and Ureta (2003) show that remittances increase schooling in El Salvador, and that these remittances have a much larger impact on the hazard rate of leaving school— around 10 times higher in urban and 2.6 times higher in rural areas—than other sources of income. Duryea, López Córdova, and Olmedo (2005) find that an increase in the share of households receiving remittances in a municipality results in better schooling and health.

In chapter 2 on Guatemala, Adams analyzes how the receipt of internal and international remittances (from the United States) affects the marginal spending behavior of households on various consumption and investment goods. Adams finds that households receiving remittances spend more on investments (such as education, health, and housing) and less on consumption (food and consumer goods, durables) than do households receiving no remittances. In particular, spending on education, which is a key issue in development efforts, shows important variation. Households receiving internal and international remittances spend at the margin 45 and 58 percent more, respectively, than do households with no remittances. Adams finds that remittance-receiving households spend more at the margin on housing.

Most studies in the literature suffer from a severe endogeneity bias. Even if we observe a positive correlation between migration and remittances on the one hand and investment on the other, we do not know a priori whether investment increased because of migration and remittances—that is, whether migration and remittances cause investment—or whether migration and remittances reflect a prior decision to increase investment, with the migrants selected from a biased sample of households that face better investment opportunities—that is, whether investment causes migration and remittances. One resolution of this dilemma is to study exogenous changes in migration or remittance flows. The major exchange rate changes of the 1997–98 Asian crises provide such an opportunity, and chapter 3 by Yang and Martínez, which is based on a survey of Filipino households, exploits it successfully. They find that unanticipated increases in remittances lead to enhanced human capital accumulation and entrepreneurship in origin households, with less child labor, greater child schooling, more hours worked in self-employment, and a higher rate of entry into capital-intensive enterprises. The latter is greater for lower-income than for higher-income households, suggesting that this effect is related to alleviation of credit constraints.

Whether such investment stimulates growth remains unproven as yet. Endogenous growth theory is based on the hypothesis that human capital (such as education and health) generates positive externalities (Lucas 1988) and further discussion of this issue is provided in the next section of this overview. Some migration research also suggests that it does generate these positive externalities (Adams and Page forthcoming), while other work suggests that remittances induce reductions in recipients' labor supply (Chami, Fullenkamp, and Jahjah 2005), which the authors interpret as lowering the rate of growth.[5] However, the decline in labor supply because of remittances may lead to higher productivity, as shown by Rozelle, Taylor, and de Brauw (1999) and Lucas (1987).

In chapter 4, McKenzie also looks at the impact of migration, rather than remittances, on education attainment in Mexico, with endogenous migration flows instrumented by historic migration rates, which are shown to be exogenous. Contrary to some of existing studies and other chapters in this volume, he finds that children ages 16 to 18 in migrant households have lower levels of schooling compared with nonmigrant households. McKenzie's result is similar to Mora and Taylor's finding in chapter 1, namely that schooling has no effect on incentives for international migration from rural Mexico. Both results are likely to be due to the special situation of Mexican immigrants in the U.S. labor market. These immigrants tend to be placed in low-skill jobs that do not require education. Thus, people with a greater potential to migrate to the United States have less incentive to invest in education.[6] Whether these results apply to other developing countries that are major sources of migration or whether they are specific to the case of Mexico is an issue that has to be more carefully examined in the future.

What Are the Regional Differences and the Dynamics of the Brain Drain?

Part 2 of the volume focuses on the effects of migration of educated and skilled people from developing to developed countries (the brain drain). The brain drain is one of the most recognizable phrases in the development literature and policy debates. With economic research providing increased evidence on the importance of human capital in the development process, the brain drain has become one of the more important areas of concern. At the heart of this concern is the view that highly educated workers generate positive externalities for society and these are lost when they emigrate.

Among the positive externalities that are lost with the emigration of educated workers are (a) the positive effects on the productivity of colleagues, employees, and other workers; (b) the provision of key public services with positive externalities, such as education and health, particularly for transmissible diseases; (c) the fiscal externalities associated with the fact that the taxes they pay are larger than the value of the public services they consume and the public funds invested in their education; and (d) their contribution to the debate on important social issues and their impact on policy and institutions.

Reliable and extensive data with which to find answers to the theoretical questions and policy debates on the brain drain have only just become available. A major contribution of the World Bank International Migration and Development Research Program to the brain-drain literature is the new database created by Docquier and Marfouk. This database is presented in chapter 5. Their work represents the most comprehensive and rigorous database on the brain drain to date and provides consistent measures of the brain drain from individual sending countries to individual destination countries—that is, bilateral measures of the brain drain—as well as regional and global aggregations. It is based on census and survey data collected from all OECD destination countries and provides brain-drain figures by education attainment for 1990 and 2000, covering 174 countries for 1990 and 195 countries for 2000 as well as 36 dependent territories.[7] An early version of this database was published in Docquier and Marfouk (2004) and was followed by a brain-drain study by Dumont and Lemaître (2004) for 2000, which covers a smaller number of countries and uses somewhat different definitions of international migration.[8]

The debate on the brain drain and its impact on source and destination countries is an old one and it has been mostly based on theoretical analysis and anecdotal evidence. A database on the 1990 brain drain to the United States was published by Carrington and Detragiache in 1999. Docquier and Marfouk's vastly expanded database in chapter 5 provides comprehensive measures that will enable researchers and policy makers to improve their analysis of the brain drain, obtain valuable insights into its social and economic impact, and improve the design of policies to deal with these issues.

Initial analysis reveals that there are large differences in the regional distributions of the brain drain and their dynamics. For example, the largest number of educated migrants comes from Europe and South and East Asia. The highest migration rates, in terms of the proportion of the total educated force, are from Africa, the Caribbean, and Central America. Some of the numbers are truly staggering, especially for small and isolated countries. For example, many Central American and island nations in the Caribbean had more than 50 percent of their university-educated citizens living abroad in 2000. Although the share of skilled workers in the total labor force in Sub-Saharan Africa is only 4 percent, these workers comprise more than 40 percent of all migrants. As a result, close to 20 percent of all skilled workers have emigrated out of Sub-Saharan African countries, excluding South Africa.

The situation in Asia is slightly different. Skilled workers account for nearly 50 percent of all migrants. However, because the overall migration rate is much lower for a variety of reasons, only 6 percent of all educated workers have migrated abroad. Chapter 5 also provides interesting insights into the labor markets of receiving OECD countries. For example, in Australia, Canada, and New Zealand, migrants form around 20 percent of the labor force (the percentages are 11.7 percent for the United States and 6.7 percent for the EU). The ratio of immigrants with tertiary education is much higher in the first three countries when compared with the native population, whereas the gap is narrower for the United States and the EU. Another interesting although mostly overlooked fact is that a large number of educated citizens from OECD countries are also migrants. For instance, millions of people from EU countries live abroad, mostly within other EU countries. As a result, the net brain migration to the EU is close to zero, whereas it is quite high for the United States, Canada, Australia, and New Zealand.

What Is the Impact of Migration on the Brain-Drain Induced "Brain Gain"?

In chapter 6, Maurice Schiff provides a critical examination of the main findings of the new brain-drain literature. The new brain-drain literature argues that, because skilled wages are typically higher in destination countries, the brain drain raises the expected benefit from education and induces additional investment in education. The increase in the average level of education is referred to as the "brain gain." A key issue in that literature is the identification of the conditions under which the brain gain dominates the brain drain and results in a net increase in the level of education. This is referred to as a "beneficial brain drain," which is thought to lead to an increase in welfare and growth. Some of the seminal papers in that literature include Mountford (1997); Stark, Helmenstein, and Prskawetz (1997, 1998); and Beine, Docquier, and Rapoport (2001, 2003).

The results of the new brain-drain literature are based on static partial equilibrium analysis and on the assumptions that (a) only skilled individuals migrate, (b) migrants obtain the same jobs and are paid the same wages as natives with comparable skills, (c) risk-neutral preferences exist; and, for most studies, (d) abilities are homogeneous. Based on partial equilibrium analysis, chapter 6 by Schiff finds that the brain gain is smaller than that obtained in the new brain-drain literature. The reasons for this difference include the following: unskilled individuals also benefit from migration, migrants earn less than natives, individuals are likely to be averse to risk, and abilities are likely to be heterogeneous.

The situation in which migrants earn less than natives with the same skills has been referred to as a "brain waste," a topic that is examined by Özden in chapter 7. An extreme case of brain waste, whereby an increase in education has no impact on the income earned in the destination country, is examined by McKenzie in chapter 4. McKenzie shows that such a situation results in a negative brain gain or net brain loss (over and above the loss because of the brain drain itself).

In chapter 6, Schiff also examines the brain-gain issue from a general equilibrium viewpoint, which also finds a smaller impact on the brain gain and on welfare and growth. This is due to the fact that a brain gain implies that additional resources are allocated to education and fewer resources are available for other uses, including health, so that the human capital gain is likely to be smaller than the brain gain and might even be negative. Moreover, even if the human capital gain is unchanged, some of the other uses such as public goods, and for which fewer resources are available, may also generate positive externalities, implying a smaller impact on welfare and growth. Finally, dynamic partial and general equilibrium analyses show that a beneficial brain drain cannot prevail in the steady state.

Are the Skills of the Skilled Migrants Fully Utilized in the Destination Countries or Is Migration Leading to Brain Waste?

To obtain a deeper understanding of the brain-drain phenomenon, cross-country studies should be complemented by country-level studies. Chapter 7 by Özden deals with the brain drain to the United States. He finds striking differences in the labor market placement among highly educated immigrants from different countries, even after controlling for their age, experience, and education. Specifically, immigrants from Latin America and Eastern Europe are more likely to end up in unskilled jobs in the United States compared with immigrants from Asia, the Middle East, and Sub-Saharan Africa. The placement of educated immigrants in unskilled jobs is referred to as the brain waste. A large part of the variation in the brain waste can be explained by variables that influence human capital in the home country of the immigrants, such as education expenditure.

A second set of factors also affects the skill distribution of migrants. U.S. migration policies and proximity to the United States enable educated Latin American workers—mainly from Mexico and Central America—to migrate although they might not qualify for skilled jobs. Migration to Western Europe tends to be easier for Africans and Eastern Europeans. As a result, only highly qualified (or the most qualified) migrants—that is, those who can obtain skilled jobs in the United States—from distant countries, will find it in their interest to migrate to the United States because skilled wages and upward mobility are typically higher than in other OECD countries. Conversely, a large share of immigrants, especially those from Latin America who can migrate at a relatively low cost, may not be qualified for skilled jobs in the United States even if they have college degrees. They nevertheless choose to migrate because unskilled wages in the United States are typically higher than skilled wages in their home countries. This observation, employment of educated migrants in unskilled jobs in the destination countries, naturally has important policy implications.

In an extension paper, Mattoo, Neagu, and Özden (2005) argue that another part of the brain waste can be explained by informational asymmetry—that is, by the fact that employers in the United States have limited information about the quality of education in a number of sending countries—and by excessive restrictions to entry in various professions, including medicine and nursing. They recommend that information on the quality of education in the sending countries be improved and disseminated more widely, and that the excessive restrictions imposed by various professional associations be relaxed.

What Are the Contributions of Skilled Migrants and Foreign Students to the Destination Country?

In chapter 8, Gnanaraj Chellaraj, Keith E. Maskus, and Aaditya Mattoo examine the impact of international students and skilled immigration in the United States on innovative activity. The main specification is based on a three-equation model of idea generation in which the dependent variables are total patent applications, patents awarded to U.S. universities, and patents awarded to other U.S. entities, each scaled by the domestic labor force. Results indicate that international graduate students have a significant and positive impact on future patent applications, as well as on future patents awarded to university and nonuniversity institutions, and that skilled immigrants have a similar although substantially smaller impact.

The central estimates indicate that a 10 percent increase in the number of foreign graduate students raises patent applications by 4.7 percent, university patent grants by 5.3 percent, and nonuniversity patent grants by 6.7 percent. Thus, reductions in the inflow of foreign graduate students and skilled migrants to the United States—partly because of increased security concerns following the September 11, 2001, terrorist attacks—are most likely to have significantly negative effects on future U.S. innovative activity.

Implications

This volume covers a diverse range of issues and provides a large number of results that aim to answer some of the questions that are high on the international migration research and policy agenda.

Part 1 of the volume shows that migration and remittances (a) reduce poverty of recipient households, (b) increase investment in human capital (education and health) and other productive activities, (c) reduce child labor and raise child education, and (d) increase entrepreneurship. Additional findings include the fact that (a) the impact of remittances on investment in human capital and other productive activities is greater than that from other sources of income, and (b) income gains may also accrue to households without migrants. Based on these studies, migration and remittances appear to have a positive impact on the development and welfare of the sending countries. Another set of findings pertain to the importance of networks and other community variables as determinants of internal and international migration. This suggests that the design of sending countries' migration policies needs to take these community effects into account.

Part 2 of the book deals with various aspects of the brain drain. Skilled individuals tend to generate benefits for their household and the rest of the society. The research presented in this volume contributes to the debate on the brain drain at many levels: (a) the first and most comprehensive database on the migration patterns by level of education is presented, and the data reveal extremely high brain-drain levels for some of the poorest and more isolated small countries in Sub-Saharan Africa and the Caribbean; (b) the hypothesis of the new brain-drain literature that a brain drain may increase the sending country's level of education and welfare is shown to be unlikely to hold; (c) the skill levels of the jobs held by a large share of the educated migrants are shown to be lower than expected from their level of education, mainly because of the relatively lower quality of their education as well as entry restrictions imposed by various professional associations in the destination country; and (d) foreign students and workers with the appropriate human capital for holding high-skill jobs provide significant positive effects on innovative activity in the United States.

The findings in this volume have a number of implications. Relaxation of restrictions on migration should generate significant welfare gains for both sending and destination countries. Among them is an increased investment in human capital in source countries, a key determinant of long-term development and growth. Excessive restrictions are likely to be very costly, especially for source countries when applied to unskilled migrants, and for destination countries when applied to skilled migrants and students. Given the important gains from migration and remittances for sending countries, governments should aim to reduce or remove the transactions costs and other barriers to sending remittances, which can be quite substantial.

Linkages between education and migration appear in almost every chapter in this volume, from the impact on education spending in the source country to the brain drain. Given the extent of the brain drain in a number of the poorest developing countries and the large negative impact that the departure of (highly) skilled labor may generate, destination countries that are concerned with these issues should cooperate with these source countries to find solutions to some of these problems.

Once the migrants arrive in the destination country, it is important that their human capital be properly employed for both sending and destination countries, as well as for the migrants themselves. Source countries should improve the quality of the information on their education programs and, in cooperation with destination countries, disseminate that information more widely to potential employers. Doing so would improve the quality of the jobs that educated migrants obtain in destination countries. Also, destination countries and migrants with the appropriate skills would benefit from the relaxation of entry restrictions imposed by various professional associations.

As is true in other areas of the international economic arena, such as trade and capital flows, cooperation and coordination on policy issues by governments is necessary to realize the potential welfare gains for all parties involved. Migration is one area in which there is ample room for improvement.

Future Research

The studies in this volume have addressed two of the major issues—the determinants and impact of migration and remittances, and the brain drain—examined in the International Migration and Development Research Program of the World Bank. Other issues addressed by the World Bank Research Program include temporary migration and Mode IV; the links among FDI, migration, and trade; the brain drain of health care providers; migrants in the destination countries and return migration; and social protection issues. These studies will be published in future volumes.

An important lacuna within the migration and development literature is the absence of high-quality data. Household surveys are among the main data sources used in migration research. The chapters in the first part of this volume rely on data from household surveys conducted by official statistical agencies or as part of the World Bank's Living Standards Measurement Study (LSMS). Although the latter studies include questions on remittances, they were not designed to deal specifically with migration issues. A major item on the agenda of the World Bank Research Program is the expansion of the migration database. The research program has already generated a more extensive data set of country-level data on the brain drain (chapter 5), and household surveys that include a separate migration module will be conducted in a number of developing countries.

Endnotes

1. This brain drain is generally viewed as having a negative impact on sending countries, although alternative views exist. These are addressed in Part II of the volume.

2. Because of unrecorded remittance flows through formal and informal channels, their true size is likely to be much higher. Note that remittances are generally viewed as having a positive impact on migrant-sending countries, although some have expressed concern about their impact on inequality and the degree to which they are invested. The latter may in part be due to the definition of investment, because it typically excludes investment in human capital (such as education, health, and food in the case of malnutrition).

3. Additional research is being conducted on (a) the economic and other conditions of migrants in the receiving countries; (b) the economic conditions (that is, type of activity, income) of return migrants in their country of origin compared with similar nonmigrants; (c) the brain drain of health care providers; and (d) the links among migration, trade, and FDI. The results of these studies will be published in additional volumes. Other areas of research are carried out in other World Bank units, including security (money laundering and financing terrorism), social protection issues and governance, implications for migration of differential population growth rates in source and destination countries, and social security in destination countries.

4. In a classic paper, Mundell (1957) showed that international trade and migration are substitutes, with barriers to trade generating the same outcomes as equivalent barriers to migration. More recent contributions have shown conditions under which complementarity obtains. Markusen (1983) obtains such results by sequentially changing the basic assumptions of the Heckscher-Ohlin model one by one. Once migration costs are incorporated in the Heckscher-Ohlin model, trade is likely to be a complement to migration (Schiff 1996) or a complement for unskilled labor and a complement for skilled labor migration (Lopez and Schiff 1998). Complementarity is obtained by Rauch and coauthors in a series of papers on the impact of ethnic diasporas on international trade, and it is also obtained when the international provision of services requires establishment (see Rauch 2001 for an extensive review).

5. A reduction in income should not be confused with a reduction in welfare. With leisure being a normal good, an increase in income associated with migration and remittances will result in an increase in the amount of leisure and a reduction in labor supply. Moreover, a reduction in income is a level effect, and it is not clear why or how it should affect the growth rate.

6. The impact of migration on the brain gain in this case is examined in chapter 6.

7. Seminal work by Carrington and Detragiache (1999) resulted in a new data set on the brain drain for 1990. It was, however, limited to the United States as a destination country—with the authors assuming that the brain-drain data for the United States applied to the other OECD countries as well—and to a smaller number of source countries.

8. Docquier and Marfouk's bilateral brain-drain data are available from the editors upon request.

References

Adams, Jr., Richard, and John Page. Forthcoming. "Do International Migration and Remittances Reduce Poverty in Developing Countries." *World Development*.

Beine, Michel, Frédéric Docquier, and Hillel Rapoport. 2001. "Brain Drain and Economic Growth: Theory and Evidence." *Journal of Development Economics* 64(1): 275–89.

———. 2003. "Brain Drain and LDCs' Growth: Winners and Losers." IZA Discussion Paper, no. 819. Institute for the Study of Labor, Bonn.

Borjas, George J. 1999. "The Economic Analysis of Migration." In *Handbook of Labor Economics*, vol. 3A, ed. Orley Ashenfelter and David Card, 1,697–760. Amsterdam, New York, and Oxford: Elsevier Science North-Holland.

Carrington, William, and Enrica Detragiache. 1999. "How Extensive is the Brain Drain?" *Finance and Development* 36(2): 46–49.

Chami, Ralph, Connel Fullenkamp, and Samir Jahjah. 2005. "Are Immigrant Remittance Flows a Source of Capital for Development?" *IMF Staff Papers* 52(1): 55–81. International Monetary Fund, Washington, DC.

Cox-Edwards, Alexandra, and Manuelita Ureta. 2003. "International Migration, Remittances and Schooling: Evidence from El Salvador." *Journal of Development Economics* 72(2): 429–61.

Docquier, Frédéric, and Abdeslam Marfouk. 2004. "Measuring the International Mobility of Skilled Workers – Release 1.0." World Bank Policy Research Working Paper, no. 3382. World Bank, Washington, DC.

Dumont, Jean-Christophe, and George Lemaître. 2004. "Counting Immigrants and Expatriates in OECD Countries: a New Perspective." Mimeo. Organisation for Economic Co-operation and Development, Paris.

Duryea, Suzanne, Ernesto López Córdova, and Alexandra Olmedo. 2005. "Migrant Remittances and Infant Mortality: Evidence from Mexico." Mimeo, February 3. Inter-American Development Bank, Washington, DC.

Glytsos, Nicholas P. 2002. "A Macroeconometric Model of the Effects of Migrant Remittances in Mediterranean Countries." In *Human Capital: Population Economics in the Middle East*, ed. Ismail Abdel-Hamid Sirageldin. Cairo: American University in Cairo Press.

Gustafsson, Bjorn, and Negatu Makonnen. 1993. "Poverty and Remittances in Lesotho." *Journal of African Economies* 2(1): 49–73.

Ibarraran, Pablo, and Darren Lubotsky. 2005. "Mexican Immigration and Self-Selection: New Evidence from the 2000 Mexican Census." NBER Working Paper, no. 11456. National Bureau of Economic Research, Washington, DC.

LaLonde, Robert J., and Robert H. Topel. 1997. "Economic Impact of International Migration and the Economic Performance on Migrants." In *Handbook of Population and Family Economics*, vol. 14, ed. M.R. Rosenzweig and O. Stark, 799–850. Amsterdam, New York, and Oxford: Elsevier Science North-Holland.

Leon-Ledesma, Miguel, and Matloob Piracha. 2004. "International Migration and the Role of Remittances in Eastern Europe." *International Migration* 42(4): 65–83.

Lopez, Ramon, and Maurice Schiff. 1998. "Migration and the Skill Composition of the Labor Force: The Impact of Trade Liberalization in LDCs." *Canadian Journal of Economics* 31(2): 318–36.

López Córdova, Ernesto. 2005. "Globalization, Migration and Development: The Role of Mexican Migrant Remittances." Mimeo, August 31. Inter-American Development Bank, Washington, DC.

Lucas, Robert E. B. 1987. "Emigration to South Africa's Mines." *The American Economic Review* 77(3): 313–30.

Lucas, Robert E. Jr. 1988. "On the Mechanics of Economic Development." *Journal of Monetary Economics* 22(1): 3–42.

Markusen, James R. 1983. "Factor Movements and Commodity Trade as Complements." *Journal of International Economics* 14(3–4): 341–56.

Mattoo, Aaditya, Ileana Cristina Neagu, and Çaglar Özden. 2005. "Brain Waste? Educated Immigrants in the U.S. Labor Market." World Bank Policy Research Working Paper. no. 3581. World Bank, Washington, DC.

McCormick, Barry, and Jackline Wahba. 2003. "Return International Migration and Geographical Inequality: The Case of Egypt." *Journal of African Economies* 12(4): 500–32.

Mora, Jorge, and J. Edward Taylor. 2004. "Remittances, Inequality and Poverty: Evidence from Rural Mexico." International Migration and Development Research Program, Development Economics Research Group. Mimeo. World Bank, Washington, DC.

Mountford, Andrew. 1997. "Can a Brain Drain Be Good for Growth in the Source Economy?" *Journal of Development Economics* 53(2): 287–303.

Mundell, Robert A. 1957. "International Trade and Factor Mobility." *The American Economic Review* 47(3): 321–35.

Ratha, Dilip. 2005. "Workers' Remittances: An Important and Stable Source of External Development Finance." Chapter 1 in *Remittances: Development Impact and Future Prospects*, eds. Samuel Maimbo and Dilip Ratha. Washington, DC: World Bank.

Rauch, James. E. 2001. "Business and Social Networks in International Trade." *Journal of Economic Literature* 39(4): 1,177–203.

Rozelle, Scott, J. Edward Taylor, and Alan DeBraw. 1999. "Migration, Remittances and Productivity in China." *The American Economic Review* 89(2): 287–91.

Schiff, Maurice. 1996. "Trade Policy and International Migration: Substitute or Complements." In *Development Strategy, Employment and Migration*, ed. J.E. Taylor. Paris: OECD.

Stark, Oded, Christian Helmenstein, and Alexia Prskawetz. 1997. "A Brain Gain with a Brain Drain." *Economics Letters* 55(2): 227–34.

———. 1998. "Human Capital Depletion, Human Capital Formation, and Migration: a Blessing or a 'Curse'?" *Economics Letters 60(3): 363–67.*

United Nations. 2002. *International Migration Report 2002.* Department of Economic and Social Affairs, Population Division, New York: United Nations.

Walmsley, T., and L.A. Winters. Forthcoming. "An Analysis of the Removal of Restrictions on the Temporary Movement of Natural Persons." *Journal of Economic Integration.*

Woodruff, Christopher, and Rene Zenteno. 2001. "Remittances and Microenterprises in Mexico." Unpublished manuscript. University of California San Diego.

World Bank. Forthcoming. *Global Economic Prospects 2006: International Remittances and Migration.* Washington, DC: World Bank.

Yang, Dean. 2005. "International Migration, Human Capital, and Entrepreneurship: Evidence from Philippine Migrants' Exchange Rate Shocks." World Bank Policy Research Working Paper, no. 3578. World Bank, Washington, DC.

PART I

MIGRATION AND REMITTANCES

DETERMINANTS OF MIGRATION, DESTINATION, AND SECTOR CHOICE: DISENTANGLING INDIVIDUAL, HOUSEHOLD, AND COMMUNITY EFFECTS

Jorge Mora and J. Edward Taylor

Introduction

Migration is a selective process. Individual, family, and community characteristics of migrants are different than of those who stay behind. The premise of this chapter is that the selectivity of migration is different for distinct migrant destinations as well as for different sectors of employment at those destinations. For example, it is often assumed that educated people have a higher propensity to migrate internationally than less educated people. Human capital theory might predict such an outcome if schooling makes workers relatively more productive abroad than at home or if information about foreign labor markets is more available and migration costs are lower for the educated. A number of empirical studies support this assumption (see Adams 2003). However, it is not necessarily the case for unauthorized migration to low-skill labor markets abroad.

The present study includes two novel extensions of past empirical migration research. First, it incorporates both alternative destinations (internal versus international) and sectors of employment (farm versus nonfarm) into a common theoretical and empirical framework. This is important because, as we shall see, different types of individuals are selected into migration to different destination and sector regimes. Second, the study includes both family and community variables, with potentially distinct impacts on migration to specific labor markets. Including family variables in the analysis reflects insights from the new economics of migration theory that migration decisions take place within larger social units (that is, households). Community variables include access to markets, which may influence the economic returns from local production. Past research on migration and market integration has had a country focus, and findings largely have been anecdotal (Martin 1993) or else based on applied theoretical or simulation models (Hinojosa-Ojeda and Robinson 1992; Levy and Wijnberger 1992). To our knowledge, this is the first study that tests for effects of indicators of local market integration on migration behavior.

We employ limited-dependent variable methods and data from the 2003 Mexico National Rural Household Survey (*Encuesta Nacional a Hogares Rurales de México*, or ENHRUM) to model the selectivity of internal and international migration to farm and nonfarm jobs. The ENHRUM is unique in providing detailed sociodemographic and economic information on a nationally representative sample of rural households in Mexico. Current and retrospective migration data, including migrants' sector of employment, were gathered for all household members as well as for children of household heads or their spouses who were living outside of the household at the time of the survey.

Mexico is an ideal site to study the selectivity of migration and its implications. Mexico's rural economies are being transformed as migrants integrate households and communities with labor markets in Mexico and the United States. Findings from the 2003 ENHRUM reveal that people are leaving Mexico's villages at an unprecedented rate. Figure 1.1, constructed from retrospective migration data gathered in the survey, shows that the percentage of Mexico's village populations working at internal and international migrant destinations increased sharply at the end of the twentieth century.[1] More than half of all migrants leaving Mexican villages go to destinations in Mexico; however, villagers' propensity to migrate to U.S. jobs more than doubled from 1990 to 2002. This surge in migration mirrors an unexpectedly large increase in the number of Mexico-born people living in the United States revealed by the U.S. 2000 Census.[2] To date, most of our understanding of the selectivity and economic impacts of migration in rural Mexico comes from a limited number of nonrandom community case studies.[3] The ENHRUM data are nationally representative of Mexico's rural households.

Background

Understanding the selectivity of migration is important for several reasons. Characteristics of migrants, their households, and their communities of origin can shape migrants' success at their destinations as well as their impacts at home. They

FIGURE 1.1   Labor Migrants as Percentage of Mexican Village Populations, by Migrant Destination, 1980–2002

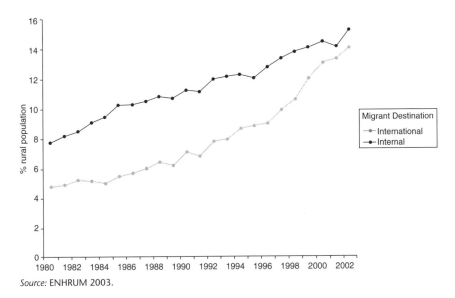

Source: ENHRUM 2003.

determine which households and communities bear the costs of human capital "lost" to migration, as well as the distribution of migration's potential benefits through remittances and the income multipliers they may create. Immigration policies attempt to influence the characteristics of legal migration, but they have less influence over the characteristics of unauthorized migrants. Because of migrant selectivity, market integration can alter the characteristics of rural populations through its influence on migration. Different theoretical models of migration imply different selectivity patterns, and these models can provide guidance for policy interventions to influence migration and its impacts, including remittance-induced development. Some sectors of migrant-destination countries rely heavily on foreign labor. For example, migrants from Mexico represented 77 percent of the U.S. farm workforce in 1997–98, up from 57 percent in 1990 (U.S. Department of Labor 1991, 2000). The determinants of migration are critical to the livelihood of these sectors.

Different migration theories imply different sets of variables shaping migration decisions and different impacts of migration on rural economies. A well-developed body of literature addresses the question of migrant selectivity by merging theories on individuals' migration decisions with human capital theory arising from the early work of Mincer (1974), Becker (1975), and others. Wages at prospective migrant origins and destinations are assumed to be a function of individuals' skills affecting their productivity at origin and destination. In the Todaro (1969) model, human capital characteristics of individuals may influence both their wages and their likelihood of obtaining a job once they migrate. Characteristics of individuals may also affect migration costs. The human capital view of migration has the key implication that the types of individuals selected into migration are those for whom, over time, the discounted income (or expected income, net of migration costs) differential between migration and nonmigration is greatest or migration costs are lowest. Perhaps the most sophisticated application of human capital theory to migration is by Vijverberg 1995), who uses a discrete choice structural model to predict the effect of earnings at various locations on migration, while controlling for observed and unobserved variables. Unlike the present research, however, this theory does not include a farm-nonfarm dichotomy. This is important because the determinants of migration are likely to differ across sectors as well as across locations.

An excellent example of this concerns education. It is often assumed that the most educated people migrate. Such an assumption is supported by human capital theory only if schooling has a greater positive effect on earnings at the migrant destination than at origin or if that education lowers migration costs and risks. Chiquiar and Hanson (2005) find a positive correlation between education and migration from Mexico to the United States. However, their study refers to migration from all of Mexico. A positive effect of schooling is likely to be the case for internal migration to nonfarm jobs or legal international migration, but it is not necessarily the case for internal migration to agricultural jobs or unauthorized international migration to any job.

The new economics of labor migration (NELM) brings a household perspective to the analysis of migration behavior. Household variables, including assets and the human capital of household members other than migrants, are hypothesized to influence migration decisions via their effect on migration costs (including the opportunity cost to households of allocating their members to migration work) as well as the impacts of remittances and the income security that migrants provide on the expected utility of the household as a whole.

Economic and market conditions in rural areas, particularly access to markets for inputs and outputs, are likely to shape the benefits and costs of migration for rural households. We are not aware of any research that tests for the effects of *local* market integration on migration. This is surprising in light of interest at the aggregate level in interactions between market reforms and international migration.[4] We find evidence on a local level that trade and migration may be complementary to each other.

If family and community as well as traditional human capital variables shape migration decisions, omitting any of these variables from the analysis is likely to result in biased estimates of migration model parameters.

Conceptual Framework

Migration is the result of individuals and households weighing the utility that is attainable under different migration regimes with the utility from not migrating. A migration regime is defined as a combination of place (the village of origin in the case of nonmigration, internal migrant destinations, or foreign destinations) and sector of employment. There are five potential regimes in our empirical model: nonmigration, two destination types (internal and international), and two employment sectors in each (farm and nonfarm).

Migration entails a discrete, dichotomous, or polychotomous choice. A reduced-form approach, in which income or expected-income is replaced by a vector of exogenous (that is, human capital and, in the case of NELM models, household capital) variables, has been used in a number of studies using probit or logit estimation techniques (see, for example, Taylor 1986, and Emerson 1989). Multinomial logit, probit, tobit, two-stage (Heckman), and various maximum-likelihood techniques for estimating discrete-continuous models, not available or accessible two decades ago, today are widely used to estimate migration-decision models at a microlevel (individual or household). Recent studies include Perloff, Lynch, and Gabbard (1998), Emerson (1989), Taylor (1987, 1992), Stark and Taylor (1989, 1991), Lucas and Stark (1985), and Barham and Boucher (1998). Explicitly or implicitly, these empirical studies are grounded in a random-utility theoretic model in which it is assumed that households make migration decisions that maximize their welfare.

Household utility is assumed to be affected positively by income, including the income person i's household receives independent of individual i's regime choice and the income the individual generates under alternative migration regimes. Household income is the sum of net incomes from all household production and labor activities, excluding individual i. This income depends on person i's family characteristics, ZF^i, including assets that affect the productivity of investments on and off the farm and migrant networks (Massey, Alarcón, and others 1987; Massey, Arango, and others 1993) that influence remittances from other family members besides person i. Income also may be influenced by community context variables, ZC^i, which affect the economic returns to family resources inside and outside the village. An example of ZC^i might be access to outside markets for family farm production or wage labor.

Nonmigrants have the option of supplying labor to local labor markets or to family farm production. Those who participate in the labor market receive a wage that depends on their human capital, ZH^i, and context variables that influence the returns to human capital in local labor markets. Nonmigrants who work in family farm or nonfarm production activities produce a value product that depends on family, community, and human capital variables. Migrants receive a wage that depends on their human capital as well as family and community variables influencing migration success (for example, migration networks; see Taylor 1986; Munshi 2003).

Individual, family, and human capital characteristics may affect remittance behavior, migrants' wages, and migrants' willingness to share their earnings with the household through remittances. Finally, individual, family, and community variables may influence migration costs, as well as the ability to finance these costs. Wealth and migration networks may play a particularly important role in this regard (Taylor 1987; López and Schiff 1998).

The impact of a given variable on migration probabilities is a mixture of the variable's expected influences on incomes at origin and destination and on migration costs.[5] We do not attempt to isolate these influences. Our goal in this study is to estimate the differential net effects of individual, family, and community variables on observed migration outcomes, using a reduced-form approach. The influence of a particular variable may be different for different migrant destinations and different sectors of employment, reflecting in part the differential returns to human and migration capital. Our empirical models, described below, are multinomial logits, in which the probability that individual j is paired with migration destination-and-sector regime d is given by the following.

$$prob(U_d^i \geq U_j^i \forall j \neq d) = \frac{e^{\beta_d Z^i}}{\sum_{j=0}^{J} e^{\beta_j Z^i}} \tag{1.1}$$

where Z^i is a vector of individual i's individual, family, and community characteristics; that is, $Z^i = [ZH^i, ZF^i, ZC^i]$.

Data and Variables

Data to estimate the model are from the ENHRUM. This survey provides detailed data on assets, sociodemographic characteristics, production, income sources, and migration from a nationally representative sample of rural households surveyed in January and February 2003. The sample includes 7,298 individuals from

1,782 households in 14 states. Having individuals as the units of observation permits us to fully exploit the information contained in the ENHRUM data. Our dependent variable is the migration-employment regime in which individuals were observed in 2002.

Instituto Nacional de Estadística, Geografía e Informática (INEGI), Mexico's national information and census office, designed the sampling frame to provide a statistically reliable characterization of Mexico's population living in rural areas, or communities with fewer than 2,500 inhabitants. For reasons of cost and tractability, individuals in hamlets or disperse populations with fewer than 500 inhabitants were not included in the survey. The result is a sample that is representative of more than 80 percent of the population that the Mexican government considers as rural.

Complete migration histories were assembled from 1980 through 2002 for (a) the household head, (b) the spouse of the head, (c) all individuals who lived in the household three months or more in 2002, and (d) a random sample of all sons and daughters of either the head or his/her spouse who lived outside the household longer than three months in 2002. These retrospective data were used to construct our migration network variables.

Survey teams visited each community twice, first in summer 2002, to conduct a survey of community characteristics via interviews with local leaders, service providers, and school teachers, and again in January and February 2003, to carry out the household survey. The household survey is the source of all information on individual and family characteristics. Community variables were constructed from the community survey.

The human capital, family, and community variables in our analysis are summarized in tables 1.1 and 1.2 and described below.

Individual Characteristics

Individual variables include the standard Mincer (1974) variables: years of completed schooling; age, which captures both life cycle and experience; age squared; gender (a dummy variable equal to 1 if male, 0 if female); status in household (1 if household head, 0 otherwise); and marital status (1 if married, 0 otherwise). The average adult (12 or older) household size is 5.6, nearly evenly divided between males and females (table 1.1). The data reveal low levels of human capital. Average schooling of household members is just under 6 years, but schooling of household heads averages just over 4 years. Average schooling is highest for internal migrants in nonfarm jobs (7.3 years). It is lowest for internal migrants in farm jobs (3.8 years; see table 1.2).

Twenty-six percent of nonmigrants are household heads, compared with 18 percent of internal and 23 percent of international migrants. Most international

TABLE 1.1. Descriptive Statistics

Variable	Mean	Standard deviation	Min.	Max.
Individual Characteristics				
Household head (Dummy)	0.25	0.43	0.00	1.00
Sex (Dummy, 1 = male)	0.49	0.50	0.00	1.00
Age	34.93	17.77	12.00	100.00
Marital status (Dummy, 1 = married)	0.61	0.49	0.00	1.00
Years of completed schooling	5.91	3.66	0.00	20.00
Family Characteristics				
Number of males over 15 years in the family0	2.74	1.82	0.00	11.0
Number of females over 15 years in the family	2.83	1.85	0.00	11.00
Number of males in family with secondary education	0.91	1.17	0.00	8.00
Number of females in family with secondary education	0.87	1.15	0.00	7.00
Schooling of household head	4.03	3.54	0.00	20.00
Land value/100,000	1.16	6.56	0.00	144.00
Livestock (number of large animals in 2001)[a]	3.65	14.68	0.00	252.00
Tractors owned by household in 2001	0.06	0.24	0.00	2.00
Wealth index	0.05	2.01	−6.28	4.48
Wealth index-squared	4.03	5.08	0.00	39.46
Number of family members at internal migrant destination in 1990	0.21	0.57	0.00	5.00
Number of family members at U.S. migrant destination in 1990	0.13	0.44	0.00	5.00
Community Characteristics				
Frequency of transport	8.53	5.83	0.00	24.00
Inaccessibility during weather shocks (Dummy)	0.14	0.35	0.00	1.00
Nonagricultural enterprise in village (Dummy)	0.25	0.43	0.00	1.00

Source: ENHRUM 2003.

Note: Sample size = 7,298.

a. Livestock includes oxen, cattle, and horses.

migrants from rural Mexico work in nonfarm rather than farm jobs. In the ENHRUM sample, 78 percent of all international migrants were observed in nonfarm jobs in 2002.[6] Farm labor migration is dominated by males. The female share is highest (35 percent) for internal migration to nonfarm jobs and lowest (5 percent) for international migration to farm jobs. A higher percentage of migrants (62 percent of internal, 72 percent of international) than nonmigrants (60 percent) are married.

Family Characteristics

Family characteristics include physical capital: land, livestock holdings, and equipment. Landholdings are measured in value terms, to reflect both quality and quantity. Livestock is proxied by the number of large animals (oxen, horses, cows) owned by the household. Equipment is proxied by the number of tractors owned by the household. Family characteristics also include human capital of family members other than person i, which is measured by the number of males and females with secondary education, years of completed schooling of the household head, migration networks, and an index of family wealth.

The wealth index was constructed using the method of principal components with data on household assets, principally housing characteristics (number of rooms; materials used for the construction of floors, walls, and roofs; dummy variables indicating whether the house had running water, electricity, and sewerage) and other services and durables (telephone, television, and a refrigerator). The procedure closely follows the one used by McKenzie and Rapoport (2004). A positive value of this indicates that a household's wealth is above the average for the sample, while a negative value indicates below-average wealth. We constructed two migration network variables, calculated as the number of family members working in the United States and at internal migrant destinations in 1990. We chose 1990 to minimize potential endogeneity of migration networks.

On average, households had landholdings valued at 116,000 pesos (approximately US$11,600), 3.6 large animals, 0.21 family migrants at internal destinations, and 0.13 migrants in the United States. Few households own tractors; the average per household is 0.06. The data show that there are wide disparities in each of these variables.

Households of nonmigrants in 2002 had few migrants in 1990, an average of 0.17 internal migrants and 0.10 working abroad. Internal migrants' households had more family members at internal destinations (0.65) and few in the United States (0.05). International migrants' households had above-average numbers of family members at both international and internal destinations (0.56 and 0.19, respectively).

Summary statistics reveal that households of international migrants had above-average wealth, indicated by a positive wealth index, while internal migrant households had below-average wealth. The wealth index for nonmigrant households (0.05) is identical to the average wealth index for the full sample. The average value of landholdings is higher in households of nonmigrants (122,000 pesos)

TABLE 1.2 Variable Means by Migrant Destination and Sector of Employment

Variable	Non-migration	Migration destination		Migration-Sector regime			
		Internal migration	International migration	Mexico, farm	Mexico, nonfarm	U.S. farm	U.S. nonfarm
Individual Characteristics							
Household head (Dummy)	0.26	0.18	0.23	0.44	0.17	0.33	0.20
Sex (Dummy, 1 = male)	0.45	0.66	0.84	0.80	0.65	0.95	0.81
Age	35.45	30.81	32.57	31.08	30.80	33.04	32.44
Marital status (Dummy, 1 = married)	0.60	0.62	0.72	0.80	0.61	0.69	0.73
Years of completed schooling	5.75	7.13	6.65	3.84	7.30	6.15	6.79
Family Characteristics							
Number of males over 15 years in the family	2.66	3.01	3.52	2.12	3.05	3.60	3.50
Number of females over 15 years in the family	2.80	3.00	3.11	1.76	3.06	2.77	3.20
Number of males in family with secondary education	0.89	0.98	1.03	0.44	1.00	1.18	0.99
Number of females in family with secondary education	0.86	0.98	0.86	0.12	1.02	0.73	0.90
Schooling of household head	4.11	3.45	3.58	3.40	3.45	3.22	3.69
Land value/100,000	1.22	0.67	0.88	0.10	0.70	0.75	0.91
Livestock (number of large animals in 2001)[a]	3.60	2.26	5.83	0.32	2.36	4.47	6.22
Tractors owned by household in 2001	0.05	0.04	0.13	0.00	0.04	0.05	0.15
Wealth index	0.05	-0.85	1.03	-1.81	-0.80	0.73	1.12
Wealth index-squared	4.01	4.75	3.61	7.74	4.60	4.07	3.48

Number of family members at internal migrant destination in 1990	0.17	0.65	0.19	0.48	0.66	0.14	0.21
Number of family members at U.S. migrant destination in 1990	0.10	0.05	0.56	0.00	0.05	0.48	0.58
Community Characteristics							
Frequency of transport	8.44	9.74	8.39	8.64	9.79	8.58	8.34
Inaccessibility during weather shocks (Dummy)	0.13	0.26	0.14	0.56	0.24	0.18	0.12
Nonagricultural enterprise in village (Dummy)	0.26	0.15	0.24	0.24	0.15	0.21	0.25
N	6297	510	491	25	485	110	381

Source: ENHRUM 2003.

Note: Sample size = 7,298.

a. Livestock includes oxen, cattle, and horses.

than of internal or international migrants (67,000 and 88,000 pesos, respectively). International migrants' households average 5.8 head of livestock (oxen, cattle, and horses), compared with 3.6 for nonmigrants' households and 2.3 for households of internal migrants.

Average schooling of heads is 4.1 years in households of nonmigrants, 3.4 years in households of internal migrants, and 3.6 years in households of international migrants.

Community Characteristics

There are several candidates for indicators of access to markets and access risk. We include two indicators in our econometric model. The first is frequency of transport availability between the village and commercial centers with which villagers transact. To construct the frequency of transport variable, we (a) created a list of commercial centers (node) with which each village interacted; (b) constructed an index of frequency of regularly scheduled transportation between the village and each of these nodes, ranging from zero (less than one trip per day) to three (more than six trips per day); and (c) summed this frequency index across commercial nodes. The higher the value of this index, the greater the frequency of transport and number of outside communities with which the village is linked via regularly scheduled transportation.[7] The second indicator is a proxy for security of market access, a dummy variable equal to 1 if the village is accessible in the case of natural disasters and 0 otherwise (for example, it is located at the end of a road or across a bridge that may become inaccessible). Our list of community variables also includes the presence of local nonfarm enterprises, which may offer employment alternatives to migration.

The frequency of transport index averages 8.5 but ranges from 0 to 24. Fourteen percent of villages lack access to transport during weather shocks, and one in four has a nonagricultural enterprise. Both frequency of transport and insecurity of market access are highest for households of internal migrants. The share in villages with nonagricultural enterprises is highest for nonmigrants (0.26) and lowest for internal migrants (0.15).

Correlations among this complex set of variables limit the usefulness of summary statistics to identify migration determinants. A multivariate regression approach that controls for these correlations is required to obtain reliable estimates of the effects of individual, family, and community characteristics on migrant destination and employment sector choice.

Estimation and Results

Figure 1.2 illustrates trends in the percentage of rural Mexicans employed as internal and international migrants in farm and nonfarm jobs from 1980 through

FIGURE 1.2   Labor Migrants as Percentage of Mexican Village Populations, by Migrant Destination and Sector of Employment, 1980–2002

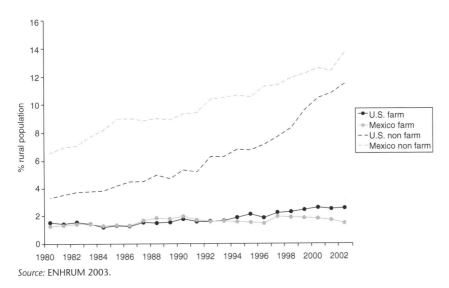

Source: ENHRUM 2003.

2002. It shows a sharp upward trend in the percentage of villagers working as internal and international migrants in nonfarm jobs, a mildly upward trend in the percentage in U.S. farm jobs, and a declining trend in the percentage in agricultural jobs in Mexico. The decrease in internal migrants employed in farm jobs reflects a decline in Mexico's agricultural employment in the 1990s.[8] In 2002, an average of 14 percent of the Mexican village population was working in the United States. This figure is higher than for the percentage of the total Mexican population; approximately 9 percent of all Mexicans were in the United States in 2002.[9] Most international migrants from rural Mexico (82 percent) were employed in U.S. nonfarm jobs. On average, 15 percent of village populations were observed as internal migrants. Of these, 90 percent were in nonfarm jobs.

We first estimated a two-regime logit model for migration and nonmigration[10] and a three-regime multinomial model for nonmigration, international migration, and internal migration. We then expanded the model to the five destination-sector (agriculture and nonagriculture) regimes. All three models were estimated using maximum likelihood in Stata.

Table 1.3 reports the estimation results for the two- and three-regime migration models, and table 1.4 reports the results for the five-choice migration-sector regime model. The columns in these two tables correspond to migrant destinations

TABLE 1.3   One- and Two-Destination Multinomial Logit Model Results

Variable	Migration destination		
	All migration	Internal migration	International migration
Individual Characteristics			
Household head (Dummy)	−0.580	−0.652	−0.572
	(−4.55)***	(−3.79)***	(−3.25)***
Sex (Dummy, 1 = Male)	1.659	1.220	2.302
	(17.31)***	(10.1)***	(15.21)***
Age	0.180	0.163	0.201
	(10.57)***	(7.48)***	(7.96)***
Age squared	−0.002	−0.002	−0.003
	(−11.36)***	(−7.52)***	(−8.99)***
Marital status (Dummy, 1 = married)	0.324	0.129	0.599
	(3.13)***	(0.97)	(4.00)***
Years of completed schooling	0.080	0.144	0.010
	(5.71)***	(7.82)***	(0.55)
Family Characteristics			
Number of males over 15 years in the family	0.043	0.042	0.051
	(1.53)	1.09	(1.37)
Number of females over 15 years in the family	0.032	−0.025	0.065
	(1.16)	−0.65	(1.75)*
Number of males in family with secondary education	−0.105	−0.126	−0.098
	(−2.54)**	(−2.28)**	(−1.74)*
Number of females in family with secondary education	0.037	0.115	−0.029
	(0.89)	(2.08)**	(−0.5)
Schooling of household head	−0.074	−0.078	−0.061
	(−5.38)***	(−4.17)***	(−3.21)***
Land value/100,000	−0.039	−0.048	−0.035
	(−2.53)**	(−1.85)*	(−1.92)*
Livestock (number of large animals in 2001)	−0.002	−0.009	−0.001
	(−0.62)	(−1.18)	(−0.49)
Tractors owned by household in 2001	0.478	0.141	0.695
	(2.96)***	(0.52)	(3.6)***
Wealth index	−0.010	−0.239	0.264
	(−0.43)	(−6.6)***	(7.2)***
Wealth index−squared	0.010	−0.016	−0.009
	(1.22)	(−1.36)	(−0.68)

TABLE 1.3 *(continued)*

	Migration destination		
Variable	All migration	Internal migration	International migration
Number of family members at internal migrant destination in 1990	0.557 (10.24)***	0.716 (11.91)***	0.107 (1.03)
Number of family members at U.S. migrant destination in 1990	0.813 (10.1)***	−0.221 (−1.11)	1.154 (12.3)***
Community Characteristics			
Frequency of transport	0.019 (2.89)***	0.029 (3.59)***	0.009 (0.91)
Inaccessible during weather shocks (Dummy)	0.548 (5.18)***	0.465 (3.63)***	0.633 (3.92)***
Nonagricultural enterprise (Dummy)	−0.297 (−3.09)***	−0.506 (−3.64)***	−0.061 (−0.48)

Source: ENHRUM 2003.
Note: Sample Size = 7,298. Likelihood Ratio χ^2 (42) = 1,642.86. t-statistics in parentheses. Default category: In village.
*** significant at 1 percent, ** significant at 5 percent, * significant at 10 percent.

and sectors of employment, the rows to explanatory variables. Asymptotic t-statistics appear in parentheses underneath the parameter estimates. The estimates presented in these tables are of the vector β_d in equation 1.1. As noted earlier, they represent the utility returns to each characteristic in regime d. These have the same signs and significance as the marginal effects of explanatory variables on migration probabilities. To obtain estimates of the probabilities of participating in migration or migration/sector regimes, these must be used together with variable means as shown in equation 1.1. Estimated effects of explanatory variables on migration and sector probabilities are presented in tables 1.5 and 1.6.

Each table reports results for the three sets of explanatory variables in the model: individual, family, and community characteristics. In most cases, all three play a significant role in shaping migration decisions. However, in many cases, the effects of these variables differ qualitatively and quantitatively between migration types and sectors of employment.

TABLE 1.4 Two-Destination, Two-Sector Multinomial Logit Model Results

Variable	Migration/Sector regime			
	Mexico, farm	Mexico, nonfarm	U.S. farm	U.S. nonfarm
Individual Characteristics				
Household head (Dummy)	−0.347	−0.712	−0.082	−0.742
	(−0.53)	(−3.99)***	(−0.24)	(−3.76)***
Sex (Dummy, 1 = Male)	2.007	1.2037	3.422	2.147
	(3.06)***	(9.81)***	(7.18)***	(13.4)***
Age	0.107	0.163	0.155	0.219
	(1.02)	(7.33)***	(3.54)***	(7.4)***
Age squared	−0.002	−0.002	−0.002	−0.003
	(−1.49)	(−7.25)***	(−4.34)***	(−8.17)***
Marital status (Dummy, 1 = married)	1.135	0.092	0.513	0.618
	(1.61)	(0.68)	(1.78)*	(3.73)***
Years of completed schooling	−0.258	0.158	−0.015	0.020
	(−2.65)***	(8.44)***	(−0.4)	(0.93)
Family Characteristics				
Number of males over 15 years in the family	−0.103	0.048	0.089	0.040
	(−0.5)	(1.25)	(1.29)	(0.99)
Number of females over 15 years in the family	−0.073	−0.017	−0.004	0.084
	(−0.36)	(−0.45)	(−0.06)	(2.08)**
Number of males in family with secondary education	0.325	−0.139	0.075	−0.155
	(1.02)	(−2.49)**	(0.76)	(−2.44)**
Number of females in family with secondary education	−1.119	0.123	−0.072	−0.022
	(−1.86)*	(2.21)**	(−0.61)	(−0.36)
Schooling of household head	0.023	−0.077	−0.117	−0.044
	(0.25)	(−4.04)***	(−2.95)***	(−2.15)**
Land value/100,000	−1.527	−0.044	−0.033	−0.036
	(−1.33)	(−1.74)*	(−0.85)	(−1.78)*
Livestock (number of large animals in 2001)	−0.250	−0.007	0.001	−0.002
	(−1.11)	(−1.05)	(0.14)	(−0.53)
Tractors owned by household in 2001	−28.756	0.123	−0.178	0.836
	(0.00)	(0.45)	(−0.37)	(4.15)***

TABLE 1.4 *(continued)*

	Migration/Sector regime			
Variable	Mexico, farm	Mexico, nonfarm	U.S. farm	U.S. nonfarm
Wealth index	−0.085	−0.247	0.221	0.293
	(−0.47)	(−6.68)***	(3.53)***	(6.58)***
Wealth index squared	0.020	−0.018	0.029	−0.029
	(0.43)	(−1.57)	(1.3)	(−1.7)*
Number of family members at internal migrant destination in 1990	0.861	0.713	−0.138	0.167
	(3.06)***	(11.71)***	(−0.57)	(1.49)
Number of family members at U.S. migrant destination in 1990	−30.901	−0.197	1.105	1.167
	(0.00)	(−0.99)	(7.69)***	(11.84)***
Community Characteristics				
Frequency of transport	−0.002	0.031	0.023	0.004
	(−0.06)	(3.71)***	(1.27)	(0.4)
Inaccessible during weather shocks (Dummy)	2.506	0.357	0.835	0.553
	(4.43)***	(2.69)***	(2.96)***	(2.97)***
Nonagricultural enterprise (Dummy)	0.920	−0.571	−0.225	−0.024
	(1.46)	(−3.99)***	(−0.89)	(−0.17)

Source: ENHRUM 2003.
Note: Sample Size = 7,298.Likelihood Ratio χ^2 (84) = 1777.63. t-statistics in parentheses. Default category: In village.
*** significant at 1 percent, ** significant at 5 percent, * significant at 10 percent.

Selectivity of Migration from Rural Mexico   Total migration includes a heterogeneous mixture of migration to internal and international destinations and to farm and nonfarm jobs. The first data column of table 1.3 reveals that, despite this heterogeneity, most individual, household, and community variables are significant in explaining the movement of individuals out of villages.

Household heads are significantly less likely to migrate than non-heads-of-household. This finding is consistent with the hypothesis that household heads have family farm-specific human capital and thus a high opportunity cost of migrating. Males are significantly more likely to migrate than females. The probability of migration increases with age, but at a decreasing rate. This reflects the selectivity of migration on the working-age population but not on the very young or elderly. Married villagers are significantly more likely to migrate than those who are not married, a finding that is similar to the positive effect of this variable in studies of labor-force participation.[11]

Other things being equal, the probability of migration rises significantly with years of completed schooling of the individual, suggesting that the economic returns to schooling, on average, are higher in migrant labor markets than in the village. However, migration is negatively associated with schooling of the household head. This is consistent with our expectation that household heads' schooling raises the productivity of labor in family production activities, thereby raising the opportunity cost of migration. There is evidence that migration propensities are lower in households with adult males (other than the migrant and head) who have secondary education. Interestingly, the number of males and females older than 15 in the family are not significantly related to migration propensities when we control for all other variables in the model. It appears that human, family, and community capital variables, not sheer numbers of adult family members, are the critical variables promoting migration.

As the value of family landholdings increases, the probability of migration decreases. This is what we would expect if household landholdings and land quality increase the productivity of family labor. Livestock holdings are not significantly associated with migration. Livestock production is not labor intensive and, unlike other land-based production activities, it does not appear to compete with migration for family labor. Controlling for these assets, our index of household wealth does not significantly affect migration in general (although this is not true for migration to specific destinations; see below). Both migration network indicators have an effect on migration that is positive and highly significant, supporting the contention by Massey, Alarcón, and others (1987) that migration is a network-driven process.[12]

All three community variables significantly explain total migration. Migration increases with villages' transportation access to commercial centers, which we use as a proxy for market integration. This finding may suggest that migration and market integration are complements on a local level. Nevertheless, other market-integration variables we tested were not significant.[13] Thus, our results leave room for the possibility that the effect of transportation on migration is ambiguous. Better transportation reduces transaction costs in labor markets, but it also lowers transaction costs in markets for local production activities that may compete with migration for family labor. The relationship between insecurity of market access and migration is positive and significant. Other things being equal, individuals in villages with insecure access to outside markets are more likely to migrate than individuals in villages where market access is secure. Migration decreases when nonfarm enterprises are present in the village.

Multinomial logit results (tables 1.3 and 1.4) reveal that the impacts of these explanatory variables are not uniform across migration destinations or sectors of migrant employment.

Internal Migration

The effects of schooling on migration are sector specific. Schooling has a significant positive effect on total migration (table 1.3) and on internal migration to nonfarm jobs (table 1.4), in which the economic returns to schooling obtained in Mexico are likely to be high. However, it is negatively associated with internal migration to farm jobs, in which skill requirements are minimal and thus the economic returns to education are likely to be small. A similar pattern is evident for the other major human capital variable. Age has a quadratic (inverted U) relationship with total migration, internal migration, and internal migration to nonfarm jobs. However, there is no significant evidence of an age (or experience) effect on internal migration to farm jobs. The negative effect of the household-head variable on migration probabilities is robust across migrant destinations. However, it is not significant for internal migration to farm jobs. Males are more likely than females to migrate internally to jobs in both sectors.

Most of the family characteristics that significantly explain migration also explain internal migration to nonfarm jobs. However, few are significant in explaining migration to farm jobs. The exceptions are the number of females with secondary education, which is negatively associated with internal farm labor migration, and the internal migration network instrument. Internal migration to nonfarm jobs is significantly and positively shaped by individuals' schooling. However, as schooling of the household head rises, the propensity for other household members to migrate internally to nonfarm jobs decreases. Landholdings have a significant negative effect on internal migration, although this effect is not significant for internal migration to farm jobs. Livestock holdings have no significant effect on internal migration to either sector. In contrast to total migration, the propensity for internal migration decreases significantly (linearly) with household wealth. The number of family members at internal migrant destinations (lagged 10 years) has a significant positive effect on internal migration to both farm and nonfarm jobs. There is no significant evidence of competition between U.S. migration networks and internal migration to either sector.

Community context variables also differentially influence internal-migrant destinations. Internal migration to nonfarm (but not farm) jobs is positively associated with the extent of village integration with outside markets. The presence of nonagricultural enterprises in the village appears to compete with internal migration to nonfarm (but not farm) jobs. Insecurity of market access increases the likelihood of internal migration to both sectors, a finding consistent with migration's role as a risk buffer for rural households.

International Migration

There is a striking difference in the association between schooling and migration for internal and international migration. International migration for rural Mexicans overwhelmingly entails unauthorized entry and employment in low-skill jobs requiring, at most, primary schooling. Wages in those jobs frequently are more than 10 times the minimum wage in Mexico; however, they generally do not depend on education. Few U.S. farmers, contractors, or households are aware of the schooling levels of the unauthorized Mexican immigrants they hire. In light of this, it is not surprising that individuals' years of completed schooling do not significantly affect their probability of international migration to either farm or nonfarm jobs. The number of females with secondary education also is not associated with international migration to either sector. However, as in the case of internal migration to nonfarm jobs, the household head's schooling is negatively associated with international migration to both farm and nonfarm sectors.

Like internal migrants, international migrants are significantly more likely to be males and less likely to be household heads. Age has a significant inverted-U-shaped relationship with the likelihood of international migration to both farm and nonfarm jobs, and married individuals are significantly more likely to be foreign migrants.

Migration networks, proxied by the number of family members in the United States in 1990, are by far the most statistically significant family variables influencing international migration. This is consistent with many past studies of Mexico-to-U.S. migration. It is noteworthy that migration networks have a much more significant effect on international than on internal migration. This no doubt reflects the greater costs and risks, and thus the greater value of family contacts, in international migration. It generalizes Taylor's (1986) finding that networks have differential effects on internal and international migration. (That study had access to data from only two villages.)

Controlling for migration networks and other variables, there is no evidence that local market integration discourages international migration. Frequency of transport is positively associated with international migration to both sectors, although it is not significant. Controlling for market access, villages at risk of losing their access to outside markets in times of weather shocks have higher international migration probabilities. The presence of local nonfarm enterprises does not significantly discourage international migration to either farm or nonfarm jobs.

Statistical Versus Quantitative Significance

Statistical significance reported in tables 1.3 and 1.4 does not necessarily imply that variables are important quantitatively in explaining migration. Tables 1.5 and 1.6 present estimated marginal effects of variables on migration-sector choice probabilities. They were constructed using the logit parameter estimates and probability function—equation 1.1—by increasing each variable by a small amount and then recalculating migration destination-sector probabilities, holding all other variables constant at their means. For dummy variables (household head, gender, marital status), probabilities were calculated setting the variable first to one and then to zero. Other discrete variables (schooling, age, numbers of family members, tractors, migration networks) were increased by one unit above their means. Continuous variables (wealth, land value) were increased by 1 percentage point above their means. To assess the importance of the percentage effects of each variable, it is useful to remember the baseline probability of each destination and sector choice at the means of all variables. These are given in table 1.7. The highest probabilities are for migration to nonfarm sectors abroad and in Mexico (0.067 and 0.066, respectively). The lowest is migration to farm jobs in Mexico (0.003). A change in an explanatory variable may have a small absolute effect, but a large relative effect, on the probability of migration to a destination-sector combination whose baseline probability is low (for example, international migration to farm jobs). Nevertheless, it is the absolute effects that are of most interest from the standpoint of identifying variables that influence whether individuals migrate, their destinations, and their sectors of employment.

A comparison of tables 1.3 and 1.4 with tables 1.5 and 1.6 illustrates the difference between statistical and scientific significance when modeling migration, particularly for specific destination-sector combinations. Many more variables are quantitatively important in explaining the probability of leaving the village (first data column in table 1.5) than the probability of migrating to specific destinations. Fewer are quantitatively important in explaining sector of employment at specific migrant destinations (table 1.6).

All things being equal, males have a 14 percent higher probability of leaving the village as labor migrants than females. The effects of the other dichotomous variables (household head and marital status), while statistically significant, are quantitatively smaller than that of the gender variable: married individuals are 2.4 percent more likely to migrate, while household heads are 4.4 percent less likely to migrate. Schooling is both statistically and quantitatively significant. A 1-year increase in schooling above the mean of 5.9 years raises the migration probability by 0.78 percentage points. Age has a larger quantitative effect; a 1-year increase in age is associated with a 1.3-percentage-point increase in migration probability.

TABLE 1.5   Estimated Marginal Effects on Migration Probabilities

| Variable | Migration destination | | |
	All migration (%)	Internal migration (%)	International migration (%)
Individual Characteristics			
Household head (Dummy)	−4.399***	−2.046***	−1.135***
Sex (Dummy, 1 = male)	14.234***	4.352***	6.267***
Age	1.327***	0.623***	0.499***
Age squared	−0.019***	−0.008***	−0.007***
Marital status (Dummy, 1 = married)	2.434***	0.415	1.320***
Years of completed schooling	0.767***	0.562***	0.011
Family Characteristics			
Number of males over 15 years in the family	0.391	0.150	0.118
Number of females over 15 years in the family	0.368	−0.095	0.159*
Number of males in family with secondary education	−0.943**	−0.429**	−0.209*
Number of females in family with secondary education	0.194	0.449**	−0.077
Schooling of household head	−0.639***	−0.271***	−0.132***
Land value/100,000	−0.314**	−0.002*	−0.001*
Livestock (number of large animals in 2001)	−0.017	−0.031	−0.003
Tractors owned by household in 2001	3.971***	0.450	2.263***
Wealth index	−0.072	0.000***	0.000***
Wealth index—squared	0.107	−0.002	−0.001
Number of family members at internal migrant destination in 1990	4.947***	3.664***	0.162
Number of family members at U.S. migrant destination in 1990	6.908***	−0.886	4.871***
Community Characteristics			
Frequency of transport	0.139***	0.109***	0.018
Inaccessibility during weather shocks (Dummy)	5.493***	1.897***	1.779***
Nonagricultural enterprise in village (Dummy)	−2.435***	−1.569***	−0.101

Source: ENHRUM 2003.

Note: *** significant at 1 percent, ** significant at 5 percent, * significant at 10 percent in the Multinomial Logit Model for the columns of migration destination; the marginal effects are reported for the Probit Model in the column of all migration.

TABLE 1.6   Estimated Marginal Effects on Migration-Sector Probabilities

Variable	Migration/Sector regime		
	Mexico nonfarm	U.S. farm	U.S. nonfarm
Individual Characteristics			
Household head (Dummy)	−2.117***	−0.017	−1.061***
Sex (Dummy, 1 == male)	4.110***	1.842***	4.183***
Age	0.594***	0.057***	0.407***
Age squared	−0.007***	−0.001***	−0.006***
Marital status (Dummy, 1 = married)	0.276	0.174*	1.005***
Years of completed schooling	0.595***	−0.008	0.024***
Family Characteristics			
Number of males over-15 years in the family	0.168	0.033	0.067
Number of females over 15 years in the family	−0.065	−0.002	0.152**
Number of males in family with secondary education	−0.451**	0.031	−0.242
Number of females in family with secondary education	0.460**	−0.027	−0.046
Schooling of household head	−0.256 ***	−0.039***	−0.070**
Land value/100,000	−0.002*	0.000	−0.001*
Livestock (number of large animals in 2001)	−0.025	0.000	−0.002
Tractors owned by household in 2001	0.367	−0.068	2.189***
Wealth index	0.000***	0.000***	0.000***
Wealth index-squared	−0.003	0.000	−0.002
Number of family members at internal migrant destination in 1990	3.492***	−0.060	0.238
Number of family members at U.S. migrant destination in 1990	−0.764	0.697***	3.671***
Community Characteristics			
Frequency of transport	0.111***	0.008	0.006
Inaccessibility during weather shocks	1.341***	0.403***	1.117***
Nonagricultural enterprise in village	−1.769***	−0.071	−0.008

Source: ENHRUM 2003.

Note: *** significant at 1 percent, ** significant at 5 percent, * significant at 10 percent in the Multinomial Logit Model.

TABLE 1.7   Baseline Probability for Each Migration Destination-Sector Regime

Sector of employment	Migration destination		
	Internal	International	All migrants
Farm	0.003	0.015	0.018
Nonfarm	0.066	0.052	0.119
Both	0.070	0.067	0.137
Number of migrants	510	491	1,001
Total sample size (migrants plus nonmigrants)		7,298	

Source: ENHRUM 2003.

Migration networks are important both statistically and quantitatively. The ex-ante presence of an additional family member at an internal migrant destination, all things being equal, raises the probability of migration by 5 percent, and an additional family member at a U.S. migrant destination increases the migration probability by nearly 7 percent.

Insecurity of market access appears to be the most important community variable influencing total migration and migration to each destination. The nonagricultural enterprise and frequency of transportation variables both have a quantitatively important effect on internal but not international migration.[14]

Even the most significant determinants of migration have a smaller quantitative effect on migration to specific destinations than on total migration. For example, the probability of migrating, ceteris paribus, is 14.2 percent greater for males than for females. The probability of internal migration, however, is only 4.4 percent higher for males, while that of international migration is 6.6 percent higher. From a quantitative perspective, the most significant variables explaining internal migration appear to be gender, internal-migration networks, household-head status, and inaccessibility to markets during weather shocks. The probability of internal migration increases by 0.56 percentage points per year of schooling and 0.62 percent per year of age or experience. The most important variables driving international migration from a quantitative perspective are gender, U.S. migration networks, physical capital (tractors, which are a substitute for migrant labor on the farm), and insecurity of market access. The wealth index is statistically significant in explaining migration, but the effect of a change in this variable on the probability of migration to either destination is negligible.

Because the probability of internal migration to farm jobs is very small, none of the variables have a measurable impact on the probability of internal farm labor migration. (All are less than 0.0 and thus are not shown in table 1.6). The majority of internal migrants (more than 95 percent) are employed in nonfarm jobs; thus, the effects of explanatory variables on this destination-sector combination are similar to those on the overall probability of internal migration.

There are more quantitative differences among sectors in the case of international migration. Migration to farm jobs abroad is influenced in a quantitatively important way by gender, international migration networks, and insecurity of market access. However, the effects of these three variables are much larger quantitatively for international migration to nonfarm jobs. The gender variable has a quantitatively larger effect on the probability of international migration to non-farm jobs than on the probability of any other destination-sector combination. Although education has a statistically significant effect on international migration to nonfarm (but not farm) jobs, this effect is quantitatively small—less than 0.02 percent per year of completed schooling. This reflects a low economic return from schooling for migrant workers from rural Mexico in U.S. farm and nonfarm jobs.

Measurement Issues and Unobserved Variables

Some variables may be affected by migration and remittances. This is a difficult methodological problem that bedevils many migration and remittances studies. For example, family investments in education, physical capital, and housing are likely to be affected by the presence of a migrant or the receipt of remittances (see Adams 1991). If the economic value of a skill is higher than the cost of acquiring it, economic logic suggests that an individual should invest in schooling. This calculus may hinge on access to migrant labor markets, which is reflected in household migration history. Individuals who do not view themselves as having a high probability of migration or access to migrant labor markets are likely to use the economic returns to schooling within the village as their reference when making schooling decisions. If returns to schooling are higher in migrant labor markets than in the village, then a positive probability of migrating may stimulate investments in schooling. This is the rationale behind recent research on the so-called "brain gain." If the individual has a positive probability of migrating to a destination where wages are high, but the returns to schooling are low, there may be a disincentive to invest in schooling. This might be the case for unauthorized migration to low-skilled labor markets abroad.

Wealth, tractor ownership, value of landholdings, and education variables are for 2001, the year in which migration decisions are modeled in our analysis. That is, they are predetermined variables. A significant portion of household landholdings are comprised of *ejido*, or reform-sector, parcels distributed to households decades earlier. Nevertheless, it may still be argued that these variables are not truly exogenous, inasmuch as both they and current migration are correlated with past migration decisions. They may be correlated with migration choices over time, in ways that cannot be modeled explicitly using cross-section data.

The main econometric concern surrounding endogeneity is that the inclusion of "contaminated" explanatory variables may bias findings with respect to other explanatory variables in the model. To explore this possibility, we reestimated the model, omitting the explanatory variables most likely to be influenced by past migration behavior: physical assets (proxied by ownership of tractors), wealth (reflecting housing characteristics), the value of landholdings, and family schooling. None of the key results of our analysis change when these variables are excluded from the regressions.[15] One might also argue that migration networks are endogenous. We used migration networks in 1990, 12 years before the survey, as proxies for networks in an effort to minimize this potential bias. Other instruments for migration networks in 2002 were not available.

Unobserved variables also may influence migration decisions. This may bias econometric results if omitted variables are correlated with the included, explanatory variables in the model. Individual-level fixed effects estimation cannot be used to address this problem using cross-sectional data, and there are limitations to the use of fixed effects methods in limited dependent variable models generally (Greene 2004). We reestimated the model using regional dummy variables to control for unobserved regional characteristics that might affect migration decisions. None of our findings changed qualitatively, and the inclusion of location fixed effects resulted in only minor quantitative changes. All things being equal, international migration probabilities tend to be higher and internal migration probabilities tend to be lower in the central and northern regions than in the southern (default) region. The west-central regional dummy variable is significant in explaining international migration to farm jobs, but none of the regional dummy variables is significant in explaining internal migration to farm jobs. We also included distance to the Mexico-U.S. border among the community characteristics in the regression. The coefficient on this variable was just significant at the 0.10 level for internal farm migration but insignificant for all other migration-sector combinations, and the findings with respect to other variables in the model did not change.

Conclusions

The econometric results presented in this chapter indicate that migration is highly selective of individuals, families, and communities. However, this selectivity differs significantly by migrant destination and sector of employment. For example, individuals' schooling has a significant positive effect on internal migration to nonfarm—but not farm—jobs. Schooling has no significant effect on international migration, which usually entails unauthorized entry and work in low-skill labor markets where the returns to schooling obtained in Mexico are likely to be small. Family contacts in the United States significantly affect international migration to both farm and nonfarm jobs. Networks in Mexico significantly affect internal migration, but much less for farm than for nonfarm jobs. Work experience has a significant positive effect on international migration to both farm and nonfarm jobs, but its effect on internal migration is significant only for nonfarm migration. Family landholdings do not significant affect internal migration. However, they have a significant positive effect on international migration to farm jobs. Household wealth has a significant negative effect on internal migration to nonfarm jobs but a positive effect on international migration to both sectors.

A few variables appear to have relatively uniform effects across migration-sector regimes. Schooling of household heads appears to raise the opportunity cost of migrating for other household members. Males are significantly more likely to migrate to all destination-sector combinations than are females. Insecurity of market access during weather shocks uniformly stimulates migration. The presence of nonagricultural enterprises in villages discourages migration but is statistically and quantitatively significant only for internal migration to nonfarm jobs.

Our findings have implications for modeling, theory, and policy. Migration and sector choice are interrelated. The model presented here brings both migration destinations and sectors of migrant employment into an integrated modeling framework. Not only individual but also family and community characteristics are significant in shaping migration. In particular, migrant networks, access to markets, and access risks at the community level influence migration and sector choice. As access to migrant labor markets and market integration in rural Mexico increase, migration patterns are likely to change. Moreover, as market integration and other policies, including U.S. immigration policies, change, the mix of characteristics in rural areas will be affected via the selectivity of migration to different locales and sectors.

The significant effect of network variables in internal and international migration reflects a migration momentum that can be reinforced by legalization and guest worker programs in the United States and policies and events that encourage migration within Mexico. Our findings support the conclusion of several past studies that networks of existing contacts at migrant destinations are key determinants of the magnitude of migration and sector of employment for future migrants (Taylor 1987; Munshi 2003), but there are other key determinants, as well.

We find that, at a local level, there is no evidence that integration with outside markets discourages migration. Other things being equal, the level of transportation infrastructure is positively related to migration, particularly to internal destinations. However, when access to markets outside the village is insecure, migration propensities increase. This is consistent with migration's role as a risk management tool in rural households. In the final analysis, market openness, ceteris paribus, may simply make it easier to migrate, and exposure to market risks may create new migration incentives.

In the short run, market integration and U.S. immigrant legalization policies, which strengthened migration networks, may have accelerated the movement of populations out of rural Mexico. In the long run, the migration of people out of rural areas surely will continue in Mexico, as it has in virtually all countries experiencing income growth. The selectivity of migration on specific variables suggests that changes in the magnitude and patterns of migration will alter the characteristics of rural households and communities over time.

Endnotes

1. The ENHRUM survey assembled complete migration histories from 1980 through 2002 for (a) the household head, (b) the spouse of the head, (c) all individuals who lived in the household three months or more in 2002, and (d) a random sample of sons and daughters of either the head or his/her spouse who lived outside the household longer than three months in 2002. The size of both villager and migrant populations in the synthetic cohorts created using retrospective data is biased downward as one goes back in time, because as individuals die, they are removed from the population and thus are not available to be counted in 2003. Permanent migration does not pose a problem, because information about migrants was provided by other family members in the village. In the relatively rare case in which entire families migrated, overall migration estimates may be biased downward; however, it is not clear whether this would produce an upward or downward bias in the *slope* of the migration trend.

2. The Mexico-born population in the United States increased from 6.7 million to 10.6 million between 1990 and 2000 (Chiquiar and Hanson 2005).

3. These include sociodemographic surveys by the Mexico Migration Project (MMP) (Population Studies Center, University of Pennsylvania, Philadelphia; www.pop.upenn.edu/mexmig/welcome.html) and various economic surveys of communities conducted in the 1980s and 1990s by the University of California, Davis, and El Colegio de Mexico (Taylor 1986, 1987; Taylor and Yúnez-Naude 2000). Although households were sampled randomly within villages, selection of villages was not random and the surveys spanned a number of years. MMP surveys tend to focus on relatively high-migration communities in central Mexico.

4. In one of his classic papers, Mundell (1957) shows that trade and migration are substitutes in the Heckscher-Ohlin model. More recent papers have used a variety of models and have reached different conclusions. Markusen (1983) examines variants of the Heckscher-Ohlin model and finds that the two variables are complements. López and Schiff (1998) find that they are substitutes (complements) in the case of skilled (unskilled) labor. Ethier (1996) and Schiff (1996) review some of the literature's findings on substitution and complementarity.

5. Some variables, for example, education, also may affect household attitudes and tastes.

6. Although most Mexican migration is to nonfarm jobs, as mentioned previously, the majority of U.S. farm jobs are filled by Mexican workers. This is a not contradiction; agriculture accounts for a small share of total U.S. employment.

7. Note that, although treating the number of trips in categories might pose a problem in general, it does not have a perverse effect in the current case.

8. The total nonfarm payroll in Mexico increased by 73 percent from 1990 through 2001 in real terms, while the farm payroll decreased by 5.2 percent (INEGI 2003).

9. The Current Population Survey shows that there were a total of 9.82 million Mexicans in the United States in 2002. In that same year, the population of Mexico was estimated at 103 million. This means that approximately 9 percent of all Mexicans were living in the United States.

10. We also estimated a two-choice probit with identical qualitative results.

11. Most (but not all) household heads in the sample are married, but most married individuals in the sample are not heads of households. This is because the sample includes all sons and daughters of either the household head or his/her spouse. Taken together, the findings on the household head and marital status variables indicate that, other things (including marital status) being equal, household heads are significantly more likely to migrate than non-heads-of-household. Also, other things (including status as a household head) being equal, married individuals are more likely to engage in migration. Descriptive statistics (not shown) reveal that most household heads do not migrate.

12. The result on networks might be subject to an endogeneity problem. The two migration network indicators we used are for 1990, that is, measured with a 13-year lag. This was done under the assumption that it would help resolve (part of) the endogeneity problem, with the 'part' depending on the degree of serial correlation of the two indicators. Although a better alternative might have been to estimate a dynamic model, we do not have the data to do that (although we should after the household survey's second round).

13. We experimented with other proxies for market access, including distance to the nearest commercial center and quality of roads, but these variables were not found to be statistically significant.

14. It is important to remember the units in which variables are measured when comparing impacts of changes in variables on migration probabilities. In general, one would expect to find quantitatively larger effects of dummy variables, such as inaccessibility during weather shocks or gender, which take on a value of 0 or 1, than of variables that can take on a larger range of values like frequency of transport (0 to 24) and age (12 to 100).

15. When all of these variables are excluded, the nonagricultural enterprise dummy becomes statistically significant in the internal farm migration equation and, in the U.S. farm migration equation, the marital status dummy becomes insignificant while the number of males older than 15 becomes significant. There are no other qualitative changes and only minimal quantitative changes.

References

Adams, Jr., Richard H. 1991. "The Effects of International Remittances on Poverty, Inequality and Development in Rural Egypt." Research Report, no. 86. International Food Policy Research Institute, Washington DC.

———. 2003. "International Migration, Remittances and the Brain Drain: A Study of 24 Labor-Exporting Countries." World Bank Policy Research Working Paper, no. 3069, June. World Bank, Washington, DC.

Barham, Bradford, and Stephen Boucher. 1998. "Migration, Remittances, and Inequality: Estimating the Net Effects of Migration on Income Distribution," *Journal of Development Economics* 55(2): 307–31.

Becker, G.S. 1975. *Human Capital*, 2nd edition. New York: Columbia University Press.

Chiquiar, D., and G. H. Hanson. 2005. "International Migration, Self-Selection, and the Distribution of Wages: Evidence from Mexico and the United States." *Journal of Political Economy* 113(2): 239–81.

Emerson, Robert D. 1989. "Migratory Labor and Agriculture." *American Journal of Agricultural Economics* 71(3): 617–629.

ENHRUM (*Encuesta Nacional a Hogares Rurales de México*). 2003.

Ethier, Wilfred J. 1996. "Theories about Trade Liberalisation and Migration: Substitutes or Complements?" In *International Trade and Migration in the APEC Region*, ed. P.J. Lloyd and L.S. Williams, 50–68. New York: Oxford University Press.

Greene, W. 2004. "The Behaviour of the Maximum Likelihood Estimator of Limited Dependent Variable Models in the Presence of Fixed Effects." *Econometric Journal* 7(1): 98–119.

Hinojosa-Ojeda, R., and S. Robinson. 1992. "Labor Issues in a North American Free Trade Area." In *North American Free Trade: Assessing the Impact*, ed. N. Lustig, B. Bosworth and R. Lawrence. Washington, DC: Brookings Institution.

INEGI (*Instituto Nacional de Estadística, Geografía e Informática*). 2003. "Anuario estadistico de los Estados Unidos Mexicanos."

Levy, S., and S. Wijnberger. 1992. "Mexican Agriculture in the Free Trade Agreement: Transition Problems in Economic Reform." OECD/Gd(92) 77 Technical Paper, no. 63. Organisation for Economic Co-operation and Development, Paris.

López, R., and M. Schiff. 1998. "Migration and the Skill Composition of the Labor Force: The Impact of Trade Liberalization." *Canadian Journal of Economics* 31(2): 318–36.

Lucas, R.E.B., and O. Stark 1985. "Motivations to Remit: Evidence from Botswana." *Journal of Political Economy* 93(5): 901–18.

Markusen, J.R. 1983. "Factor Movements and Commodity Trade as Complements." *Journal of International Economics* 14(3–4): 341–56.

Martin, P.L. 1993. *Trade and Migration: NAFTA and Agriculture*. Washington, DC: Institute for International Economics.

Massey, Douglas S., Rafael Alarcón, Jorge Durand, and Humberto González. 1987. *Return to Aztlan: The Social Process of International Migration from Western Mexico*. Berkeley and Los Angeles: University of California Press.

Massey, D. S., J. Arango, G. Hugo, A. Kouaouci, A. Pellegrino, and J.E. Taylor. 1993. "Theories of International Migration: An Integration and Appraisal." *Population and Development Review* 19(3): 431–66.

McKenzie, David, and Hillel Rapoport. 2004. "Network Effects and the Dynamics of Migration and Inequality: Theory and Evidence from Mexico." BREAD Working Paper, no. 063, April (http://www.cid.harvard.edu/bread/papers/working/063.pdf). Bureau for Research in Economic Analysis of Development, Boston.

Mincer, Jacob. 1974. *Schooling, Experience, and Earnings*. New York: Columbia University Press.

Mundell, Robert A. 1957. "International Trade and Factor Mobility." *The American Economic Review* 47(3): 321–35.

Munshi, Kaivan. 2003. "Networks in the Modern Economy: Mexican Migrants in the U.S. Labor Market." *Quarterly Journal of Economics* 18(2): 549–99.

Perloff, J.M., L. Lynch, and S.M. Gabbard. 1998. "Migration of Seasonal Agricultural Workers." *American Journal of Agricultural Economics* 80(1): 154–64.

Schiff, Maurice. 1996. "Trade Policy and International Migration: Substitutes or Complements?" In *Development Strategy, Employment and Migration: Insights from Models*, ed. J.E. Taylor. Paris: Organisation for Economic Co-operation and Development.

Stark, O., and J.E. Taylor. 1989. "Relative Deprivation and International Migration." *Demography* 26: 1–14.

———. 1991. "Migration Incentives, Migration Types: The Role of Relative Deprivation." *The Economic Journal* 101(408): 1163–78.

Taylor, J.E. 1986. "Differential Migration, Networks, Information and Risk." In *Migration Theory, Human Capital and Development*, ed. O. Stark, 147–71. Greenwich, CT: JAI Press.

———. 1987. "Undocumented Mexico-U.S. Migration and the Returns to Households in Rural Mexico." *American Journal of Agricultural Economics* 69: 626–38.

———. 1992. "Earnings and Mobility of Legal and Illegal Immigrant Workers in Agriculture," *American Journal of Agricultural Economics* 74(4): 889–896.

Taylor J.E., and Yúnez-Naude. 2000. "The Returns from Schooling in a Diversified Rural Economy." *American Journal of Agricultural Economics* 82(2): 287–97.

Todaro, Michael P. 1969. "A Model of Migration and Urban Unemployment in Less-Developed Countries." *The American Economic Review* 59(1): 138–48.

United States Department of Labor. 1991. Findings from the National Agricultural Workers Survey (NAWS) 1990: A Demographic and Employment Profile of Perishable Crop Farm Workers. Office of the Assistant Secretary for Policy, Program Economics, Research Report no. 8. Washington, DC

———. 2000. Findings from the National Agricultural Workers Survey (NAWS) 1997–1998: A Demographic and Employment Profile of United States Farmworkers. Office of the Assistant Secretary for Policy, Office of Program Economics, Research Report no. 8. Washington, DC

Vijverberg, W.P.M. 1995. "Dual Selection Criteria with Multiple Alternatives: Migration, Work Status and Wages." *International Economic Review* 36(1): 159–85.

2

REMITTANCES, POVERTY, AND INVESTMENT IN GUATEMALA

Richard H. Adams, Jr.

Introduction

In the developing world, internal and international migrants tend to remit or send a sizeable portion of their increased income earnings to families back home. Yet despite the ever-increasing size of these internal and international remittances,[1] little attention has been paid to analyzing the impact of these financial transfers on poverty and investment in the developing world. Three factors seem to be responsible for this lacuna. The first is an absence of remittances data: few household surveys collect useful data on the size of remittance transfers to households in origin communities. The second is a lack of poverty data: it is quite difficult to estimate accurate poverty levels in developing countries. The final factor relates to how remittances are spent or used. In the past, many researchers and policy makers have assumed that households spend most of their remittance income on consumption, with only a small fraction of such income being spent on investment.[2]

This chapter analyzes the impact of internal and international remittances on poverty and investment in one developing country: Guatemala.[3] Guatemala represents a good case study because it produces a large number of internal migrants (to urban areas) and international migrants (to the United States). The presence of a new, detailed nationally representative household survey in Guatemala makes it possible to analyze the impact of these two types of remittances in that country.

At the outset, it should be noted that any effort to examine the impact of remittances (internal or international) on poverty and investment involves several important methodological issues. On the one hand, it is possible to treat remittances as a simple exogenous transfer of income by migrants. When treated as an exogenous transfer, the economic question is as follows: How do remittances, in total or at the margin, affect the observed level of poverty or investment in a developing country?[4] On the other hand, it is also possible to treat remittances as a potential substitute for domestic (home) earnings. When treated as a potential substitute for home earnings, the economic question is as follows: How does the observed level of poverty or investment in a country compare with a counterfactual scenario without migration and remittances but including an imputation for the home earnings of migrants had those people stayed and worked at home? This latter treatment seems to represent the more interesting (and challenging) economic question because it compares poverty and investment in a country with and without remittances.[5]

One of the unique contributions of this chapter is that it develops counterfactual income estimates for migrant and nonmigrant households by using econometric estimations to predict the incomes of households with and without remittances. However, this approach has its own methodological difficulties. Most notably, the attempt to predict (estimate) the incomes of migrant households on the basis of the observed incomes of nonmigrant households becomes problematic if the two groups of households differ systematically in their expected incomes. In other words, if migrant and nonmigrant households differ systematically in their characteristics, there will be selection bias in any estimates of income that are based on nonmigrant households. To test for this possible selection bias, this chapter employs a Heckman-type selection correction procedure, where the selection rules model the decision of the household to produce migrants and receive remittances using a multinomial logit-ordinary least squares (OLS) two-stage estimation of income.

The chapter includes eight sections. The first section presents the data set. The second and third sections operationalize and estimate a two-stage Heckman-type selection model to test for sample selection bias. The results of these sections suggest that the subsample of nonmigrant households is randomly selected from the population and that therefore the bias resulting from estimating predicted income equations using OLS without selection controls would be small. The fourth and fifth sections discuss how counterfactual income estimates for households can be developed by using predicted income equations to identify the incomes of households with and without remittances. These sections find that both internal and international remittances reduce the level, depth, and severity of poverty in Guatemala. Turning to the analysis of how remittances are spent or used, the sixth and seventh sections develop and estimate a model for examining the marginal expenditure patterns of households on consumption and investment. The results show that at the margin households receiving remittances spend less on consumption goods—food—and more on investment—education and housing— than do households receiving no remittances. The final section summarizes the main findings.

Data

Data for the study come from a national household survey conducted by the Instituto Nacional de Estadistica in Guatemala (INEG) during the period July to December 2000.[6] The survey included 7,276 urban and rural households and was designed to be statistically representative at the national level and for urban and rural areas. The survey was comprehensive, collecting detailed information on a wide range of topics, including income, expenditure, education, financial assets, and remittances.[7]

It should, however, be emphasized that this survey was not designed as a migration or remittances survey. In fact, the survey collected limited information on these topics. With respect to migration, the survey collected no information on the characteristics of the individual migrant: age, education, income earned outside the home, or length of time away. This means that no data are available on the characteristics of migrants—either remitting or nonremitting migrants—who are currently living outside of the household. With respect to remittances, the survey only asked three basic questions: (a) Does your household receive remittances from family or friends? (b) Where do the people sending remittances live?[8] and (c) How much (remittance) money did your household receive in the past 12 months? While the lack of data on individual migrant characteristics is unfortunate, the presence of detailed information on household income and expenditure makes it possible to use responses to these three questions to examine the impact of remittances on poverty in Guatemala.

Table 2.1 presents summary data from the survey. This table shows that 5,665 households (77.8 percent of all households) received no remittances, 1,063 households (14.6 percent) received internal remittances (from Guatemala), and 593 households (8.1 percent) received international remittances (from the United States). According to the data, 88 households received internal and international remittances and these 88 households are counted in both columns of remittance-receivers in table 2.1.[9]

The data in table 2.1 reveal several interesting contrasts among the three groups of households, that is, those receiving no remittances, those receiving internal remittances (from Guatemala), and those receiving international remittances (from the United States). On average, when compared with nonremittance households, households receiving remittances (internal or international) have more members with secondary education, older household heads, fewer children under age 5, and more wealth (value of house). In a broad sense, these findings tend to accord with human capital theory, which suggests that educated people are more likely to migrate because educated people enjoy greater employment and income opportunities in destination areas.

TABLE 2.1   Summary Data on Nonremittance Households and Remittance-Receiving Households, Guatemala, 2000

Variable	Receive no remittances	Receive internal remittances (from Guatemala)	Receive international remittances (from the United States)	t-test (no remittances versus internal remittances)	t-test (no remittances versus international remittances)
Human Capital					
Number of members over age 15 with primary education	1.18 (1.11)	1.08 (1.15)	1.18 (1.13)	3.51**	—
Number of members over age 15 with secondary education	0.46 (0.85)	0.59 (0.94)	0.69 (1.06)	-4.67**	-7.32**
Number of members over age 15 with university education	0.15 (0.52)	0.17 (0.55)	0.14 (0.46)	-2.54**	-0.19
Parents' education					
Father's years of schooling	4.46 (4.32)	3.88 (4.23)	4.05 (4.09)	3.14**	0.96
Mother's years of schooling	3.40 (3.97)	3.40 (4.22)	3.58 (3.88)	—	3.30**
Household Characteristics					
Age of household head (years)	42.74 (14.24)	50.96 (16.66)	48.34 (16.12)	-17.03**	-9.32**
Household size	5.32 (2.46)	4.74 (2.69)	5.18 (2.68)	6.50**	0.52

Number of males over age 15	1.35	1.19	1.21	6.67**	3.52**
	(0.84)	(0.98)	(1.00)		
Number of females over age 15	1.42	1.59	1.65	−7.18**	−7.73**
	(0.80)	(0.91)	(0.92)		
Number of children under age 5	0.88	0.62	0.69	8.14**	5.49**
	(0.96)	(0.89)	(0.96)		
Networks					
Head of household is nonindigenous (1 = yes)	0.59	0.67	0.68	−5.62**	−5.86**
	(0.49)	(0.47)	(0.46)		
Wealth					
Value of house (quetzals)	3,906.08	4,802.16	4,691.63	−4.82**	−3.69**
	(7,963.60)	(7,364.90)	(5,840.0)		
Area					
Area (1 = urban, 2 = rural)	1.58	1.49	1.52	6.51**	5.02**
	(0.49)	(0.50)	(0.49)		
N	5,665	1,063	593	—	—

Source: ENCOVI 2000.

Note: N = 7,276 households; 88 households receive both internal remittances (from Guatemala) and international remittances (from the United States). All values are weighted; standard deviations are in parentheses. In 2000, 1 Guatemalan quetzal = US$0.128. —denotes not available.

* significant at the 0.05 level. ** significant at the 0.01 level.

An Econometric Model of Household Incomes with Selection Controls

It is possible to construct a counterfactual scenario without migration and remittances by treating households with no remittances as a random draw from the population, estimating a mean regression of incomes for these nonremittance households, and then using the resulting parameter estimates to predict the incomes of households with internal and international remittances. This approach becomes problematic, however, if households with and without remittances differ systematically in their incomes, because then the regression results will be biased. The purpose of this section is to examine the extent of selection bias, if any, using a multinomial logit-OLS two-stage selection control model.

To operationalize such a model, it is necessary to identify variables that are distinct for migration and the receipt of remittances in the first-stage equation, and for the determination of household income in the second-stage equation. The model is identifiable if there is at least one independent variable in the first-stage choice function that is not in the second-stage income function. Factors that affect migration and the receipt of remittances in the choice function, but do not affect household income in the income function, would then identify the model.

The first-stage choice function of the probability of a household that has a migrant and receives remittances can be estimated as follows.

Prob (Y = migration and receive remittances) = f [Human Capital (Number of household members with preparatory, primary, secondary or university education), Household Characteristics (Age of household head, Household size, Number of males or females over age 15), Migration Network, Household Wealth (Value of house)]   (2.1)

The rationale for including these variables in the choice equation follows the standard literature on migration and remittances. According to the basic human capital model, human capital variables are likely to affect migration, because better educated people enjoy greater employment and expected income-earning possibilities in destination areas (Todaro 1976; Schultz 1982).[10] In the literature, household characteristics—such as age of household head and number of male and female members—are also hypothesized to affect the probability of migration. In particular, some analysts (Lipton 1980; Adams, 1993) have suggested that migration is a life-cycle event in which households with older heads and more males and females over age 15 are more likely to participate. With respect to networks, the sociological literature has stressed the importance of family and village networks in encouraging migration (Massey 1987; Massey, Goldring, and

Durand 1994). Because nonindigenous people in Guatemala have a longer tradition of migration and stronger migration networks in destination communities (especially in the United States), equation 2.1 hypothesizes that households with a nonindigenous head will be more likely to produce migrants and receive remittances. Finally, because of the significant initial costs in financing migration, the economic literature often suggests that households with more wealth are likely to produce migrants (Barham and Boucher 1998; Lanzona 1998). The choice function in equation 2.1 therefore includes a wealth variable—value of house and value of house squared—with the expectation that middle-wealth households will have the highest probability of producing migrants and receiving remittances.

The second-stage income function can be estimated as follows.

$$\text{Household income} = g\,[\text{Human capital (Number of household members}$$
$$\text{with secondary or university education), Household Characteristics (Age}$$
$$\text{of household head, Household size, Number of males or females over}$$
$$\text{age 15), Ethnic Variable]} \qquad (2.2)$$

In equation 2.2, one of the household characteristic variables—age of household head—will identify the model. In other words, it is hypothesized that age of household head will affect household migration and the receipt of remittances, but that it will not have an impact on household income.[11] The reasoning for this is as follows. According to the literature, households with older heads are likely to produce more migrants because they have more household members in the "prime age span" for migration: ages 15 to 30. However, in equation 2.2 households with older heads are not expected to receive more income because, although income generally increases with level of education, older household heads in Guatemala tend to be less educated.

Estimating the Econometric Model with Selection Controls

Table 2.2 shows the regression coefficients and t-values from estimating the first-stage choice function. Several of the outcomes are unexpected. For internal remittances, there is a slight tendency for households with more educated members to have a higher propensity to receive internal remittances. However, for international remittances, no such tendency exists: the results suggest that households with the lowest level of education—preparatory education—actually have the highest propensity to receive remittances. Moreover, for internal and international remittances, the coefficients for the highest level of education—university education—are

TABLE 2.2   Multinomial Logit Model for Guatemala

Variable	Receive internal remittances (from Guatemala)	Receive international remittances (from the United States)
Human capital		
Number of members over age 15 with preparatory education	−0.216 (−0.83)	0.620 (3.70)**
Number of members over age 15 with primary education	0.057 (1.21)	0.169 (2.94)**
Number of members over age 15 with secondary education	0.174 (3.20)**	0.336 (5.34)**
Number of members over age 15 with university education	−0.009 (−0.11)	−0.051 (−0.46)
Household characteristics		
Age of household head	0.034 (12.84)**	0.292 (8.97)**
Household size	−0.043 (−2.07)*	0.037 (1.52)
Number of males over age 15	−0.442 (−6.83)**	−0.588 (−7.54)**
Number of females over age 15	0.143 (2.23)*	−0.048 (−0.65)
Networks		
Head of household is nonindigenous (1=Yes)	0.171 (2.06)*	0.194 (1.96)*
Wealth		
Value of house	0.001 (1.85)	0.001 (4.46)**
Value of house squared	−0.001 (−2.12)*	−0.001 (−4.05)**
Constant	−3.144 (−19.60)**	−3.792 (−19.76)**
Log likelihood	−4,560.71	
Restricted log likelihood	−4,831.25	
Chi−squared (22)	541.08	
Significance level	0.000	
N	7,276	

Source: Calculated from ENCOVI 2000.

Note: Figures in parentheses are t-values.

* significant at the 0.05 level, ** significant at the 0.01 level.

negative and statistically insignificant. In other words, the most educated households in Guatemala are not receiving more remittances because the relationship among education, migration, and remittances is not the strong, positive one hypothesized by human capital theory.

Table 2.3 presents results for the OLS and the sample selection-corrected household income estimates. Many of the coefficients have the expected sign. As hypothesized, the coefficient for age of household head is statistically insignificant in all cases, meaning that this variable has no effect on household income. Also as hypothesized, the coefficients for number of household members with secondary or university education are positive and usually highly significant.

The most important finding in table 2.3 is that the two selection control variables are statistically insignificant. The insignificant t-values on the selection control variables, and the fact that the other coefficient estimates in the table are generally similar in the two specifications, suggest that the subsample of nonmigrant households is randomly selected from the population. This means that, under the assumptions imposed, the bias resulting from estimating the equations by OLS without selection controls would be small.[12]

This finding of "no selection bias" is similar to the one reported by Barham and Boucher (1998) in their examination of selection bias among migrant households in Nicaragua. However, because this finding runs contrary to the common assumption in the literature that migrants are a "select" group (with respect to education, income, skill),[13] it is important to list some of the reasons for this no selection bias finding in Guatemala, two of which are provided below.

The first reason for the finding has already been broached, namely, that households receiving internal and international remittances in Guatemala are not positively selected with respect to education.[14] The results of the choice function model in table 2.2 show that households with the most educated members—university education—do not have the highest propensity to receive remittances. The second reason for the no-selection-bias finding relates to the nature of the data set. The Guatemala data are based on information collected from households in a labor-sending country, and thus they include data on households that are producing legal and illegal international migrants. It is likely that illegal international migrants come from poorer and less educated households than legal international migrants. As Taylor (1987) found for Mexico, many illegal migrants from Guatemala work in low-skill, low-income jobs in the United States, which are not attractive to members of wealthier and more educated households. For this reason, any study—like the present one—that includes information on legal and illegal migrants (and their remittances) is less likely to find selection bias than studies that are confined to legal migrants (and their remittances). In other words,

TABLE 2.3 Household Income Estimates (Selection Corrected) for Guatemala

Variable	Receive internal remittances[a]		Receive international remittances	
	OLS	Selection corrected	OLS	Selection corrected
Number of members over age 15 with secondary education	1,749.558 (6.64)**	1,641.541 (4.57)**	1,316.405 (2.78)**	939.245 (1.36)
Number of members over age 15 with university education	5,263.583 (12.57)**	6,220.215 (13.91)**	5,215.057 (5.78)**	6,933.377 (6.03)**
Age of household head	−30.548 (−1.07)	−68.026 (−1.04)	3.590 (0.13)	−8.081 (−0.16)
Household size	−933.157 (−7.01)**	−1,022.448 (−6.18)**	−985.309 (−4.11)**	−1,236.357 (−4.06)**
Number of males over age 15	631.744 (2.13)*	1,123.712 (1.39)	599.205 (1.02)	1,216.985 (1.25)
Number of females over age 15	55.971 (0.16)	543.890 (1.17)	−562.313 (0.88)	−980.547 (−1.18)
Head of household is nonindigenous (1=Yes)	2,658.155 (5.46)**	2,337.357 (3.85)**	1,985.362 (2.05)*	1,431.718 (1.05)
Lambda (Selection control)	—	−2,290.172 (−0.47)	—	−1,508.352 (−0.37)
Constant	7,762.936 (1.05)	12,650.837 (1.23)	8,755.980 (1.11)	13,996.067 (1.42)
Adjusted R^2	0.279	0.317	0.157	0.133
F−test	59.72	57.62	15.60	12.34
N	1,063	1,063	593	593

Source: Calculated from ENCOVI 2000.

Note: Dependent variable is annual per capita household income (excluding remittances). All values are weighted. Figures in parentheses are t-values. OLS = ordinary least squares.

a. From Guatemala

b. From the United States

* significant at the 0.05 level, ** significant at the 0.01 level.

including illegal international migrants in the data set reduces the likelihood that migrants are positively selected with respect to income, education, or skill.

Estimating Predicted Income Functions for the No-Migration/Remittance Counterfactual

This section discusses how counterfactual income estimates for households in the no-migration/remittance situation can be developed by using predicted income equations to identify the incomes of households with and without remittances. These counterfactual income estimates can be developed by using the following three-step procedure. First, the parameters predicting per capita household expenditure (excluding remittances) are estimated from the 5,665 households that do not receive remittances. The results of the preceding section showed that these parameters can be reliably estimated, without significant selection bias, from the 5,665 households not receiving remittances using OLS. Second, the parameters estimated from the 5,665 households with no remittances are applied to the 1,063 households that receive internal remittances (from Guatemala). Third, the parameters from the 5,665 households with no remittances are applied to the 593 households that receive international remittances (from the United States). This enables us to predict per capita household expenditures in the excluding remittances situation for the three groups of households: those receiving no remittances, those receiving internal remittances, and those receiving international remittances.

Given the data at hand, it can be hypothesized that per capita household expenditure (excluding remittances) in Guatemala can be predicted as the function of the following variables.

$$PREX_i = \alpha_0 + \alpha_1 EDPREP_i + \alpha_2 EDPRIM_i + \alpha_3 EDSEC_i + \alpha_4 EDUNIV_i$$
$$+ \alpha_5 SCHF_i + \alpha_6 SCHM_i + \alpha_7 HS_i$$
$$+ \alpha_8 MALE15_i + \alpha_9 FEM15_i + \alpha_{10}CHILD5_i$$
$$+ \alpha_{11}NON\_IND_i + \alpha_{12} AR_i + \sum_{j=1}^{7} \beta_{ij}REG_{ij} + \varepsilon_i \qquad (2.3)$$

where for household i, PREX is per capita household expenditure (excluding remittances),[15] EDPREP is the number of household members over age 15 with preparatory education, EDPRIM is the number of household members over age 15 with primary education, EDSEC is the number of household members over age 15 with secondary education, EDUNIV is the number of household members over age 15 with higher (university) education, SCHF is years of schooling of father, SCHM is years of schooling of mother, HS is household size, MALE15 is number of males in household over age 15, FEM15 is number of females in household over age 15, CHILD5 is number of children in household under age 5, NON_IND is head of household is nonindigenous (1 if yes, otherwise 0), AR is area of residence (one if urban, 2 if rural), and REG is seven regional dummy variables (with metropolitan region omitted).

It is important to discuss the reasons for including each of the regressors in equation 2.3. Following the logic of the previous section, four human capital and two parental education variables are included in the model. It is expected that each of these variables will be positive and significant. Four household characteristic variables also appear in the model. The household size variable captures the impact of family size on household expenditure and is expected to be negative. The other three household characteristic variables relate to the life-cycle factors discussed above: it is expected that the first two of these variables will have a positive impact on household expenditure and that the child variable will have a negative impact. Because ethnicity of the household is likely to affect household expenditures, an ethnic variable—1 if head of household is nonindigenous—is included in equation 2.3. Finally, in developing countries like Guatemala, average household expenditures are generally larger in urban than rural areas. For this reason, an area variable (1 if urban, 2 if rural) is included in the model; this variable is expected to have a negative sign.[16]

Table 2.4 reports the results obtained from using equation 2.3 to predict per capita household expenditure (excluding remittances). While many of the coefficients have the right sign and level of significance, several of the outcomes are unexpected. For example, with respect to human capital, the findings show that only the highest level of education—university education—has a positive and significant impact on household expenditure. This unexpected result suggests that returns to education in the local employment market are rather low (and possibly negative) for the lowest levels of education, such as primary education.[17] Similarly, although the level of schooling of the father has the expected positive and significant impact on household expenditure, the level of schooling of the mother does not. The latter outcome probably reflects both the low average level of schooling for the mother, as well as the rather limited job- and income-earning opportunities for older, uneducated women in Guatemala.

The parameter results from table 2.4 can be used to predict per capita household expenditure in the excluding remittances situation for the three groups of households: (a) those receiving no remittances, (b) those receiving internal remittances (from Guatemala), and (c) those receiving international remittances (from the United States).

TABLE 2.4   Regression to Estimate Predicted Per Capita Household Expenditure (Excluding Remittances)

Variable	Regression coefficient	t-ratio
Human capital		
Number of members over age 15 with preparatory education	−434.39	−1.04
Number of members over age 15 with primary education	−656.36	−5.57**
Number of members over age 15 with secondary education	−64.67	−0.41
Number of members over age 15 with university education	3,466.38	13.14**
Parents' education		
Father's years of schooling	610.53	18.59**
Mother's years of schooling	−89.80	−2.93**
Household characteristics		
Household size	−739.59	−13.06**
Number of males over age 15	303.56	1.93
Number of females over age 15	366.51	2.32*
Number of children under age 5	−781.66	−6.79**
Ethnicity		
Head of household is nonindigenous (1=Yes)	1,236.37	6.02**
Area		
Area (1 = urban, 2 = rural)	−1,429.23	−7.08**
Constant	14,566.37	29.43**
Adj. R^2 = 0.471		
F-statistic = 264.24		

Source: Calculated from ENCOVI 2000.

Note: Regression is based on those 5,665 households that receive no remittances. The parameters are used to predict per capita household expenditures (excluding remittances) for households that receive internal remittances (from Guatemala) or international remittances (from the United States). Seven regional dummy variables are included in the equation, but not reported in the table.

* significant at the 0.05 level, ** significant at the 0.01 level.

Once counterfactual household expenditures have been predicted for the three groups of households in the excluding remittances situation, household expenditures in the including remittances situation can be calculated as follows. First, for those households receiving internal or international remittances, the predicted income contribution of the migrant as estimated from equation 2.3 can be set to 0. Second, the actual amounts of internal or international remittances received by households from migrants can be added to the level of household expenditures. For households receiving remittances, these internal and international remittances average 1,431.4 and 2,259.2 quetzals per capita per year, respectively.

Table 2.5 summarizes our efforts to predict per capita household expenditure for the three groups of households in the two situations: (a) excluding remittances and (b) including remittances. Three key findings emerge from this table. First, when predicted equations are used to impute the home (domestic) earnings of migrants, households receiving remittances are richer than households not receiving remittances. Because migration, especially international migration, can be a costly endeavor, it is perhaps logical that migration represents a more viable option for households with more income (expenditure). However, the second finding from table 2.5 tends to bring a cautionary note to the preceding finding. Although migration may have its costs, it is rather paradoxical to note that, in the excluding remittances situation, households receiving internal remittances have higher mean incomes (expenditures) than do households receiving international remittances. Because internal migration should generally be less expensive than international migration, this outcome is unexpected. Perhaps the best explanation for this paradoxical outcome is that, while migration may have its costs, the economic costs of migration are not the only factor "explaining" the willingness of people to work in another place. The final finding in table 2.5 is quite expected, namely that remittances greatly increase the level of household expenditure. In the including remittances situation, the average level of expenditures for households receiving internal and international remittances is 37.1 and 39.5 percent higher, respectively, than that for households not receiving remittances.

Remittances and Poverty

Now that per capita household expenditures have been predicted in the two situations—excluding and including remittances—for the three groups of households, it is possible to examine the impact of these financial transfers on poverty in Guatemala. This is done in table 2.6.

Table 2.6 is based on the World Bank poverty line for Guatemala in 2000 of 4,319 quetzels per person per year.[18] Table 2.6 reports three different poverty measures using this poverty line. The first measure—poverty headcount—shows the percent of the population living beneath the poverty line. The second measure—poverty gap—focuses on the depth of poverty by showing in percentage terms how far the average expenditures of the poor fall short of the poverty line. The third poverty measure—squared poverty gap—indicates the severity of poverty. The squared poverty gap index possesses useful analytical properties, because it is sensitive to changes in distribution among the poor.

TABLE 2.5   Predicted Per Capita Expenditures for Nonremittance Households and Remittance-Receiving Households, Guatemala, 2000

	Receive no remittances	Receive internal remittances (from Guatemala)	Receive international remittances (from the United States)	Percent change (no remittances versus internal remittances)	Percent change (no remittances versus international remittances)
			(in quetzals)		
Predicted mean annual per capita expenditures (excluding remittances)	7,399.26	8,710.49	8,062.03	+17.72	+8.95
Predicted mean annual per capita expenditures (including remittances)	7,399.26	10,141.88	10,321.26	+37.06	+39.49
N	5,665	1,063	593		

Source: Calculated from ENCOVI 2000.

Note: N = 7,276 households; 88 households receive both internal remittances (from Guatemala) and international remittances (from the United States). All values are predicted from equation 2.3; see text. All values are weighted. In 2000, 1 Guatemalan quetzal = US$0.128.

Columns (1)–(4) of table 2.6 report the results for the different poverty measures when remittances are excluded or included in predicted household expenditure. With only one exception, the various poverty measures show that the inclusion of remittances—either internal or international—in household expenditure reduces the level, depth, and severity of poverty in Guatemala. However, the size of the poverty reduction greatly depends on how poverty is measured. According to the poverty headcount measure, including internal remittances in household expenditure reduces the level of poverty by only 1 percent and including international remittances in such expenditure actually increases the level of poverty by 1.6 percent. However, poverty is reduced much more when measured by indicators focusing on the depth and severity of poverty, such as the poverty gap and squared poverty gap. For example, the squared poverty gap measure shows that including internal or international remittances in household expenditure reduces poverty by 23.5 or 21.9 percent, respectively. In other words, including remittances—internal or international—in household expenditure has a greater impact on reducing the severity of poverty in Guatemala than it does on reducing the proportion of people living in poverty.

Columns (1) to (4) of table 2.6 reveal that the inclusion of internal or international remittances in household expenditure has little impact on income inequality, as measured by the Gini coefficient.[19] With the receipt of either internal or international remittances, inequality remains relatively stable with a Gini coefficient of about 0.50. This means that most of the poverty-reducing effect of remittances in Guatemala comes from increases in mean household income (expenditure) rather than from any progressive change in income inequality caused by these income flows.

Remittances and Investment: Selecting a Functional Form for Analysis

This section examines how internal and international remittances are spent or used in Guatemala. To do this, it is necessary to compare the marginal spending behavior for the three groups of households on six different categories of expenditure: food,[20] consumer goods/durables, housing, education, health, and other. The goal is to see whether households receiving internal or international remittances spend their income differently from those households that do not receive remittances.

It is necessary to choose a proper functional form to analyze the marginal spending behavior of these different groups of households. The selected functional form must do several things. First, it should provide a good statistical fit to household expenditure on a wide range of goods. Second, because of the focus on expenditure-consumption relationships, the chosen form must have a slope that

TABLE 2.6 Effect of Remittances on Poverty for Nonremittance-Receiving and Remittance-Receiving Households, Guatemala, 2000

	Receive no remittances (1)	Receive internal remittances (from Guatemala) (2)	Receive international remittances (from the United States) (3)	Receive internal and international remittances (4)	% change (no remittances versus internal remittances) (5)	% change (no remittances versus international remittances) (6)	% change (no remittances vs. internal and international remittances) (7)
Poverty headcount (percent)	55.28	54.74	56.19	54.17	(−0.98)	+1.65	(−2.01)
Poverty gap (percent)	25.89	23.63	22.62	24.95	(−8.73)	(−12.64)	(−3.64)
Squared poverty gap (percent)	18.82	14.40	14.69	17.43	(−23.49)	(−21.95)	(−7.39)
Gini coefficient	0.505	0.490	0.486	0.504	(−2.98)	(−3.77)	(−0.20)
Predicted mean per capita household expenditure[a]	7,625.85	7,921.35	7,721.43	7,984.55	+3.87	+1.25	+4.70
N	7,276	7,276	7,276	7,276			

Source: Calculated from ENCOVI 2000.

Note: Column 1 uses predicted income equations to measure the situation excluding remittances for all 7,276 households. Column 2 measures the situation for all households when only internal remittances (from Guatemala) are included in predicted household expenditure. Column 3 measures the situation for all households when only international remittances (from the United States) are included in predicted household expenditure. Column 4 measures the situation for all households when both internal and international remittances are included in predicted household expenditure. Poverty calculations made using 2000 World Bank poverty line of 4,319 quetzals/ person/ year. For predicted income equation, see text. All values are weighted. In 2000, 1 Guatemalan quetzal = US$0.128.

a. Includes remittances in quetzals.

is free to change with expenditure. What is needed is a functional form that mathematically allows for rising, falling, or constant marginal propensities to spend over a broad range of goods and expenditure levels. Third, the chosen form should conform to the criterion of additivity. To be internally consistent, the sum of the marginal propensities for all goods should equal unity.

One functional form that meets all of these criteria is the Working-Leser model, which relates budget shares linearly to the logarithm of total expenditure. A modified version of the Working-Leser model represents the basic form that will be used in this analysis.[21] In expenditure share form, this model can be written as follows.

$$C_i /\text{EXP} = \beta_i + a_i /\text{EXP} + \gamma_i (\log \text{EXP}) \qquad (2.4)$$

where C_i/EXP is the share of expenditure on good i in total expenditure EXP. Adding up requires that $\Sigma\, C_i/\text{EXP} = 1$.

In comparing the expenditure behavior of households with different levels of income, various socioeconomic and locational factors other than expenditure must be taken into account. Part of the observed differences in expenditure behavior, for example, may be caused by differences in household composition (family size, number of children, and so on), education, urban or rural residence, geographic region, or (in this sample) receipt of internal or international remittances. These household characteristic variables need to be included in the Engel functions in a way that allows them to shift both the intercept and the slope of the Engel functions. Let Z_j denote the household characteristic variable j and let μ_{ij} and λ_{ij} be constants. The complete model in semi-log ratio form is then as follows.

$$C_i/\text{EXP} = \beta_i + a_i /\text{EXP} + \gamma_i (\log \text{EXP}) + \Sigma_j[(\mu_{ij})Z_j/\text{EXP} + \lambda_{ij}(Z_j)] \quad (2.5)$$

To estimate equation 2.5, the various household characteristic variables need to be specified and identified. Therefore, in addition to the variables that have already been defined in equation 2.3, AGEHD is the variable for age of household head. The complete model to be estimated is then as follows.

$$
\begin{aligned}
C_i/\text{EXP} = {} & \beta_1 + \alpha_i/\text{EXP} + \gamma_1(\log \text{EXP}) + \gamma_2\text{INTREM} + \gamma_3(\text{INTREM})(\log \text{EXP}) \\
& + \gamma_4\text{EXTREM} + \gamma_5(\text{EXTREM})(\log \text{EXP}) + \mu_1\text{HS}/\text{EXP} + \lambda_1\text{HS} \\
& + \mu_2\text{AGEHD}/\text{EXP} + \lambda_2\text{AGEHD} + \mu_3\text{CHILD5}/\text{EXP} \\
& + \lambda_3\text{CHILD5} + \mu_4\text{EDPREP}/\text{EXP} + \lambda_4\text{EDPREP} + \mu_5\text{EDPRIM}/\text{EXP} \qquad (2.6) \\
& + \lambda_5\text{EDPRIM} + \mu_6\text{EDSEC}/\text{EXP} + \lambda_6\text{EDSEC} + \mu_7\text{EDUNIV}/\text{EXP} \\
& + \lambda_7\text{EDUNIV} + \delta_1\text{AR} + \delta_2\sum_{j=1}^{7}\lambda_j\,\text{REG}_j + \varepsilon_i
\end{aligned}
$$

where:

C_i = annual per capita household expenditure on one of six expenditure
categories defined above (food, consumer goods/durables, housing,
education, health, or other)

EXP = total annual per capita household expenditure

INTREM = internal remittances dummy variable (1 if household receives
internal remittances, 0 otherwise)

EXTREM = international remittances dummy variable (1 if household receives
international remittances, 0 otherwise)

In equation 2.6 the dummy variables for the receipt of internal and international remittances (INTREM and EXTREM) are entered separately and linearly, and each of these dummy variables is also interacted with the log of total annual expenditures (log EXP) to affect both the intercept and the slope of the Engel functions. This means that the marginal budget share for good i can be derived using the equations in Adams (2005a, 11).

Empirical Results: Remittances and Household Expenditure Behavior

Equation 2.6 was estimated on all 7,276 survey households and results are shown in tables 2.7 and 2.8. Table 2.7 shows the results without remittance variables, and table 2.8 shows the results with both remittance variables.

In table 2.8, when the relevant coefficients (log EXP and INTREM*log EXP) are summed up, the results show that households receiving internal remittances spend less on food, and more on consumer goods/durables, housing, health, and other. These latter findings are encouraging because, although food represents a consumption good (except in cases of malnutrition), health is more like an investment item. The results for international remittances are identical to those for internal remittances.

The results of equation 2.6 can be used to calculate marginal budget shares for the three groups of households on the six different categories of expenditure. This makes it possible to identify at the margin how the receipt of internal or international remittances affects the expenditure patterns of households in Guatemala.

Table 2.9 presents the marginal budget shares for the households on the various categories of expenditure. Three results are noteworthy. First, households receiving remittances spend less at the margin on food than non-remittance-receiving households. At the margin, households receiving internal and international remittances spend 11.9 and 14.8 percent less, respectively, on food than do

TABLE 2.7   OLS Regression Analysis of Household Expenditure in Guatemala, without Remittance Variables

Variable	Food	Consumer goods, durables	Housing	Education	Health	Other
Reciprocal of total per capita expenditure (α_i/EXP)	−371.096 (−9.81)**	1.243 (−0.05)	149.316 (5.75)**	−25.314 (−1.67)	47.858 (3.89)**	200.479 (8.05)**
Log total annual per capita household expenditure (log EXP)	−0.115 (−20.24)**	0.048 (12.68)**	0.011 (2.92)**	−0.001 (−0.08)	0.015 (8.59)**	0.039 (10.52)**
Household size (HS)	0.001 (0.07)	0.007 (7.19)**	−0.015 (−14.86)**	0.011 (19.79)**	−0.001 (−2.14)**	−0.003 (−2.97)**
Household size/total expenditure	16.284 (4.37)**	−3.864 (−1.54)	10.546 (4.12)**	−14.709 (−9.82)**	0.036 (0.03)	−8.293 (−3.38)**
Age of household head (AGEHD)	−0.001 (−1.21)	−0.001 (−13.39)**	0.002 (15.58)**	−0.001 (−7.86)*	0.001 (3.50)**	0.001 (2.35)*
Age household head/total expenditure	0.577 (1.14)	2.054 (6.03)**	−3.036 (−8.74)**	0.621 (3.06)**	−0.046 (−0.28)	−0.171 (−0.51)
Number of children in household less than 5 years (CHILD5)	−0.001 (−0.10)	0.005 (2.26)*	0.010 (4.41)**	−0.029 (−21.81)**	0.009 (8.01)**	0.006 (2.59)**
Number children/total expenditure	1.227 (0.13)	−11.980 (−1.94)	−12.103 (−1.92)	45.895 (12.46)**	−14.000 (−4.70)**	−9.033 (−1.50)
Number household members with preparatory education (EDPREP)	−0.017 (−1.33)	0.011 (1.35)	0.001 (0.02)	−0.003 (−0.67)	0.006 (1.40)	0.002 (0.33)
Number preparatory education/total expenditure	24.187 (0.68)	−33.506 (−1.40)	23.405 (0.96)	23.405 (−0.01)	−9.805 (−0.85)	−4.178 (−0.18)
Number household members with primary education (EDPRIM)	−0.006 (−2.47)*	0.008 (4.80)**	−0.001 (−0.42)	−0.005 (−5.24)**	0.002 (2.55)*	0.002 (1.21)

Number primary education/total expenditure	−7.521 (−1.14)	−11.422 (−2.56)*	9.216 (2.03)*	7.809 (2.94)**	0.566 (−0.26)	2.483 (0.57)
Number household members with secondary education (EDSEC)	−0.024 (−8.13)**	0.008 (3.82)**	0.001 (0.16)	0.011 (9.40)**	0.004 (3.99)**	0.001 (0.56)
Number secondary education/total expenditure	−46.460 (−3.25)**	−15.262 (−1.59)	18.477 (1.88)	35.409 (6.17)**	−3.672 (−0.79)	11.507 (1.22)
Number household members with university education (EDUNIV)	−0.035 (−6.74)**	0.007 (2.02)*	−0.001 (−0.41)	0.017 (8.36)**	0.006 (3.65)**	0.006 (1.69)
Number university education/total expenditure	−33.853 (−0.77)	−39.506 (−1.33)	−52.189 (1.73)	−7.388 (−0.42)	0.109 (0.01)	28.448 (0.98)
Constant	1.474 (25.48)**	−0.262 (−6.72)**	0.079 (1.99)*	0.039 (0.90)	−0.128 (−6.82)**	−0.202 (−5.32)**
Adj. R^2	0.411	0.154	0.200	0.328	0.087	0.080
F-statistic	212.5	56.4	76.8	149.3	31.6	27.4

Source: Calculated from ENCOVI 2000.

Note: N = 7,276 households. Numbers in parentheses are t-statistics (two-tailed). One area dummy variable and seven regional variables are included in the equation, but are not reported in the table. All expenditure categories defined in table 2.2. OLS = ordinary least squares.

*significant at the 0.05 level, **significant at the 0.01 level.

TABLE 2.8 OLS Regression Analysis of Household Expenditure in Guatemala, with Remittance Variables

Variable	Food	Consumer goods, durables	Housing	Education	Health	Other
Reciprocal of total per capita expenditure (α_i/EXP)	−375.350 (−9.87)**	−1.961 (−0.08)	146.228 (5.60)**	−27.216 (−1.78)	47.748 (3.86)**	206.628 (8.25)**
Log total annual per capita household expenditure (log EXP)	−0.115 (−19.93)**	0.049 (12.54)**	0.011 (2.66)**	−0.001 (−0.41)	0.016 (8.45)**	0.041 (10.73)**
Internal remittances dummy (INTREM)	0.004 (0.11)	0.058 (2.04)*	−0.080 (−2.74)**	−0.008 (−0.48)	−0.012 (−0.93)	0.038 (1.35)
(Internal remittances dummy) x (Total household expenditure) (INTREM)(log EXP)	−0.001 (−0.32)	−0.007 (−2.17)*	0.010 (3.13)**	0.001 (0.78)	0.001 (1.04)	−0.004 (−1.54)*
International remittances dummy (EXTREM)	−0.131 (−2.17)*	0.007 (0.18)	0.051 (1.24)	−0.013 (−0.53)	0.008 (0.42)	0.077 (1.94)
(International remittances dummy) x (Total household expenditure) (EXTREM)(log EXP)	0.012 (1.88)	0.001 (0.09)	−0.005 (−1.20)	0.002 (0.89)	−0.001 (−0.59)	−0.008 (−1.96)*
Household size (HS)	0.001 (0.23)	0.006 (6.91)**	−0.014 (−14.74)**	0.011 (19.61)**	−0.001 (−1.96)*	−0.002 (−3.05)**
Household size/total expenditure	16.114 (4.32)**	−3.482 (−1.39)	10.264 (4.01)**	−14.588 (−9.74)**	−0.082 (−0.07)	−0.082 (−3.35)**
Age of household head (AGEHD)	−0.001 (−0.71)	−0.001 (−13.05)**	−0.001 (14.62)**	0.001 (−8.49)**	0.001 (3.35)**	0.001 (2.72)**
Age household head/total expenditure	0.524 (1.03)	1.985 (5.80)**	−2.895 (−8.30)**	0.673 (3.31)**	−0.032 (−0.19)	−0.256 (−0.77)

Number of children in household less than 5 years (CHILD5)	-0.001 (-0.17)	0.010 (4.35)**	-0.029 (-21.79)**	0.008 (7.93)**	0.006 (2.65)**
Number children/total expenditure	2.285 (0.25)	-12.005 (-1.91)	45.550 (12.38)**	-13.817 (-4.63)**	-9.309 (-1.54)
Number household members with preparatory education (EDPREP)	-0.016 (-1.30)	0.001 (0.04)	-0.003 (-0.71)	0.006 (1.45)	0.002 (0.33)
Number preparatory education/total expenditure	23.597 (0.67)	23.207 (0.95)	0.294 (0.02)	-10.119 (-0.88)	-4.212 (-0.18)
Number household members with primary education (EDPRIM)	-0.006 (-2.53)*	-0.001 (-0.39)	-0.005 (-5.18)**	0.002 (2.54)*	0.002 (1.20)
Number primary education/total expenditure	-7.732 (-1.17)	9.265 (2.04)*	7.864 (2.97)**	-0.582 (-0.27)	2.528 (0.58)
Number household members with secondary education (EDSEC)	-0.024 (-8.10)**	0.001 (0.02)	0.011 (9.26)**	0.003 (3.97)**	0.001 (0.70)
Number secondary education/total expenditure	-46.957 (-3.29)**	19.540 (1.99)*	36.102 (6.30)**	-3.625 (-0.78)	10.552 (1.12)
Number household members with university education (EDUNIV)	-0.035 (-6.82)**	-0.001 (-0.49)	0.018 (8.58)**	0.006 (3.50)**	0.005 (1.64)
Number university education/total expenditure	-34.324 (-0.78)	53.874 (1.78)	-8.666 (-0.49)	0.865 (0.06)	29.648 (1.02)
Constant	1.481 (25.13)**	-0.266 (-6.71)**	0.046 (1.97)*	-0.129 (-6.74)**	-0.218 (-5.63)**
Adj. R^2	0.412	0.155	0.331	0.092	0.080
F-statistic	183.3	48.9	129.4	27.3	23.8

Source: Calculated from ENCOVI 2000.

Note: N=7,276 households. Numbers in parentheses are t-statistics (two-tailed). One area dummy variable and seven regional variables are included in the equation, but are not reported in the table. All expenditure categories defined in table 2.2.

*significant at the 0.05 level, **significant at the 0.01 level.

TABLE 2.9   Marginal Budget Shares on Expenditure for Nonremittance Households and Remittance-Receiving Households, Guatemala, 2000

Expenditure category	Households receiving no remittances (N=5665)	Households receiving internal remittances from Guatemala) (N=1063)	Households receiving international remittances (from the (N=593)	% change (no remittances versus internal remittances) internal remittances)	% change (no remittances versus international remittances)
Food	0.386	0.340	0.330	(−11.92)	(− 14.77)
Consumer goods, durables	0.203	0.202	0.229	(−0.50)	+ 12.81
Housing	0.183	0.211	0.187	+15.30	+ 2.18
Education	0.031	0.045	0.04	+45.16	+58.06
Health	0.023	0.028	0.023	+21.74	—
Other	0.173	0.188	0.177	+ 8.67	+ 2.31

Source: Calculated from ENCOVI 2000.

Note: Some figures do not sum to unity because of rounding. All expenditure categories defined in Adams (2005a, table 2.2).

non-remittance-receiving households. There is no evidence here that remittance-receiving households "waste" their increased earnings on "conspicuous" food consumption. Second, households receiving remittances spend more of their increments to expenditure on housing than do non-remittance-receiving households. The percentage increases for marginal spending on housing are 15.3 percent for households receiving internal remittances and 2.2 percent for households receiving international remittances (with the difference statistically significant). Like other studies, this suggests that remittance-receiving households are devoting much of their increments to expenditure on housing, an investment from the standpoint of the individual migrant who provides an expected stream of utility or of financial return. Third, while the absolute levels of expenditure are quite small, remittance-receiving households are spending considerably more at the margin on education. The percentage increases for marginal spending on education, which are the largest in the table, are 45.2 percent for households receiving internal remittances and 58.1 percent for households receiving international remittances. As discussed in Adams (2005a, 18), when these marginal expenditures on education are disaggregated by level of education, most of these incremental expenditures on education go to higher education. For example, at the secondary level, households receiving internal and international remittances spend 19.6 and 142.4 percent more, respectively, on secondary education than do non-remittance-receiving households. These large marginal increases in spending on higher education are important because increased expenditure on education can raise the level of human capital in the country as a whole. Because the level of human capital is an important component of economic growth, increased expenditure on education by remittance-receiving households may provide the means for raising the rate of economic growth in a country.

Conclusion

Three key findings emerge from this analysis of the impact of internal and international remittances on poverty and investment in Guatemala.

First, using predicted equations to develop counterfactual income estimates for households with and without remittances, the chapter finds that both internal and international remittances reduce the level, depth, and severity of poverty in Guatemala. However, the size of the poverty reduction greatly depends on how poverty is measured. According to the poverty headcount measure, the inclusion of internal remittances in household expenditure reduces the level of poverty by only 1 percent and the inclusion of international remittances in such expenditure actually increases the level of poverty by 1.6 percent. However, poverty is reduced much more when measured by indicators focusing on the depth and severity of poverty. For example, the squared poverty gap (which measures the severity of poverty) shows that including internal or international remittances in household expenditure reduces poverty by 23.5 or 21.9 percent, respectively.

Second, contrary to other studies, this analysis finds that the majority of remittance earnings are not spent on consumption goods. In fact, at the mean level of expenditure, this study finds that although households without remittances spend 58.9 percent of their increments to expenditure on consumption goods—food and consumer goods, durables— households receiving internal and international remittances spend 54.2 and 55.9 percent, respectively, on consumption goods. In other words, at the margin, households receiving remittances actually spend less (not more) on consumption than do households without remittances.

Third, instead of spending more on consumption, households receiving remittances tend to view their remittance earnings as a temporary (and possibly uncertain) stream of income, one to be spent more on investment than consumption goods. For example, at the margin, households receiving internal and international remittances spend 45.2 and 58.1 percent more, respectively, on education than households that do not receive remittances. This increased marginal spending on education underscores the way that households prefer to invest—rather than spend—their remittance earnings.

Endnotes

1. While no estimates are available regarding the size of internal remittances, Ratha (2004) has recently estimated that official international remittances to the developing world now total $93 billion per year, making them the second most important source of external funding in developing countries.

2. See, for example, Chami, Fullenkamp, and Jahjah (2003).

3. This paper represents a shortened and condensed version of Adams (2005a, 2005b).

4. Several researchers have examined remittances as an exogenous transfer of resources on income inequality in developing countries. See, for example, Stark, Taylor, and Yitzhaki (1986).

5. For other attempts to treat remittances as a substitute for home earnings and to predict (estimate) the incomes of households with and without migration, see Barham and Boucher (1998) and Adams (1991).

6. This 2000 Guatemala household survey was implemented as part of the "Program for the Improvement of Surveys and Measurement of Living Conditions in Latin America and the Caribbean" (ENCOVI), which was sponsored by the Inter-American Development Bank (IDB), the World Bank and the Economic Committee for Latin America and the Caribbean (CEPAL).

7. For more details on this 2000 Guatemala household survey, see World Bank (2003).

8. Following are the five possible responses to the question "where do these people sending (your household) remittances live?" (a) Guatemala; (b) United States; (c) Mexico; (d) Central America; and (e) other countries.

9. A smaller number of survey households (43) received remittances from other countries, and are not counted as remittance-receiving households in this study.

10. While early work on the human capital model found that education had a positive impact on migration (Todaro 1976; Shultz 1982;), more recent empirical work in the Arab Republic of Egypt

(Adams 1991, 1993) and Mexico (Taylor 1987; Mora and Taylor 2005) has found that migrants are not necessarily positively selected with respect to education.

11. Other work has found that, although age of household head will affect household migration, this variable will have no impact on premigration household income. See, for example, Adams (2005c) in Ghana.

12. This finding is robust to alternative ways of specifying the choice and income functions in equations (1) and (2). For more information, contact the author.

13. See, for example, Chiswick (2000) and Carrington and Detragiache (1998).

14. In a recent study of the determinants of international migration from rural Mexico, Mora and Taylor (2005) also find that international migrants to the United States are not positively selected on the basis of education.

15. In equation (2.3), the dependent variable is per capita household expenditure (excluding remittances), rather than per capita household income (excluding remittances). There are three reasons for using expenditure rather than income data here. First, because people tend to use savings to smooth fluctuations in income, many economists believe that expenditures provide a more accurate measure of an individual's welfare over time. Second, in developing countries, like Guatemala, expenditures are often easier to measure than income because of the many problems involved in measuring income for the self-employed in agriculture. Third, the poverty line used in this paper is based on expenditure rather than income data. To be consistent, it is therefore preferable to work with expenditure data in the predicting equation.

16. Seven regional dummy variables (referenced to the capital city) are also included in equation (2.3).

17. In fact, a recent World Bank study (2003, table 7.3) found that returns to primary school education are relatively low in Guatemala. When compared with people with no education, people who had completed primary education received 15 percent more in hourly wages, while those who had completed university education received 74 percent more.

18. This poverty line is defined as the level of per capita expenditures needed to meet the costs of attaining minimum food requirements of 2,172 kilocalories per person per day. The costs of meeting minimum nonfood expenditures are also added to this food line. The result is a national poverty line—including food and nonfood costs—for Guatemala in 2000. For more details on this poverty line, see World Bank (2003, annex 3).

19. These results are different from those reported by Adams (1995) for rural Pakistan, where internal remittances were found to reduce income inequality, and international remittances represented an inequality-increasing source of income.

20. Food expenditures include the value of both purchased and own-produced (and consumed) food. See World Bank (2003, 229–30).

21. The functional form used in this analysis differs from the Working-Leser model because it includes an intercept. In theory, C_i should always equal zero whenever total expenditure EXP is zero, and this restriction should be built into the function. But zero observations on EXP invariably lie well outside the sample range. Also, observing this restriction with the Working-Leser model can lead to poorer statistical fits. Including the intercept term in the model has little effect on the estimation of marginal budget shares for the average person, but it can make a significant difference for income distribution results.

References

Adams, Jr., R. 1991. "The Effects of International Remittances on Poverty, Inequality and Development in Rural Egypt." Research Report, no. 86. International Food Policy Research Institute, Washington, DC.

———. 1993. "The Economic and Demographic Determinants of International Migration in Rural Egypt." *Journal of Development Studies* 30(1): 146–67.

———. 1995. "Sources of Income Inequality and Poverty in Rural Pakistan." Research Report, no. 102. International Food Policy Research Institute, Washington, DC.

———. 2005a. "Remittances, Household Expenditure and Investment in Guatemala." World Bank Policy Research Working Paper, no. 3532. World Bank, Washington, DC.

———. 2005b. "Remittances, Selection Bias and Poverty in Guatemala." Unpublished manuscript. World Bank, Washington, DC.

———. 2005c. "Remittances and Poverty in Ghana." Unpublished manuscript. World Bank, Washington, DC.

Barham, B., and S. Boucher. 1998. "Migration, Remittances and Inequality: Estimating the Net Effects of Migration on Income Distribution." *Journal of Development Economics* 55(2): 307–31.

Carrington, W., and E. Detragiache. 1998. "How Big is the Brain Drain?" IMF Working Paper 98/102. International Monetary Fund, Washington, DC.

Chami, R., C. Fullenkamp, and S. Jahjah. 2003. "Are Immigrant Remittance Flows a Source of Capital for Development?" IMF Working Paper 03/189. International Monetary Fund, Washington, DC.

Chiswick, B. 2000. "Are Immigrants Favorably Self-Selected: An Economic Analysis." In *Migration Theory: Talking Across Disciplines*, ed. E. Brettell and J. Hollifield. New York: Routledge.

Lanzona, L. 1998. "Migration, Self-Selection and Earnings in Philippine Rural Communities." *Journal of Development Economics* 56(1): 27–50.

Lipton, M. 1980. "Migration from Rural Areas of Poor Countries: The Impact on Rural Productivity and Income Distribution." *World Development* 8(1): 1–24.

Massey, D. 1987. *Return to Aztalan: The Social Process of International Migration from Western Mexico.* Berkeley, CA: University of California.

Massey, D., L. Goldring, and J. Durand. 1994. "Continuities in Transnational Migration: An Analysis of Nineteen Mexican Communities." *American Journal of Sociology* 99(6): 1,492–533.

Mora, J., and J. E. Taylor. 2005. "Determinants of International Migration, Destination, and Sector Choice: Disentangling Individual, Household, and Community Effects." Chapter 1 in this volume.

Ratha, D. 2004. "Enhancing the Developmental Effect of Workers' Remittances to Developing Countries." *Global Development Finance*: 169–73. Washington, DC: World Bank.

Schultz, T. P. 1982. "Notes on the Estimation of Migration Functions." In *Migration and the Labour Market in Developing Countries*, ed. R. Sabot. Boulder, CO: Westview Press.

Stark, O., J. E. Taylor, and S. Yitzhaki. 1986. "Remittances and Inequality." *The Economic Journal* 96(383): 722-40.

Taylor, J. E. 1987. "Undocumented Mexico-US Migration and the Returns to Households in Rural Mexico." *American Journal of Agricultural Economics* 69(3): 626–38.

Todaro, M. 1976. *Internal Migration in Developing Countries.* Geneva. Switzerland: International Labour Office.

World Bank. 2003. *Poverty in Guatemala.* Washington, DC: World Bank.

3

REMITTANCES AND POVERTY IN MIGRANTS' HOME AREAS: EVIDENCE FROM THE PHILIPPINES

Dean Yang and Claudia A. Martínez

Introduction

Between 1965 and 2000, individuals living outside their countries of birth grew from 2.2 percent to 2.9 percent of world population, reaching a total of 175 million people in 2001.[1] The remittances that these migrants send to origin countries are an important but poorly understood type of international financial flow. In 2002, remittance receipts of developing countries amounted to $79 billion.[2] This figure exceeded total official development aid ($51 billion), and amounted to roughly four-tenths of foreign direct investment inflows ($189 billion) received by developing countries in that year.[3]

What effect do remittance flows have on poverty and inequality in migrants' origin households, and in their home areas more broadly? The answer to this question is central to any assessment of the effect of international migration on origin countries,[4] and of the benefits to origin countries of developed-country policies liberalizing inward migration—for example, as proposed in Rodrik (2002) and Bhagwati (2003). Remittance flows have their most direct effect on incomes in migrants' origin households. More generally, remittances may have broader effects on economic activity in migrants' home areas, leading to changes in poverty and inequality even in households without migrant members. In addition, remittance inflows to certain regions may reduce poverty more broadly if remittance-receiving households make direct transfers to nonrecipient households.

A major obstacle to examining the causal impact of remittance flows on aggregate poverty and inequality is the fact that remittances are not randomly assigned across areas, so that any observed relationship between remittances and an aggregate outcome of interest may not reflect the causal impact of remittances. Reverse causation is a serious concern. For example, if remittances serve as insurance for recipient households, worsening economic conditions could lead to increases in remittance flows (as documented in Yang and Choi 2005), leading to a positive relationship between poverty and remittances. Omitted variables could also be at work. For instance, sound macroeconomic policies could lead to reductions in poverty and simultaneously attract remittances intended for investment in the local economy, so that poverty and remittances would be negatively correlated.

This chapter exploits a unique natural experiment that helps identify the causal impact of remittances on poverty in migrants' origin households and, more broadly, in remittance-receiving areas. In identifying the causal impact of remittances, it is useful to have a source of random or arbitrary variation in remittance flows to more readily put aside concerns about reverse causation and omitted variables. In June 1997, 6 percent of Philippine households had one or more members working overseas. These overseas members were working in dozens of foreign countries, many of which experienced sudden changes in exchange rates because of the 1997 Asian financial crisis. Crucially for the empirical analysis, there was substantial variation in the size of the exchange rate shock experienced by migrants. Between July 1997 and October 1998, the U.S. dollar and currencies in the Middle Eastern destinations of Filipino workers rose 52 percent in value against the Philippine peso. Over the same time period, by contrast, the currencies of Taiwan (China), Singapore, and Japan rose by only 26 percent, 29 percent, and 32 percent, while those of Malaysia and Republic of Korea actually fell slightly against the peso.[5]

These sudden and heterogeneous changes in the exchange rates faced by migrants allow us to estimate the causal impact of the shocks on remittances, household income, and poverty in the migrants' origin households. Appreciation of a migrant's currency against the Philippine peso leads to increases in household remittance receipts and in total household income. In migrants' origin households, a 10 percent improvement in the exchange rate leads to a 0.6 percentage point decline in the poverty rate. The instrumental variables estimate indicates that an increase in migrant households' remittance receipts equivalent to 10 percent of precrisis household income reduces the poverty rate among such households by 2.8 percentage points.

In addition, different regions within the Philippines sent migrants to somewhat different overseas locations, so that the *mean* exchange rate shock experienced by a region's migrants also varied considerably across the country. For example, the mean exchange rate shock faced by migrants from Northern Mindanao was 34 percent, while the mean shock for migrants from the Cordillera Administrative Region was 46 percent, and the average across all migrants in the country was 41 percent. To understand the regional impact of aggregate remittance flows to certain regions, we ask how changes in the mean exchange rate shock influence changes in region-level poverty and inequality. We find evidence of favorable spillovers to households without migrant members. In regions with more favorable mean exchange rate shocks, aggregate poverty rates decline. However, there is no strong evidence that the region-level mean exchange rate shock affects measures of aggregate inequality. This aggregate decline in poverty may be due to increases in economic activity driven by remittance flows, as well as by direct transfers from migrants' origin households to households that do not have migrant members.

The results in this chapter relate to the immediate impact of changes in remittances (driven by exchange rate changes) on poverty in migrants' origin households and home areas. In addition, the changes in exchange rates could also have more persistent effects on households, if their newfound resources allowed them to make longer-term investments in child human capital and in entrepreneurial enterprises (that outlast the exchange rate shocks or the length of migrant members' overseas stays). Yang (2004) examines this issue in detail, finding that favorable exchange rate shocks lead to greater child schooling, reduced child labor, and increased education expenditure in migrants' origin households. Favorable exchange rate shocks raise hours worked in self-employment and lead to greater entry into relatively capital-intensive enterprises by migrants' origin households. At the end of the empirical section below, we provide a summary of the results in Yang (2004).

This chapter is related to an existing body of research on the impact of migration and remittances on aggregate economic outcomes (such as poverty and inequality) in migrants' origin areas. One approach used in previous research has been to compare the actual income distribution (including remittances) with the income distribution when remittances are subtracted from household income. The difference is then interpreted as the impact of remittances.[6] Such an approach assumes that domestic nonremittance income is invariant with respect to remittance receipts and thus is likely to yield biased estimates of the impact of remittances. With this concern in mind, other research constructs counterfactual measures of poverty and income distribution based on predicting the income of remittance recipients in the absence of remittances.[7] In contrast to existing work on the topic, we believe this is the first study to examine the impact of remittances on poverty and inequality in migrants' home areas using exogenous variation in an important determinant of remittances (exchange rates in migrants' overseas locations).

This chapter is organized as follows. The first section describes the dispersion of Filipino household members overseas and discusses the nature of the exchange rate shocks at the household and regional levels. The second section describes the data used and presents the empirical results. The third section concludes the findings. Further details on the household data sets are provided in annex 3.A.

Overseas Filipinos: Characteristics and Exposure to Shocks

Characteristics of Overseas Filipinos

To ameliorate rising unemployment and aggregate balance of payments problems, in 1974 the Philippine government initiated an Overseas Employment Program to facilitate the placement of Filipino workers in overseas jobs. At the outset, the government directly managed the placement of workers with employers overseas, but it soon yielded the function to private recruitment agencies and assumed a more limited oversight role. The annual number of Filipinos going overseas on officially processed work contracts rose sixfold from 36,035 to 214,590 between 1975 and 1980, and more than tripled again by 1997 to 701,272.[8] Today, the government authorizes some 1,300 private recruitment agencies to place Filipinos in overseas jobs (Diamond 2002). Contracts for most overseas positions typically have an initial duration of two years and usually are open to renewal. For the majority of positions, overseas workers cannot bring family members with them and must go alone.

Data on overseas Filipinos are collected in the Survey on Overseas Filipinos (SOF), which is conducted in October of each year by the National Statistics Office of the Philippines. The SOF asks a nationally representative sample of households in the Philippines about household members who moved overseas within the last five years.

In June 1997 (one month before the Asian financial crisis), 5.9 percent of Philippine households had one or more household members overseas, in a variety of foreign countries. Table 3.1 displays the distribution of household members working overseas by country in June 1997.[9] Filipino workers are remarkably dispersed worldwide. Saudi Arabia is the largest single destination, with 28.4 percent of the total, and Hong Kong (China) comes in second with 11.5 percent. No other destination accounts for more than 10 percent of the total. The only other economies accounting for 6 percent or more are Taiwan (China), Japan, Singapore, and the United States. The top 20 destinations listed in the table account for 91.9 percent of overseas Filipino workers; the remaining 8.1 percent are distributed among 38 other identified countries or have an unspecified location.

TABLE 3.1   Locations of Overseas Workers from Sample Households, June 1997

Location	Number of overseas workers	% of total	Exchange rate shock (June 1997–Oct 1998)
Saudi Arabia	521	28.4%	0.52
Hong Kong, China	210	11.5%	0.52
Taiwan, China	148	8.1%	0.26
Singapore	124	6.8%	0.29
Japan	116	6.3%	0.32
United States	116	6.3%	0.52
Malaysia	65	3.5%	−0.01
Italy	52	2.8%	0.38
Kuwait	51	2.8%	0.50
United Arab Emirates	49	2.7%	0.52
Greece	44	2.4%	0.30
Korea, Rep.	36	2.0%	−0.04
Northern Mariana Islands	30	1.6%	0.52
Canada	29	1.6%	0.42
Brunei	22	1.2%	0.30
United Kingdom	15	0.8%	0.55
Qatar	15	0.8%	0.52
Norway	14	0.8%	0.35
Australia	14	0.8%	0.24
Bahrain	13	0.7%	0.52
Other	148	8.1%	
Total	1,832	100.0%	

Source: Data are from October 1997 Survey on Overseas Filipinos.

Note: "Other" includes 38 additional countries plus a category for "unspecified" (total 58 countries explicitly reported). Overseas workers in table are those in households included in sample for empirical analysis (see Data Appendix for details on sample definition). Exchange rate shock: Change in Philippine pesos per currency unit where overseas worker was located in Jun 1997. Change is average of 12 months leading to Oct 1998 minus average of 12 months leading to Jun 1997, divided by the latter (e.g., 10% increase is 0.1).

Table 3.2 displays summary statistics on the characteristics of overseas Filipino workers in the same survey. In the households included in the empirical analysis, 1,832 workers were overseas in June 1997 (see annex 3.A for details on the construction of the household sample). The overseas workers have a mean age of 34.5 years; 38 percent are single and 53 percent are male. The two largest occupational categories are (a) production and related workers and (b) domestic servants, each

TABLE 3.2   Characteristics of Overseas Workers from Sample Households

	Mean	Standard deviation	10th percentile	Median	90th percentile
Age	34.49	9.00	24.00	33.00	47.00
Marital status is single (indicator)	0.38				
Gender is male (indicator)	0.53				
Occupation (indicators)					
Production and related workers	0.13				
Domestic servants	0.31				
Ship's officers and crew	0.12				
Professional and technical workers	0.11				
Clerical and related workers	0.04				
Other services	0.10				
Other	0.01				
Highest education level (indictors)					
Less than high school	0.15				
High school	0.25				
Some college	0.31				
College or more	0.30				
Postition in household (indicators)					
Male head of household	0.28				
Female head or spouse of head	0.12				
Daughter of head	0.28				
Son of head	0.15				
Other relation to head	0.16				
Months overseas as of Jun 1997 (indicators)					
0–11 months	0.30				
12–23 months	0.24				
24–35 months	0.16				
36–47 months	0.15				
48 months or more	0.16				
Number of individuals 1,832					

Source: October 1997 Survey on Overseas Filipinos, National Statistics Office of the Philippines.

Note: "Other" occupational category includes "administrative, executive, and managerial workers" and "agricultural workers." Overseas workers in table are those in households included in sample for empirical analysis (see Data Appendix for details on sample definition).

accounting for 31 percent of the total. Thirty-one percent of overseas workers in the sample have achieved some college education, and an additional 30 percent have a college degree. In terms of position in the household, the most common categories are male heads-of-household and daughters of household heads, each accounting for 28 percent of overseas workers. Sons of household heads account for 15 percent, female household heads or spouses of household heads account for 12 percent, and other relations account for 16 percent of overseas workers. As of June 1997, the bulk of overseas workers had been away for relatively short periods: 30 percent had been overseas for just 0–11 months, 24 percent for 12–23 months, 16 percent for 24–35 months, 15 percent for 36–47 months, and 16 percent for 48 months or more.

Shocks Generated by the Asian Financial Crisis

The geographic dispersion of overseas Filipinos meant that there was considerable variety in the exchange rate shocks they experienced in the wake of the Asian financial crisis, starting in July 1997. The devaluation of the Thai baht in that

FIGURE 3.1 Exchange Rates in Selected Locations of Overseas Filipinos, July 1996 to October 1998 (Philippine pesos per unit of foreign currency, normalized to 1 in July 1996)

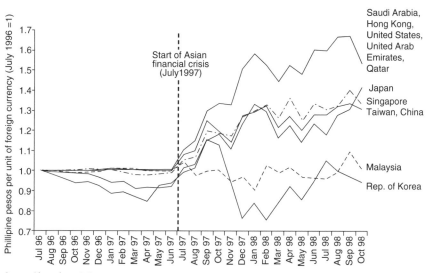

Source: Bloomberg L.P.
Note: Exchange rates are as of last day of each month.

month set off a wave of speculative attacks on national currencies, primarily (but not exclusively) in East and Southeast Asia.

Figure 3.1 displays monthly exchange rates for selected major locations of overseas Filipinos (expressed in Philippine pesos per unit of foreign currency, normalized to 1 in July 1996). [10] The sharp trend shift for nearly all countries after July 1997 is the most striking feature of this graph. An increase in a particular country's exchange rate should be considered a favorable shock to an overseas household member in that country: each unit of foreign currency earned would convert to more Philippine pesos once remitted.

For each country j, we construct the exchange rate change between the average level during October 1997–September 1998 and the average level during July 1997–June 1996: following measure of the exchange rate change.

$$\text{ERCHANGE}_j = \frac{Average country j exchange rate from Oct. 1997 to Sep. 1998}{Average country j exchange rate from Jul. 1996 to Jun. 1997} - 1. \quad (3.1)$$

A 50 percent improvement would be expressed as 0.5, a 50 percent decline as -0.5. Exchange rate changes for the 20 major destinations of Filipino workers are listed in the third column of table 3.1. The changes for the major Middle Eastern destinations and the United States were all at least 0.50. By contrast, the exchange rate shocks for Taiwan (China), Singapore, and Japan were 0.26, 0.29, and 0.32, respectively, while those for Malaysia and Korea were negative: -0.01 and -0.04, respectively. Workers in Indonesia experienced the worst exchange rate change (-0.54), while workers in Libya experienced the most favorable change (0.57) (not shown in table).

Household-level exchange rate shock

We construct a household-level exchange rate shock variable as follows. Let the countries in the world where overseas Filipinos work be indexed by $j\varepsilon\{1,2,...,J\}$. Let n_{ij} indicate the number of overseas workers a household i has in a particular country j in June 1997 (so that $\sum_{j=1}^{J} n_{ij}$ is its total number of household workers overseas in that month). The exchange rate shock measure for household i is as follows.

$$\text{ERSHOCK}_i = \frac{\sum_{j=1}^{J} n_{ij} \text{ERCHANGE}_j}{\sum_{j=1}^{J} n_{ij}} \quad (3.2)$$

In other words, for a household with just one worker overseas in a country j in June 1997, the exchange rate shock associated with that household is simply ERCHANGE$_j$. For households with workers in more than one foreign country in June 1997, the exchange rate shock associated with that household is the weighted average exchange rate change across those countries, with each country's exchange rate being weighted by the number of household workers in that country.[11] Because this variable is undefined for households without overseas migrants, when examining the impact of ERSHOCK$_i$, we restrict the sample to households with one or more members working overseas one month before the Asian financial crisis (in June 1997). To eliminate concerns about reverse causation, it is crucial that ERSHOCK$_i$ is defined solely on the basis of migrants' locations before the crisis. For example, households experiencing positive shocks to their Philippine income source might be better positioned to send members to work in places that experienced better exchange rate shocks.

Region-level exchange rate shock. For analysis of poverty in nonmigrant households, and of inequality across all households, we calculate the mean exchange rate shock across migrants within 16 geographic regions of the Philippines.[12] This measure varies across regions because of regional differences in the locations of overseas workers.

For Philippine region k, the region-level migrant exchange rate shock is as follows.

$$\text{REGSHOCK}_k = \frac{\sum_{j=1}^{J} N_{kj} \, \text{ERCHANGE}_j}{\sum_{j=1}^{J} N_{kj}} \tag{3.3}$$

As before, countries in the world where overseas Filipinos work are indexed by $j\varepsilon\{1,2,...,J\}$, and ERCHANGE$_j$ is the exchange rate shock for a migrant in country j as defined in equation 3.1 above. N_{kj} is the number of overseas workers a region k has in a particular country j in June 1997 (so that $\sum_{j=1}^{J} N_{kj}$ is the total number of the region's workers overseas in that month). As with the household-level shock measure, it is important that REGSHOCK$_k$ is defined solely on the basis of migrants' locations before the crisis.

Across regions in the Philippines, REGSHOCK$_k$ has a mean of 0.40 and a standard deviation of 0.03. The lowest value of REGSHOCK$_k$ is 0.34 (Northern Mindanao) and the highest value is 0.46 (Cordillera Administrative Region).

Empirical Analysis

In this section, we first describe the data and sample construction and the characteristics of sample households. We then discuss the regression specification and various empirical issues, and present estimates of the impact of exchange rate shocks on poverty and inequality. At the end of the empirical section, we summarize related results (from Yang 2004) on the impact of the exchange rate shocks on human capital investment and entrepreneurial activity in these same households.

Data

Household surveys.   The empirical analysis uses data from a set of linked household surveys conducted by the National Statistics Office of the Philippine government, covering a nationally representative household sample: the Labor Force Survey (LFS), the Survey on Overseas Filipinos (SOF), the Family Income and Expenditure Survey (FIES), and the Annual Poverty Indicators Survey (APIS).

The LFS is administered quarterly to inhabitants of a rotating panel of dwellings in January, April, July, and October; the other three surveys are administered less often as riders to the LFS. Usually, one-fourth of dwellings are rotated out of the sample in each quarter, but the rotation was postponed for five quarters starting in July 1997. Thus, three-quarters of dwellings included in the July 1997 round were still in the sample in October 1998 (one-fourth of the dwellings had just been rotated out of the sample). The analysis of this study takes advantage of this fortuitous postponement of the rotation schedule to examine changes in households over the 15-month period from July 1997 to October 1998.

Survey enumerators note whether the household currently living in the dwelling is the same as the household surveyed in the previous round; only dwellings inhabited continuously by the same household from July 1997 to October 1998 are included in the sample for analysis. Because the exchange rate shocks are likely to have different effects on households depending on whether they have migrant members, we separately analyzed households that reported having one or more members overseas in June 1997 and households that did not report having migrant members in that month.

Before being used as dependent variables, all variables denominated in currency terms are converted into real 1997 terms using the 1997–98 change in the regional consumer price index. See annex 3.A for other details regarding the contents of the household surveys and the construction of the sample for analysis.

Poverty statistics.   Poverty variables take household per capita income as the basis, where overseas household members are not included in the per capita income calculations. However, remittances received from the overseas members are included in household income. This procedure acknowledges the lack of information on the earnings of overseas migrants and is consistent with that used in constructing the Philippine government's poverty statistics (Virola and others 2005). To construct poverty measures, we used poverty lines for 1997 and 1998, by locality, from the Philippine government's National Statistical Coordination Board (NSCB).[13]

The empirical analysis focuses on three poverty measures. First, a *poverty indicator* for household i in period t, POV_{it}.

$$POV_{it} = \begin{cases} 1 \text{ if } Y_{it} < \tilde{Y}_{it} \\ 0 \text{ otherwise} \end{cases} \qquad (3.4)$$

where Y_{it} is household per capita income, and Y_{it} is the per capita poverty line for household i and period t. The second poverty measure is the *poverty gap*, expressed in pesos.

$$POVGAP_{it} = \begin{cases} \tilde{Y}_{it} - Y_{it} \text{ if } Y_{it} < \tilde{Y}_{it} \\ 0 \text{ otherwise} \end{cases} \qquad (3.5)$$

The third poverty measure is the *poverty gap (as fraction of the poverty line)*, expressed in pesos.

$$POVGAPFR_{it} = \begin{cases} \dfrac{\tilde{Y}_{it} - Y_{it}}{Y_{it}} \text{ if } Y_{it} < \tilde{Y}_{it} \\ 0 \text{ otherwise} \end{cases} \qquad (3.6)$$

The poverty indicator provides information on the incidence of poverty in particular households. Conversely, the measures for poverty gap provide information on the depth of poverty.

Rainfall shocks. A number of the analyses in this study examine the impact of region-level exchange rate shocks, and so it is crucial to control for the impact of other types of region-level shocks on poverty and inequality that might be correlated (coincidentally) with the region-level exchange rate shocks. Reflecting the central role of agriculture in the Philippine economy, important regional economic fluctuations derive from rainfall variation (as documented in Yang and Choi 2005).

To construct measures of rainfall shocks, we use rainfall data obtained from the Philippine Atmospheric, Geophysical, and Astronomical Services Administration (PAGASA). Daily rainfall data are available for 47 weather stations, often as far back as 1951. Rainfall variables are constructed by station separately for the two distinct weather seasons in the Philippines: the dry season from December through May, and the wet season from June through November. Monthly rainfall is calculated by summing daily rainfall totals, with daily missing values replaced by the average among the nonmissing daily totals in the given station-month, as long as the station had 20 or more daily rainfall records. When a particular station-month had less than 20 daily rainfall records, monthly rainfall for the station is taken as the monthly rainfall recorded at the nearest station with 20 or more daily rainfall records. Seasonal total rainfall for each station in each year is obtained by summing monthly rainfall for the respective months in each wet or dry season (December observations are considered to belong to the subsequent calendar year's dry season).

Households are assigned the rainfall data for the weather station geographically closest to their local area (specifically, the major city or town in their survey domain), using great circle distances calculated using latitude and longitude coordinates. Because some stations are never the closest station to a particular survey domain, the number of stations that ultimately are represented in the empirical analysis is 38.

Rainfall shock variables are then constructed as the change in rainfall between the two years relevant for household incomes in the survey reporting periods. The rainfall taken to be relevant for income in January through June 1997 (the first observation for each household) is in the wet and dry seasons of 1996, while the rainfall taken to matter for income in April through September 1998 (the second observation for each household) is in the wet and dry seasons of 1997. So the wet (dry) rainfall shock variables will be rainfall in the wet (dry) season of 1997 minus rainfall in the wet (dry) season of 1996. Yang and Choi (2005) document that these rainfall shock variables are strongly correlated with changes in income across localities in the Philippines during this same time period and using these same household data.

Characteristics of Sample Households.

Tables 3.3 and 3.4 present descriptive statistics for the households used in the empirical analysis, separately for migrant households (table 3.3, N=1,646) and nonmigrant households (table 3.4, N=26,121). Migrant households are those with at least one member working overseas in June 1997 and nonmigrant households account for all others.

The top row of each table displays summary statistics for the relevant exchange rate shock. For migrant households, the shock is at the household level, and it has a mean of 0.41 and a standard deviation of 0.16. For nonmigrant households, the shock is at the regional level, and it also has a mean of 0.41. The cross-regional variation in the size of the shock is substantially smaller than the overall variation, so the region-level exchange rate shock has a standard deviation of only 0.03.

In migrant households, the mean number of overseas workers in June 1997 was 1.11, mean remittance receipts were 36,194 pesos ($1,392) in January through June 1997, and the mean of remittances as a share of household income was 0.40. Nonmigrant households by definition have no members overseas initially. As a result, they also have substantially smaller remittances, with a mean of 1,889 pesos ($73), amounting to 2 percent of household income on average in January through June 1997.

Migrant households tend to be wealthier than other Philippine households in terms of their initial (January through June 1997) per capita income. Fifty-one percent of migrant households are in the top quartile of the national household income per capita distribution, and 28 percent are in the next-highest quartile. Nine percent of migrant households are below the poverty line, and the poverty gap (as fraction of the poverty line) has a mean of 0.02. Mean precrisis income per capita in migrant households is 20,235 pesos ($778).[14] By contrast, nonmigrant households are fairly evenly split across income quartiles and have a mean per capita income of 11,857 ($456). They have higher poverty rates (31 percent) and a higher mean poverty gap (as a fraction of the poverty line) of 0.10.

In terms of gift-giving,[15] migrant households do not appear to be dramatically different from other households: mean gifts to other households are 527 pesos ($20) and 406 pesos ($16), respectively, from January through June 1997. Gifts received do tend to be somewhat higher for migrant households, so that net gifts (gifts given minus gifts received) are more negative for migrant households.

Education levels and occupational groups of migrant household heads also indicate higher socioeconomic status. Thirty percent of migrant household heads have some college or more education, compared with just 20 percent of nonmigrant household heads. Twenty-three percent of migrant household heads work in agriculture, compared with 38 percent in all other households. In addition, 68 percent of migrant households are urban, compared with 58 percent of nonmigrant households.

Regression Specification

We are interested in the impact of migrants' exchange rate shocks on poverty in migrant households and, more broadly, in other (nonmigrant) households. For a migrant household, the shock in question is the household-level migrant exchange rate shock, ERSHOCK$_{it}$, as defined in equation 3.2. For a nonmigrant household, the shock is the region-level migrant exchange rate shock, REGSHOCK$_{kt}$, defined in equation 3.3.

TABLE 3.3   Descriptive Statistics for Households *with* Overseas Migrants

	Mean	Standard deviation	10th percentile	Median	90th percentile
Num. of observations: 1,646					
Exchange rate shock	0.41	0.16	0.26	0.52	0.52
Household financial statistics (Jan-Jun 1997)					
Total expenditures	73,596	66,529	24,600	57,544	132,793
Total income	94,272	92,826	28,093	70,906	175,000
Income per capita in household	20,235	21,403	5,510	15,236	39,212
Gifts to other households (a)	527	1,673	0	100	1,100
Gifts received (b)	4,000	25,934	0	613	9,380
Net gifts (a − b)	−3,474	25,950	−9,080	−340	480
Remittance receipts	36,194	46,836	0	26,000	87,500
Remittance receipts (as share of hh income)	0.40	0.31	0.00	0.37	0.85
Number of HH members working overseas in Jun 1997	1.11	0.36	1	1	1
HH size (including overseas members, Jul 1997)	6.16	2.42	3	6	9
Located in urban area	0.68				
HH position in national income per capita distribution, Jan–Jun 1997 (indicators)					
Top quartile	0.51				
3rd quartile	0.28				
2nd quartile	0.14				
Bottom quartile	0.07				
Poverty (based in Jan–Jun 1997 HH per capita income)					
Poverty indicator	0.09		0	0	0
Poverty gap (pesos)	1,671	7,152			
Poverty gap (fraction of poverty line)	0.02	0.09	0.00	0.00	0.00

Household head characteristics (Jul 1997):				
Age	49.9	13.9	32	50	68
Highest education level (indicators)				
Less than elementary	0.17			
Elementary	0.20			
Some high school	0.10			
High school	0.22			
Some college	0.16			
College or more	0.14			
Occupation (indicators)				
Agriculture	0.23			
Professional job	0.08			
Clerical job	0.13			
Service job	0.05			
Production job	0.14			
Other	0.38			
Does not work	0.00			
Marital status is single (indicator)	0.03			

Source: National Statistics Office, the Philippines.

Note: Surveys used: Labor Force Survey (Jul 1997 and Oct 1998), Survey on Overseas Filipinos (Oct 1997 and Oct 1998), 1997 Family Income and Expenditures Survey (for Jan–Jun 1997 income and expenditures), and 1998 Annual Poverty Indicators Survey (for Apr–Sep 1998 income and expenditures). Currency unit: Expenditure, income, and cash receipts from abroad are in Philippine pesos (26 per US$ in Jan–Jun 1997). Definition of exchange rate shock: Change in Philippine pesos per currency unit where overseas worker was located in Jun 1997. Change is average of 12 months leading to Oct 1998 minus average of 12 months leading to Jun 1997, divided by the latter (e.g., 10% increase is 0.1). If household has more than one overseas worker in Jun 1997, exchange rate shock variable is average change in exchange rate across household's overseas workers. (Exchange rate data are from Bloomberg L.P.) Sample: Households with a member working overseas in Jun 1997 (according to Oct 1997 Survey of Overseas Filipinos) and that also appear in 1998 Annual Poverty Indicators Survey, and excluding households with incomplete data (see Data Appendix for details).

TABLE 3.4   Descriptive Statistics for Households *without* Overseas Migrants

	Mean	Standard deviation	10th percentile	Median	90th percentile
Num. of observations 26,121					
Region-level exchange rate shock	0.41	0.03	0.35	0.41	0.43
Household financial statistics (Jan–Jun 1997)					
Total expenditures	47,436	54,156	13,657	32,495	93,493
Total income	56,053	77,659	13,516	35,909	113,452
Income per capita in household	11,857	15,115	2,864	7,625	24,100
Gifts to other households (a)	406	3,471	0	25	680
Gifts received (b)	1,609	7,192	0	276	3,718
Net gifts (a - b)	-1,202	7,793	-3,364	-150	290
Remittance receipts	1,889	13,183	0	0	0
Remittance receipts (as share of hh income)	0.02	0.10	0.00	0.00	0.00
Number of HH members working overseas in Jun 1997	0.00	0.00	0	0	0
HH size (including overseas members, Jul 1997)	5.23	2.26	3	5	8
Located in urban area	0.58				
HH position in national income per capita distribution, Jan–Jun 1997 (indicators)					
Top quartile	0.23				
3rd quartile	0.25				
2nd quartile	0.26				
Bottom quartile	0.26				
Poverty (based in Jan–Jun 1997 HH per capita income)					
Poverty indicator	0.31				
Poverty gap (pesos)	6,188	13,054		0	24,082
Poverty gap (fraction of poverty line)	0.10	0.18	0.00	0.00	0.41

Household head characteristics (Jul 1997):					
Age	46.7	14.1	30	45	67
Highest education level (indicators)					
Less than elementary	0.28				
Elementary	0.22				
Some high school	0.11				
High school	0.18				
Some college	0.11				
College or more	0.09				
Occupation (indicators)					
Agriculture	0.38				
Professional job	0.06				
Clerical job	0.11				
Service job	0.07				
Production job	0.26				
Other	0.12				
Does not work	0.00				
Marital status is single (indicator)	0.03				

Source: National Statistics Office, the Philippines.

Note: Surveys used: Labor Force Survey (Jul 1997 and Oct 1998), Survey on Overseas Filipinos (Oct 1997 and Oct 1998), 1997 Family Income and Expenditures Survey (for Jan–Jun 1997 income and expenditures), and 1998 Annual Poverty Indicators Survey (for Apr–Sep 1998 income and expenditures). Currency unit: Expenditure, income, and cash receipts from abroad are in Philippine pesos (26 per US$ in Jan–Jun 1997). Definition of region-level exchange rate shock: mean (within one of 16 regions) of migrant households' exchange rate shocks (see previous table). Sample: Households without a member working overseas in Jun 1997 (according to Oct 1997 Survey of Overseas Filipinos) and that also appear in 1998 Annual Poverty Indicators Survey, and excluding households with incomplete data (see Data Appendix for details).

The regression equation for migrant and nonmigrant households will be similar, with the only difference being in the shock variable. Each household in the data set is observed twice, so the analysis asks how changes in outcome variables between 1997 and 1998 are affected by intervening shocks. A first-differenced regression specification is therefore natural for a household i in region k and time period t.

$$\Delta Y_{ikt} = \beta_0 + \beta_1 SHOCK_{ik} + \varepsilon_{ikt} \tag{3.7}$$

For household i, ΔY_{ikt} is the change in an outcome of interest (such as the poverty indicator or remittance receipts). $SHOCK_{ik}$ is the relevant exchange rate shock for household i in region k (either $ERSHOCK_i$ or $REGSHOCK_k$). First-differencing of household-level variables is equivalent to the inclusion of household fixed effects in a levels regression, so that estimates are purged of time-invariant differences across households in the outcome variables. ε_{ikt} is a mean-zero error term.

The constant term, β_0, accounts for the average change in outcomes across all households. This is equivalent to including a year fixed effect in a regression where outcome variables are expressed in levels (not changes). It also accounts for the shared impact across households of the decline in Philippine economic growth after the onset of the crisis (and any other change between 1997 and 1998 common to all households).[16]

The coefficient of interest is β_1, the impact of a unit change in the exchange rate shock on the outcome variable. The identification assumption is that if the exchange rate shocks faced by households had all been of the same magnitude (instead of varying in size), then changes in outcomes would not have varied systematically across households on the basis of their overseas workers' locations.

While this parallel-trend identification assumption is not possible to test directly, a partial test is possible. An important type of violation of the parallel-trend assumption occurs (a) if households with migrants in countries with more favorable shocks vary along certain precrisis characteristics from households whose migrants had less favorable shocks, and (b) if changes in outcomes vary according to these same characteristics even in the absence of the migrant shocks. In fact, households experiencing more favorable migrant shocks do differ along a number of precrisis characteristics from households experiencing less favorable shocks. Yang (2004) documents that the household's exchange rate shock can be predicted by a number of preshock characteristics of households and their overseas workers.[17]

Any correlation between precrisis characteristics and the exchange rate shock is only problematic if precrisis characteristics are also associated with differential changes in outcomes independent of the exchange rate shocks (that is, if precrisis characteristics are correlated with the residual ε_{it} in equation 3.7.

To check whether the regression results are, in fact, contaminated by changes associated with precrisis characteristics, we also present coefficient estimates that include a vector of precrisis household characteristics X_{it-1} on the right-hand side of the estimating equation.

$$\Delta Y_{ikt} = \beta_0 + \beta_1 \, (\text{SHOCK}_{ik}) + \delta' \, (X_{it-1}) + \varepsilon_{ikt} \qquad (3.8)$$

X_{it-1} includes a range of precrisis household and head-of-household characteristics. Household-level controls are as follows: income variables as reported in January through June 1997 (log of per capita household income; indicators for being in the second, third, and top quartile of the sample distribution of household per capita income), and an indicator for urban location. Other controls include demographic and occupational variables as reported in July 1997: number of household members (including overseas members); five indicators for the household head's highest level of education completed (elementary, some high school, high school, some college, and college or more; less than elementary omitted); the household head's age; an indicator for whether "household head's marital status is single"; and six indicators for the household head's occupation (professional, clerical, service, production, other, not working; agricultural omitted).

It is possible to use more control variables for migrant households than for nonmigrant households. First of all, the exchange rate shock varies within regions for migrant households, so for these households it is possible to include 16 indicators for Philippine regions and their interactions with the indicator for urban location as controls.[18]

In addition, for migrant households, it is possible to control for characteristics of the household's migrants. The migrant controls are means of the following variables across a household's overseas workers who were away in June 1997: indicators for months away as of June 1997 (12–23, 24–35, 36–47, 48 or more; 0–11 omitted); indicators for highest education level completed (high school, some college, college or more; less than high school omitted); occupation indicators (domestic servant, ship's officer or crew, professional, clerical, other service, other occupation; production omitted); relationship to household head indicators (female household head or spouse of household head, daughter, son, other relation; male household head omitted); indicator for single marital status; and age.

Inclusion of the vector X_{it-1} controls for changes in outcome variables related to households' precrisis characteristics. Examining whether coefficient estimates on the exchange rate shock variable change when the precrisis household characteristics are included in the regression can shed light on whether changes in the outcome variables related to these characteristics are correlated with households' exchange rate shocks, constituting a partial test of the parallel-trend identification assumption.

In addition, to the extent that $\mathbf{X}_{it-1}$ includes variables that explain changes in outcomes but that are themselves uncorrelated with the exchange rate shocks, their inclusion can reduce residual variation and lead to more precise coefficient estimates. Therefore, in most results tables, we present regression results without and with the vector of controls for precrisis household characteristics, $\mathbf{X}_{it-1}$ (equations 3.7 and 3.8). As it turns out, for many outcome variables, inclusion of this vector of precrisis characteristics control variables makes the results stronger. It does this by making coefficient estimates higher in absolute value, by reducing standard error estimates, or both.

A final identification worry might be that the coefficient β_1 is biased because of a correlation between SHOCK$_{ik}$ and changes in other time-varying characteristics of regions. Of particular concern is the variation in local-level rainfall driven by El Niño (the weather phenomenon), which began in mid-1997 (nearly coincident with the onset of the Asian financial crisis). So we also present regression results that include controls for local-level rainfall shocks in the wet and dry seasons.

Spatial correlation among households sharing similar shocks is likely to bias ordinary least squares (OLS) standard error estimates downward (Moulton 1986). The concern is a correlation among error terms of households experiencing similar exchange rate shocks, so we allow for an arbitrary variance-covariance structure among observations experiencing similar shocks. For the migrant household regressions, standard errors are clustered according to the June 1997 location of the household's overseas worker.[19] For the nonmigrant household regressions, standard errors are clustered at the level of 16 regions (REGSHOCK$_i$ varies at this level).

Regression Results[20]

We now turn to an analysis of the impact of the migrant exchange rate shocks on migrant households and nonmigrant households.

Impact on migrant households.   It is natural to examine the reduced-form impact of household-level migrant exchange rate shocks (ERSHOCK$_i$) on poverty and other outcomes within the migrants' origin households. At the end of this section, we will turn to instrumental variables estimates of the impact of remittances on poverty, using the exchange rate shock as an instrument.

Table 3.5 presents descriptive statistics and reduced-form regression results for migrant households. The first two columns provide descriptive statistics for the initial (January through June 1997) values of the outcome variables and the change in these variables from 1997 to 1998. Regression column 1 provides coefficient estimates (standard errors in parentheses) on $ERSHOCK_i$ from estimation of equation 3.7 via OLS. Regression column 2 estimates equation 3.8, including controls for household and migrant characteristics before the Asian financial crisis. Regression column 3 augments equation 3.8 with controls for the wet and dry season rainfall shocks, to help control for bias caused by any correlation between local rainfall shocks and migrant exchange rate shocks.

Panel A of the table presents results for the three poverty measures. The initial (January through June 1997) mean of the poverty indicator represents the poverty rate among migrant households in the initial period, 0.09. Analogously, the mean change in the poverty indicator is the change in the poverty rate among these households: at 0.041, this a substantial increase in the poverty rate from its initial level.

The coefficient estimates on the exchange rate shock in regression columns 1 through 3 indicate that improvements in the exchange rates faced by a household's migrants lead to reductions in the incidence of household poverty: coefficient estimates in all three columns are negative. Inclusion of controls for initial household and migrant characteristics (column 2) and for local rainfall shocks (column 3) has little impact on the estimates: the coefficient in column 3 is −0.060, while the coefficient estimate in column 1 is −0.061.

The coefficient estimates in columns 1 and 3 are statistically significant at the 10 percent level. The coefficient estimate in column 3 (−0.060) indicates that a one-standard-deviation increase in the size of the exchange rate shock (0.16, a favorable change) leads to a 1 percentage point decline in the likelihood a household is in poverty. This is a large effect, relative to the mean change in poverty incidence over the time period (4.1 percentage points) and the initial poverty rate at the start of the period (9 percent).

Consistent with the negative impact on the incidence of poverty, the exchange rate shocks are also associated with reductions in the two poverty gap measures (second and third rows of panel A): coefficient estimates for those outcomes are all negative in sign, large in magnitude, and stable in the face of the inclusion of additional control variables. However, these coefficients are also imprecisely estimated, and this should only be taken as suggestive evidence that exchange rate shocks also reduce the depth of poverty in migrant households.

How do these reductions in poverty come about? Panel B examines the impact of exchange rate shocks on two likely channels through which the shocks affect household poverty. The first row presents results for which the outcome variable is the change in remittance receipts (expressed as a fraction of initial household income).[21] The initial (January through June 1997) mean of this outcome variable

TABLE 3.5 Impact of Migrant Exchange Rate Shocks, 1997-8

	Initial mean of outcome	Mean (std.dev.) of change in outcome	Coefficient on exchange rate shock (OLS)			Coefficient on remittance receipts (IV)
			(1)	(2)	(3)	
Panel A: Poverty measures						
Poverty indicator	0.09	0.041 (0.008)	−0.061 (0.031)*	−0.054 (0.035)	−0.06 (0.034)*	−0.278 (0.138)**
Poverty gap (pesos)	1,671	1,594 (270)	−1,992 (1,284)	−1,611 (1,490)	−1,853 (1,492)	−8,505 (6,684)
Poverty gap (fraction of poverty line)	0.023	0.018 (0.004)	−0.02 (0.017)	−0.017 (0.018)	−0.02 (0.018)	−0.093 (0.073)
Panel B: Remittances, household income						
Remittance receipts	0.395	0.099 (0.021)	0.152 (0.112)	0.220 (0.079)***	0.218 (0.081)***	1.083 (0.332)***
Household income	1.000	0.131 (0.027)	0.232 (0.144)	0.238 (0.114)**	0.236 (0.113)**	
Panel C: Gifts						
Gifts to other households (a)	0.007	0.001 (0.001)	0.012 (0.004)**	0.01 (0.004)**	0.01 (0.004)**	0.047 (0.021)**
Gifts received (b)	0.046	−0.029 (0.002)	−0.023 (0.010)**	−0.013 (0.014)	−0.012 (0.014)	−0.056 (0.076)
Net gifts (a − b)	−0.039	0.03 (0.003)	0.034 (0.012)***	0.023 (0.016)	0.022 (0.016)	0.103 (0.092)

Specification:			
Region*Urban controls	N	Y	Y
Controls for pre-crisis household and migrant characteristics	N	Y	Y
Rainfall shock controls	N	N	Y
Number of observations in all regressions	1,646		

Notes: Standard errors in parentheses, clustered by location country of household's eldest overseas worker. All dependent variables are first-differenced variables. For remittance and income variables, change is between Jan-Jun 1997 and Apr-Sep 1998 reporting periods, expressed as fraction of initial (Jan-Jun 1997) household income. Poverty variables based on income per capita in household (excluding overseas members), using poverty lines specific to urban and rural areas by province. Gifts changes are between Jan-Jun 1997 and Apr-Sep 1998 reporting periods, expressed as fractions of initial (Jan-Jun 1997) expenditures. (Expenditures are only for current consumption, and do not include purchases of durable goods.) See Table 3.3 for notes on sample definition and definition of exchange rate shock.

Region*Urban controls are 16 indicators for regions within the Philippines and their interactions with an indicator for urban location. Household-level controls are as follows. Income variables as reported in Jan-Jun 1997: log of per capita household income; indicators for being in 2nd, 3rd, and top quartile of sample distribution of household per capita income. Demographic and occupational variables as reported in July 1997: number of household members (including overseas members); five indicators for head's highest level of education completed (elementary, some high school, high school, some college, and college or more; less than elementary omitted); head's age; indicator for "head's marital status is single"; six indicators for head's occupation (professional, clerical, service, production, other, not working; agricultural omitted).

Migrant controls are means of the following variables across HH's overseas workers in June 1997: indicators for months away (12-23, 24-35, 36-47, 48 or more; 0-11 omitted); indicators for highest education level completed (high school, some college, college or more; less than high school omitted); occupation indicators (domestic servant, ship's officer or crew, professional, clerical, other service, other occupation; production omitted); relationship to HH head indicators (female head or spouse of head, daughter, son, other relation; male head omitted); indicator for single marital status; years of age. Rainfall shocks are changes in wet and dry season rainfall between first and second period.

* significant at 10%; ** significant at 5%; *** significant at 1%

is 0.395. Remittance receipts increased, on average, over the time period: the mean change is 0.099 (or 9.9 percent of initial household income). The coefficient estimates indicate that improvements in the exchange rate faced by migrant household members lead to substantial increases in household remittance receipts. Coefficient estimates become larger in magnitude and achieve statistical significance (at the 1 percent level) upon inclusion of the initial household and migrant characteristics control variables, and are robust to the inclusion of the rainfall shock controls. The coefficient estimate in column 3 indicates that a one-standard-deviation increase in the size of the exchange rate shock (0.16) leads to an increase in remittances amounting to 3.5 percent of initial household income.

Coefficient estimates in regressions where the outcome variable is the change in household income (as a fraction of initial household income) are similar in magnitude and statistical significance to the coefficient estimates for the change in remittances (second row of panel B). This suggests that the increase in household income comes directly as a result of the increase in remittances, rather than via second-order effects on entrepreneurial income (at least over this 15-month time frame).[22]

We are also interested in examining spillovers to nonmigrant households of the shocks experienced in migrant households. One potentially important channel through which migrant households might affect poverty in nonmigrant households is gifts (transfers). Panel C examines the impact of the exchange rate shocks on gift-giving, gift receipt, and net gifts (gifts given minus gifts received), expressed as fractions of initial household expenditures. (The gifts variables do not include remittances.)

The strongest result is for changes in gifts to other households, shown in the first row of panel C. The coefficient on the exchange rate shock is positive and statistically significantly different from zero in all specifications, and is highly robust to the inclusion of control variables and the rainfall shocks. The coefficient in column 3 (0.01) indicates that a one-standard-deviation increase in the size of the exchange rate shock (0.16) leads to an increase in gifts to other households, which amounts to 0.16 percent of initial household expenditures.

The coefficient estimates in regressions where gifts received and net gifts are the dependent variables are in the last two rows, and are consistent with the results for gifts given. Gifts received decline and net gifts rise in households experiencing more favorable migrant exchange rate shocks. That said, the coefficient estimates for these outcome variables are not statistically significantly different from zero when initial household and migrant characteristics control variables are added to the regression (columns 2 and 3). However, the coefficient for net gifts in column 3 is marginally statistically significant, with a t-statistic of 1.39 and a p-value of 0.170.

We now turn to instrumental variables estimates of the impact of remittance receipts on the various outcome variables in table 3.5, in which the exchange rate shock is used as an instrument for remittance receipts. This analysis seems workable, first of all, because the impact of the exchange rate shock on remittance receipts is strong. The F-statistic on the test of the significance of the exchange rate shock in column 3 when remittances are the outcome variable is 7.29 (with a p-value of 0.0092). Equally important, it is plausible that the IV exclusion restriction is satisfied: the impact of the exchange rate shock on the various outcomes can be reasonably assumed to work primarily via the change in remittance receipts.

The results are presented in column 4 of table 3.5, using the most inclusive list of control variables. The first result of interest is simply the impact of instrumented remittances on total household income (second row of panel B). The coefficient of 1.08 is highly statistically significant and essentially indicates a one-for-one effect of remittance receipts on household income.

Turning to the poverty results, the coefficient on the poverty indicator (-0.278) is negative and statistically significant. A 10 percentage point increase in remittance receipts (as a fraction of initial household income) leads to a reduction of 2.8 percentage points in the household's likelihood of being in poverty. The coefficients on the two poverty gap measures also are negative, although neither is statistically significantly different from zero.

Finally, the impact of instrumented remittances on the gifts measures corresponds to the findings in the reduced-form results in columns 1 through 3. There is a positive and statistically significant effect on gifts to other households. A 10 percentage point increase in remittance receipts (as a fraction of initial household income) leads to a 0.5 percentage point increase in gifts to other households. The impact of remittances on gifts received and on net gifts is negative and positive, respectively, but neither of these results are statistically significant.

Impact on nonmigrant households. Did the exchange rate shocks, which lead to increased remittances, higher incomes, and reductions in poverty in migrant households, also have effects on nonmigrant households? Potential channels for any potential spillover effects to nonmigrant households include general increases in economic activity (driven by increased expenditures by migrant households), as well as direct transfers from migrant households to nonmigrant households.

Table 3.6 presents descriptive statistics and regression results for estimates of the impact of region-level migrant exchange rate shocks—REGSHOCK$_k$, as defined in equation 3.3—on nonmigrant households. The format of the table is identical to the format of table 3.5, except that the shock variable is now REGSHOCK$_k$ instead of ERSHOCK$_j$.

The three poverty measures (in panel A) indicate increases in poverty in the period following the financial crisis. The initial (January through June 1997) poverty rate among nonmigrant households is 0.307, and this figure increases by 0.102 (roughly one-third) over the study period. Likewise, the measures of the depth of poverty also show substantial increases.

The coefficient estimates for the poverty measures indicate that increases (favorable changes) in the mean exchange rate shock across a region's migrants lead to declines in the incidence and depth of poverty. In the first row of panel A, the coefficient estimates on REGSHOCK$_k$ are all negative, and become more negative and statistically significantly different from zero in the specifications that include initial household controls and the rainfall shocks.[23] In the third row of the panel (where poverty gap as a share of the poverty line is the outcome variable), coefficient estimates on REGSHOCK$_k$ are also negative and again are statistically significantly different from zero in columns 2 and 3. The results for the poverty gap in pesos (second row of panel A) are consistent with the results for the other two poverty outcomes in terms of sign (that is, negative), but for this outcome, the coefficient estimates are not statistically significantly different from zero.

It is also worth noting the robustness of the coefficient estimates to inclusion of the rainfall shocks controls (comparing results in columns 2 and 3). The similarity of coefficient estimates across the two columns suggests that the rainfall shocks and regional exchange rate shocks are not highly correlated, providing little reason to be concerned that the coincidental timing of El Niño with the Asian financial crisis leads to substantial bias.

The size of the estimated impacts on poverty is not extremely large, but neither are they insignificant. The coefficient estimate in column 3 of panel A indicates that a one-standard-deviation increase in the size of the region-level migrant exchange rate shock (0.03) leads to a 1.4 percentage point reduction in the incidence of poverty (compare this with an initial level of 30.7 percent and an aggregate change between 1997 and 1998 of 10.2 percentage points). Such a shock also leads to a modest reduction in the depth of poverty, as measured by the poverty gap as a fraction of the poverty line, of 0.7 percentage points (compared with an initial level of 9.8 percent and a change between 1997 and 1998 of 5.2 percentage points).

The obvious question is how exchange rate shocks in migrant households translate into reductions in poverty in nonmigrant households. Regression estimates in panels B and C attempt to address this question by examining the impact of the region-level migrant exchange rate shocks on changes in remittances, household income, and gifts in nonmigrant households.

The first row of panel B presents results for which the outcome variable is the change in remittance receipts (expressed as a fraction of initial household income).

In households without migrant members, the initial (January through June 1997) mean of this outcome variable is low (0.023). Remittance receipts actually declined on average over the time period, with a mean change of −0.006. The coefficient estimates indicate that improvements in REGSHOCK$_k$ do not have an important effect on remittance receipts in nonmigrant households: the coefficient estimates are inconsistently signed, close to zero, and are not statistically significantly different from zero. Changes in remittance receipts from overseas do not help explain the reductions in poverty in nonmigrant households.

It is important to check whether reductions in poverty in nonmigrant households are accompanied by increases in their household income. The second row of panel B does so, presenting results for which the outcome variable is the change in household income (expressed as a fraction of initial household income). The coefficient on REGSHOCK$_k$ is positive in all three specifications, and it becomes substantially larger in magnitude when control variables are added in columns 2 and 3. The coefficient in column 3 (0.992) suggests that a one-standard-deviation increase in the size of the region-level migrant exchange rate shock (0.03) leads to a 3 percentage point increase in household income (as a share of initial income). However, this coefficient is imprecisely estimated, with a standard error of 0.767 (the t-statistic is 1.29, p-value 0.216). This should therefore be taken as merely suggestive evidence that household incomes increase between 1997 and 1998 in regions with more positive values of REGSHOCK$_k$.

Additionally, there is evidence that gift receipts by nonmigrant households rise in regions that experience more positive changes in the mean migrant exchange rate shock. REGSHOCK$_k$ has little relationship to gifts given to other households by nonmigrant households, as evidenced by the small size and the lack of statistical significance of the coefficient estimates in the first row of panel C. However, region-level migrant exchange rate shocks do lead to larger gift receipts: the coefficients in the second row of panel C are all positive, and the coefficient in column 3 is statistically significantly different from zero. The impact of REGSHOCK$_k$ on net gifts is negative and also statistically significant in column 3.

The coefficient on gifts received in column 3 of panel C indicates that a one-standard-deviation increase in the size of the region-level migrant exchange rate shock (0.03) leads to a 0.26 percentage point increase in gifts received (as a share of initial household expenditures).

In sum, more favorable region-level migrant exchange rate shocks lead to reductions in the incidence and depth of poverty, increases in receipt of gifts, and (possibly) increases in household income levels. The magnitude of the response of gift receipts does not appear large enough to explain the reductions in poverty, so it is likely that general increases in economic activity (translating into higher incomes for the poor) also play a role.

TABLE 3.6 Impact of Region-Level Migrant Exchange Rate Shocks on Non-Migrant Households, 1997–8

	Initial mean of outcome	Mean (std.dev.) of change in outcome	Regressions		
			(1)	(2)	(3)
Panel A: Poverty measures					
Poverty indicator	0.307	0.102 (0.009)	-0.412 (0.358)	-0.481 (0.241)*	-0.475 (0.248)*
Poverty gap (pesos)	6,188	4,325 (444)	-4,587 (15,674)	-4,913 (12,128)	-3,483 (10,923)
Poverty gap (fraction of poverty line)	0.098	0.052 (0.006)	-0.272 (0.192)	-0.244 (0.130)*	-0.233 (0.120)*
Panel B: Remittances, household income					
Remittance receipts	0.023	-0.006 (0.002)	-0.026 (0.038)	0.029 (0.055)	0.024 (0.054)
Household income	1.000	0.027 (0.016)	0.036 (0.876)	0.817 (0.875)	0.992 (0.767)
Panel C: Gifts					
Gifts to other households (a)	0.007	-0.001 0.000	-0.008 (0.014)	-0.005 (0.013)	0.024 (0.013)
Gifts received (b)	0.037	-0.021 (0.001)	0.044 (0.038)	0.07 (0.051)	0.086 (0.042)**

Net gifts (a − b)	−0.030	0.02	−0.052	−0.074	−0.091
		(0.002)	(0.044)	(0.054)	(0.045)**
Specification:					
Controls for pre-crisis characteristics			N	Y	Y
Rainfall shock controls			N	N	Y
Num. of observations in all regressions	26,121				

Notes: Each cell in regression columns 1–3 presents coefficient estimate on exchange rate shock in a separate OLS regression. Standard errors in parentheses, clustered by location country of household's eldest overseas worker. All dependent variables are first-differenced variables. Controls for pre-crisis characteristics are: household characteristics as in table 3.5, indicator for urban location, and fraction of households in province with a migrant member. See table 3.5 for other notes.

* significant at 10%; ** significant at 5%; *** significant at 1%

Region-Level Analysis

To examine region-level inequality measures, we collapse the data to the level of the Philippines' 16 regions. The outcome variables of interest are changes in three measures of inequality at the region level: the Gini index, the 90–10 percentile ratio, and the 75–25 percentile ratio. These measures are constructed on the basis of household per capita income (calculated excluding overseas members), making use of survey weights. To confirm the robustness of the household-level results in tables 3.5 and 3.6, we also examine poverty measures at the regional level that are analogous to the household-level poverty measures previously used: the regional poverty rate (the mean across households of POV_{it}) and the regional means of the two poverty gap measures ($POVGAP_{it}$ and $POVGAPFR_{it}$).

The regression equation is as follows.

$$\Delta INEQ_{jt} = \alpha_0 + \alpha_1 REGSHOCK_j + \varepsilon_{jt} \tag{3.9}$$

where $\Delta INEQ_{jt}$ is the change between January and June 1997 and April and September 1998 in a measure of income inequality. $REGSHOCK_j$ is as defined above in equation 3.3. ε_{jt} is a mean-zero error term. Each region-level regression will therefore have just 16 observations.

The first two columns of table 3.7 provide descriptive statistics for the initial (January through June 1997) values of the outcome variables and the change in these variables from 1997 to 1998. Regression column 1 provides coefficient estimates (standard errors in parentheses) on $REGSHOCK_j$ from estimation of equation 3.9 via OLS. Regression column 2 augments equation 3.9 with controls for the mean of the wet and dry season rainfall shocks across households within the region, to help control for bias caused by any correlation between the rainfall shocks and the regional exchange rate shocks.

Panel A of the table provides results for which the poverty measures are the dependent variables. The mean poverty rate across regions is 0.349 in the initial period. Poverty rates increased over the study period, with a mean change across regions of 0.106. The coefficient estimate on $REGSHOCK_j$ for this outcome in column 1 is negative (-0.546) and statistically significant at the 10 percent level. Inclusion of the rainfall shock controls (column 2) makes the coefficient slightly more negative (-0.582), and it maintains its level of statistical significance.

How large is this effect on the poverty rate? A one-standard-deviation increase in the region-level migrant exchange rate shock (0.03) leads to a 1.8 percentage point reduction in the poverty rate. Reassuringly, this estimate is quite similar to the 1.4 percentage point estimated effect of a 0.03 region-level exchange rate shock in the household regression in table 3.6.

TABLE 3.7   Impact of Region-Level Migrant Exchange Rate Shocks, 1997–8

	Initial mean of outcome	Mean (std.dev.) of change in outcome	Regressions (1)	Regressions (2)
Panel A: Regional poverty measures				
Poverty rate	0.349	0.106 (0.010)	−0.546 (0.287)*	−0.582 (0.314)*
Mean poverty gap (pesos)	7,028	4,457 (431)	−4,508 (14,428)	−5,525 (16,126)
Mean poverty gap (fraction of poverty line)	0.115	0.056 (0.006)	−0.256 (0.195)	−0.267 (0.220)
Panel B: Regional inequality measures				
Gini coefficient	0.455	0.021 (0.003)	0.055 (0.111)	0.031 (0.104)
90–10 percentile ratio	7.274	0.73 (0.167)	−2.499 (5.584)	−3.363 (6.153)
75-25 percentile ratio	2.806	0.102 (0.051)	−2.584 (1.578)	−2.295 (1.736)
Specification: Rainfall shock controls			N	Y
Num. of obs. in all regressions:	16			

Notes: Each cell in regression columns 1–2 presents coefficient estimate on region-level exchange rate shock in a separate OLS regression. Units of analysis are 16 Philippine regions. Standard errors in parentheses. All dependent variables are in first-differences. Independent variable (region-level exchange rate shock) is mean exchange rate shock across migrants within region (mean 0.40, std. dev. 0.03). Construction of poverty and inequality variables uses sample weights.
* significant at 10%; ** significant at 5%; *** significant at 1%.

The coefficient estimates of the region-level migrant exchange rate shock for the two poverty gap measures are negative in column 2 of panel A (and are consistent with the decline in the poverty rate), but they are not precisely estimated. The results on the depth of poverty must therefore be taken as suggestive in this analysis.

Descriptive statistics and regression results for the impact of region-level migrant exchange rate shocks on region-level inequality are presented in panel B of the table. All three measures of within-region income inequality rise modestly on average between 1997 and 1998: the Gini coefficient by 0.021 (from a base of 0.455), the 90–10 percentile ratio by 0.73 (from a base of 7.274), and the 75–25 percentile ratio by 0.102 (from a base of 2.806).

The coefficient estimates of the impact of $REGSHOCK_j$ on the inequality measures tell a somewhat inconclusive story. The coefficient estimates in regressions for which the Gini coefficient is the outcome variable are positive (indicating an increase in inequality). By contrast, the coefficient estimates in the regressions for the 90–10 and 75–25 percentile ratios are negative (indicating reductions in inequality). However, these coefficients are all quite small in magnitude; the coefficient in column 2 for the 90–10 percentile ratio indicates that a one-standard-deviation increase in $REGSHOCK_j$ would cause a mere 0.10 decline in this inequality measure (from a base of 7.274). What is more, none of the coefficients in the regressions for the inequality measures are statistically significantly different from zero.

In sum, this analysis confirms that region-level migrant exchange rate shocks lead to modest reductions in the region-level incidence of poverty. A 3 percent improvement in the mean exchange rate experienced by a region's migrants is associated with a 1.8 percentage point reduction in poverty (from a base of 0.349). However, there are no strong results regarding the impact of such shocks on the depth of poverty or on income inequality within regions.

Effects of Exchange Rate Shocks on Human Capital and Entrepreneurship

This chapter has concerned itself with the immediate impact of exchange rate shocks on poverty in migrants' origin households and home areas (via changes in remittances). An important question that arises is whether exchange rate shocks are likely to also have longer-term effects on the well-being of migrants' origin households. Yang (2004) addresses this question in detail, and examines the impact of migrants' exchange rate shocks on human capital investment and entrepreneurial activity in migrants' origin households, activities that are likely to have more persistent effects on household well-being and whose effects could last beyond migrant members' overseas stays.

If households have complete access to credit, transitory shocks should have no effect on household long-term investments, because borrowing allows households to make investments in advance of the future returns. But when households face credit constraints, and when household investments require fixed costs be paid in advance of the investment returns, the timing of household investments may depend on current income realizations. In particular, households may raise investments when experiencing positive income shocks. In economic models of child labor, such as Baland and Robinson (2000) or Basu and Van (1998), temporary increases in household income can allow households to reduce child labor-force participation and raise child schooling. The effect of such positive income shocks on child schooling is magnified if schooling involves large fixed costs, such as tuition. Transitory income shocks can also affect household participation in entrepreneurial activities, if such activities are capital-intensive. Rosenzweig and Wolpin (1993) document how productive assets may play dual roles as savings mechanisms and income sources when credit and formal savings mechanisms are poor or nonexistent: accumulation and decumulation of productive assets in the face of positive and negative shocks (respectively) play a role analogous to accumulation and decumulation of savings. One might expect that households experiencing favorable exchange rate shocks would accumulate productive assets.

The relevant analyses in Yang (2004) involve estimating regressions analogous to equations 3.7 and 3.8, in which the dependent variables are the changes in several variables related to child human capital investment and entrepreneurial activity. Regression analyses are for exactly the same migrant households that are analyzed in the current chapter (whose summary statistics are given in table 3.3, and for whom poverty results are presented in table 3.5).

Table 3.8 reports some key results from Yang (2004) for five dependent variables. The results presented are for regressions analogous to equation 3.7. In columns 1 and 2, the dependent variables relate to child human capital investment, and the unit of analysis is a child followed from July 1997 to October 1998. Regressions are for children ages 10–17 in July 1997; the dependent variables are not recorded for children younger than 10.

More favorable exchange rate shocks are associated with improved human capital investment in children, because they lead to increases in schooling and declines in child labor. In the first column of the table 3.8, the outcome is the change in an indicator for the child's primary activity being reported as student. In the second column, the dependent variable is the change in total hours worked in the past week. More favorable exchange rate shocks are associated with differential increases in student status and declines in child labor. The coefficients in columns 1 and 2 indicate that one-standard-deviation increase in the size of the exchange rate shock (0.16) leads to a differential increase in student status of 1.7 percentage points, and to differential declines in child labor of 0.35 hours in the past week.[24]

In columns 3 through 5 of table 3.8, the dependent variables relate to entrepreneurial activity in migrants' origin households. The unit of analysis is a household.

TABLE 3.8   Impact of Migrant Exchange Rate Shocks on Child Human Capital and Entrepreneurship, 1997–8

	Dependent variables				
	Change in student status (children aged 10–17)	Change in hours worked (children aged 10–17)	Entry into a new entrepreneurial activity	Net entry into "transportation and communication services" entrepreneurship	Net entry into "manufacturing" entrepreneurship
Coefficient on exchange rate shock	0.103 (0.041)**	−2.215 (0.905)**	0.140 (0.046)***	0.076 (0.031)**	0.058 (0.025)**
R-squared	0.27	0.15	0.06	0.04	0.06
Num. of observations	1,188	1,188	1,646	1,646	1,646

Source: Yang 2004.

Note: Each column is a separate OLS regression. Standard errors in parentheses, clustered by location country of household's eldest overseas worker. Entrepreneurial outcomes are household-level, and child outcomes are individual-level regressions. Changes between 1997 and 1998. Each regression includes household location fixed effects and controls for household and migrant characteristics (see notes to Table 3.5 for list). Regressions for child outcomes include controls for individual-level control variables (as reported in 1997): fixed effects for each year of age; gender indicator; indicator for marital status is single, indicator for primary activity is student, indicator for not in labor force, and five indicators for highest schooling level completed (elementary, some high school, high school, some college, and college or more).

* significant at 10%; ** significant at 5%; *** significant at 1%.

In the third column, the outcome is an indicator for entry into a new entrepreneurial activity between 1997 and 1998. The coefficient is positive and statistically significant, indicating that households with more favorable exchange rate shocks were more likely to enter a new entrepreneurial activity over the study period. A one-standard-deviation increase in the size of the exchange rate shock (0.16) leads to a differential 2.2 percentage point increase in the likelihood of entry into a new entrepreneurial activity.

These new entries are concentrated in two subcategories of entrepreneurship: transportation and communication services, and manufacturing. In columns 4 and 5 of the table, the outcomes are net entry into these activities (the change between periods of an indicator for participation in the said activity). In both columns, the coefficients on the exchange rate shock are positive and statistically significantly different from zero.[25] It is sensible that new entries into entrepreneurship are concentrated in these activities, because they are likely to involve nontrivial fixed costs in vehicles and equipment that could become more affordable in the wake of positive exchange rate shocks. The results for transportation and communication services most likely reflect entry into transportation services, such as taxi and minibus operation, and are consistent with other results in Yang (2004)—that positive exchange rate shocks also raise vehicle ownership. Manufacturing activities include small activities such as mat weaving, tailoring, dressmaking, and food processing.

In sum, additional evidence in Yang (2004) indicates that the exchange rate shocks raised household investment in child human capital and capital-intensive entrepreneurial activities. The fact that the exchange rate shocks stimulated such investments suggests that the shocks are likely to have persistent and positive effects on household well-being over the long term, in addition to their leading to reductions in current poverty.

Conclusion

Millions of migrants worldwide send remittances to families back home. The potential poverty-reducing impact of remittances has been widely discussed, but until now empirical evidence on the topic has been scarce. This chapter helps fill this gap, by examining the impact of exogenous shocks to remittances on poverty rates in migrants' origin households, as well as in nonmigrant households in the same geographic region.

Filipino migrants work in a variety of foreign countries, and these migrants experienced sudden changes in exchange rates because of the 1997 Asian financial crisis. Appreciation of a migrant's currency against the Philippine peso leads to increases in household remittance receipts. In migrants' origin households, a 10 percent improvement in the exchange rate leads to a 0.6 percentage point decline in the poverty rate.

We also find evidence of spillovers to households without migrant members. Because of geographic variation within the Philippines in migrants' overseas locations, there was also variation in the region-level mean migrant exchange rate shock across regions of the country. In regions with a greater number of more favorable mean exchange rate shocks, poverty rates decline even in households without migrant members. There is, however, no strong evidence of effects on region-level inequality. This broader decline in poverty may be due to increases in economic activity driven by remittance flows, as well as by direct transfers from migrants' origin households to households that do not have migrant members.

It is important to note that the period studied in this chapter (1997–98) was one of substantial economic fluctuation in the Philippines, because of the Asian financial crisis and the drought caused by El Niño. Although there is no evidence that the estimates are confounded because of a cross-regional correlation between the region-level exchange rate shocks and other shocks, concern exists that the effects of exchange rate shock on poverty reduction might appear primarily during a crisis period, and not during periods free from economic fluctuations. In other words, in a time of general increases in poverty, remittances flowing into a region might prevent households from falling into poverty (or from falling deeper into poverty), but these remittances may not have the same effect in times of economic growth. An important area of future research would be to examine the impact of migrants' exchange rate shocks (or other determinants of remittances) on poverty in home areas when the home areas in question are not suffering general declines in economic conditions.

Annex 3.A. Household Data Set

Four linked household surveys were provided by the National Statistics Office of the Philippine government: the Labor Force Survey (LFS), the Survey on Overseas Filipinos (SOF), the Family Income and Expenditure Survey (FIES), and the Annual Poverty Indicators Survey (APIS).[26]

The LFS collects data on primary activity, hours worked in the past week, and demographic characteristics of household members age 10 or older. These data refer to the household members' activities in the week before the survey. The survey defines a household as a group of people who live under the same roof and share common food. The definition also includes people currently overseas if they lived with the household before departure.

The SOF is administered in October of each year to households reporting in the LFS that any members left for overseas within the last five years. The SOF collects information on characteristics of the household's overseas members, their overseas locations and lengths of stay overseas, and the value of remittances received by the household from overseas in the last six months (April to September).

In the analysis, we use the July 1997 and October 1998 rounds of the LFS and the October 1997 and October 1998 rounds of the SOF. We obtain household income, expenditures, and gifts from the FIES for January through June 1997 and from the APIS for April through September 1998 (because no FIES was conducted in 1998). Remittance data are from the FIES for January through June 1997 and from the SOF for April through September 1998.

Data on remittances received from overseas in the second reporting period (April through September 1998) are available in both the APIS and the SOF (both conducted in October 1998). All analyses of remittances use data from the SOF for the second reporting period, because this source is likely to be more accurate (the SOF asks for information on amounts sent by each household member overseas, which are then added up to obtain total remittance receipts; by contrast, the APIS asks for total cash receipts from overseas). Total household income in April through September 1998 (obtained from the APIS) is adjusted so that the remittance component reflects data from the SOF.

The sample used in the empirical analysis consists of all households meeting the following criteria:

- The household's dwelling was also included in the October 1998 LFS/SOF. As mentioned above, one-quarter of households in the sample in July 1997 had just been rotated out of the sample in October 1998.
- The same household has occupied the dwelling between July 1997 and October 1998. This criterion is necessary because the LFS does not attempt to interview households that have changed dwellings. Usefully, the LFS data set contains a field noting whether the household currently living in the dwelling is the same as the household surveyed in the previous round.
- The household has complete data on precrisis control and outcome variables (recorded July 1997).
- The household has complete data on postcrisis outcome variables (recorded October 1998).

Of 30,744 dwellings that the National Statistics Office did not rotate out of the sample between July 1997 and October 1998 (criterion 1), 28,152 (91.6 percent) contained the same household continuously over that period (criterion 2). Of these households, 27,767 had complete data for all variables used in the empirical analysis (criteria 3 and 4).

Determining Precrisis Location of Overseas Household Members

In this subsection, we describe the rules used to determine whether a particular individual in the October 1997 SOF was overseas in June 1997, and if so, what country the person was in at that time. Among other questions, the SOF asks the following:

- Question 1. When did the family member last leave for overseas?
- Question 2. In what country did the family member intend to stay when he/she last left?
- Question 3. When did the family member return home from his/her last departure (if at all)?

These questions unambiguously identify individuals as being away in June 1997 (and their overseas locations) if they left for overseas in or before that month and returned afterward (or are still overseas). Unfortunately, the survey does not collect information on stays overseas before the most recent stay. Thus, there are individuals who most recently left for overseas between June 1997 and the survey date in October 1997, but who were likely to have been overseas before then as well. Fortunately, there is an additional question in the SOF that is of use:

- Question 4. How many months has the family member worked/been working abroad during the last five years?

Using this question, two reasonable assumptions allow us to proceed. First, assume all stays overseas are continuous (except for vacations home in the middle of a stay overseas). Second, assume no household member moves between countries overseas. With these two assumptions, the questions asked on the SOF are sufficient to identify whether a household had a member in a particular country in June 1997.

For example, a household surveyed in October 1997 might have a household member who last left for Saudi Arabia in July 1997 and had not yet returned from that stay overseas. If that household member is reported as having worked overseas for four months or more, the first assumption implies the person first left for overseas in or before June 1997. The second assumption implies that the person was in Saudi Arabia.

Using questions 1 and 3, 89.8 percent of individuals identified as being away in June 1997 (and their overseas locations) were classified as such. The remaining

10.2 percent of individuals identified as being away in June 1997 (and their locations) relied on question 4 and the two allocation assumptions just described.

Endnotes

1. Estimates of the number of individuals living outside their countries of birth are from United Nations (2002), while data on world population are from U.S. Bureau of the Census (2002).

2. The remittance figure is the sum of the "workers' remittances," "compensation of employees," and "migrants' transfers" items in the International Monetary Fund's International Financial Statistics database for all countries not listed as "high income" in the World Bank's country groupings. All dollars are U.S. dollars.

3. Aid and foreign direct investment (FDI) figures are from World Bank (2004). While the figures for official development aid and FDI are likely to be accurate, by most accounts (for example, Ratha 2003) national statistics on remittance receipts are considerably underreported. So the remittance figure may be taken as a lower bound.

4. Borjas (1999) argues that the investigation of benefits accruing to migrants' source countries is an important and virtually unexplored area in research on migration.

5. We describe the exchange rate index in the following section.

6. See, for example, Stark, Taylor, and Yitzhaki (1986); Taylor (1992); Ahlburg (1996); and Rodriguez (1998).

7. Examples of this approach include Adams (1989), Barham and Boucher (1998), and Adams (2004).

8. The source for these data is *Philippine Yearbook* (2001), table 15.4. These figures do not include Filipinos who go overseas without the help of government-authorized recruitment agencies. By all accounts (for example, Cariño and others 1998), there was a dramatic rise in the number of Filipinos going overseas in this period, so the figures should not reflect merely the collection of new data on previously undocumented worker departures.

9. For 90 percent of individuals in the SOF, their location overseas in that month is reported explicitly. For the remainder, a few reasonable assumptions must be made to determine their June 1997 location. See the annex A for the procedure used to determine the locations of overseas Filipinos in the SOF.

10. The exchange rates are as of the end of each month, and were obtained from Bloomberg L.P.

11. Of the 1,646 households included in the analysis, 1,485 (90.2 percent) had just one member working overseas in June 1997; 140 households (8.5 percent) had two, 18 households (1.1 percent) had three, and 3 households (0.2 percent) had four members working overseas in that month.

12. We use the National Statistics Office of the Philippines' region definitions as of July 1996 (version 4). The regions are the National Capital Region (NCR), Ilocos, Cagayan Valley, Central Luzon, Southern Tagalog, Bicol, Western Visayas, Central Visayas, Eastern Visayas, Western Mindanao, Northern Mindanao, Southern Mindanao, Central Mindanao, Cordillera Administrative Region (CAR), Autonomous Region of Muslim Mindanao (ARMM), and Caraga.

13. These data are available online at http://www.nscb.gov.ph/poverty/2000/povertyprov.asp. For 1997, the poverty lines were constructed separately for urban and rural areas within 83 disaggregated localities (provinces). In 1998, poverty lines were not constructed at this disaggregated level, and they are only available at the level of 16 regions.

14. Per capita figures exclude overseas members. U.S. dollars are converted from Philippine pesos based on the first-half 1997 exchange rate of roughly 26 pesos per US$1.

15. Note that gifts do not include remittances.

16. After the onset of the crisis, annual real gross domestic product (GDP) contracted by 0.8 percent in 1998, as compared with growth of 5.2 percent in 1997 and 5.8 percent in 1996 (World Bank 2004). The urban unemployment rate (unemployed as a share of total labor force) rose from 9.5 percent

to 10.8 percent between 1997 and 1998, while the rural unemployment rate went from 5.2 percent to 6.9 percent over the same period (*Philippine Yearbook* 2001, table 15.1).

17. See appendix table 1 in Yang 2004.

18. Inclusion of such controls for nonmigrant households would absorb all variation in the $REGSHOCK_k$ variable, which only varies at the region level.

19. For households that had more than one overseas worker in June 1997, the household is clustered according to the location of the eldest overseas worker. This results in 55 clusters.

20. The empirical results are subject to some limitations which may or may not have a bearing on the results. These include (a) the use of the nominal exchange rate between each destination country's currency and the Filipino peso, adjusted for Filipino inflation but not for inflation in the destination country, although the latter could also affect the decision of how much to remit; (b) the lack of information regarding the currency that is relevant for sea-based migrants, and which might be the U.S. dollar—assuming many of them are paid in that currency, rather than the currency of the country where the ship is registered; and (c) the fact that the coverage of the Filipino migrants is incomplete.

21. Dividing by precrisis household income achieves something similar to taking the log of an outcome: normalizing to take account of the fact that households in the sample have a wide range of income levels, and allowing coefficient estimates to be interpreted as fractions of initial household income.

22. Yang (2004) finds that favorable exchange rate shocks raise entrepreneurial activity and entrepreneurial investments in these same households, but they do not have strong effects on entrepreneurial income. It may be that entrepreneurial investments need more than 15 months to yield income improvements.

23. Because none of these households have migrant members initially, columns 2 and 3 do not include controls for migrant characteristics, only household characteristics.

24. Additional results presented in Yang (2004) indicate that during the 1997-98 period, child schooling declined and child labor increased, on average, across all migrant households. So these results indicate that households with a greater number of more favorable migrant exchange rate shocks saw a smaller decline in student status and a smaller increase in child labor.

25. There are no statistically significant effects of the exchange rate shock on net entry into the remaining nine categories of entrepreneurship; see Yang (2004) for details.

26. Use of the data requires a user fee, and the data sets remain the property of the Philippine government.

References

Adams, Richard H. Jr. 1989. "Worker Remittances and Inequality in Rural Egypt." *Economic Development and Cultural Change* 38(1): 45–71.

———. 2004. "Remittances and Poverty in Guatemala." World Bank Policy Research Working Paper, no. 3418, September. World Bank, Washington, DC.

Ahlburg, Dennis A. 1996. "Remittances and the Income Distribution in Tonga." *Population Research and Policy Review* 15(August): 391–400.

Baland, Jean-Marie, and James A. Robinson. 2000. "Is Child Labor Inefficient?" *Journal of Political Economy* 108(4): 663–79.

Barham, Bradford, and Stephen Boucher. 1998. "Migration, Remittances and Inequality: Estimating the Net Effects of Migration on Income Distribution." *Journal of Development Economics* 55: 307–31.

Basu, Kaushik, and Pham Hoang Van. 1998. "The Economics of Child Labor." *American Economic Review* 88(3): 412–27.

Bhagwati, Jagdish. 2003. "Borders Beyond Control." *Foreign Affairs* 82(1): 98–104.

Borjas, George. 1999. "The Economic Analysis of Immigration." In *Handbook of Labor Economics*, ed. Orley Ashenfelter and David Card, vol. 3A, 1,697–760. North-Holland.

Cariño, Benjamin. 1998. "Introduction." In *Filipino Workers on the Move: Trends, Dilemmas, and Policy Options*, ed. Benjamin Cariño. Manila: Philippine Migration Research Network.

Diamond, David. 2002. "One Nation, Overseas." *Wired Magazine*. Issue 10.06.

Moulton, Brent. 1986. "Random Group Effects and the Precision of Regression Estimates." *Journal of Econometrics* 32(3): 385–97.

Philippine Yearbook. 2001. Manila: National Statistics Office.

Ratha, Dilip. 2003. "Workers' Remittances: An Important and Stable Source of External Development Finance." In *Global Development Finance 2003: Striving for Stability in Development Finance*, 157–75. Washington, DC: International Monetary Fund.

Rodriguez, Edgard R. 1998. "International Migration and Income Distribution in the Philippines." *Economic Development and Cultural Change* 46(2): 329–50.

Rodrik, Dani. 2002. "Feasible Globalizations." NBER Working Paper, no. 9129, August. National Bureau of Economic Research, Washington, DC.

Rosenzweig, Mark, and Kenneth Wolpin. 1993. "Credit Market Constraints, Consumption Smoothing and the Accumulation of Durable Production Assets in Low-Income Countries: Investments in Bullocks in India." *Journal of Political Economy* 101: 223–44.

Stark, Oded, J. Edward Taylor, and Shlomo Yitzhaki. 1986. "Remittances and Inequality." *Economic Journal* 96(383): 722–40.

Taylor, J. Edward. 1992. "Remittances and Inequality Reconsidered: Direct, Indirect, and Intertemporal Effects." *Journal of Policy Modelling* 14(2): 187–208.

United Nations. 2002. *International Migration Report 2002.* New York: UN Population Division.

U.S. Bureau of the Census. 2002. *International Data Base.* Washington, DC.

Virola, Romulo A., Redencion M. Ignacio, Glenita V. Amoranto, and Bernadette B. Balamban. 2005. "Official Poverty Statistics in the Philippines: Methodology and 2003 Estimates." *National Statistical Coordination Board Technical Papers*, TP-200504-SS1-01, Government of the Philippines, March 4.

World Bank. 2004. *World Development Indicators on CD-ROM 2004.* Washington, DC.

Yang, Dean. 2004. "International Migration, Human Capital, and Entrepreneurship: Evidence from Philippine Migrants' Exchange Rate Shocks." Ford School of Public Policy Working Paper Series, no. 02-011. University of Michigan, Ann Arbor.

Yang, Dean, and HwaJung Choi. 2005. "Are Remittances Insurance? Evidence from Rainfall Shocks in the Philippines." Ford School of Public Policy Working Paper Series, no. 2005-005. University of Michigan, Ann Arbor.

4

BEYOND REMITTANCES: THE EFFECTS OF MIGRATION ON MEXICAN HOUSEHOLDS

David J. McKenzie

Introduction

The number of international migrants in the world increased by 21 million between 1990 and 2000, a 14 percent increase, resulting in 175 million people living in a country outside their birth (United Nations 2002). Remittances from migrants have grown rapidly over the same time, with developing countries receiving $126 billion in 2004 (Ratha 2005). The United States holds the largest stock of immigrants and is the source of the largest share of remittances. Mexicans are by far the largest immigrant group in the United States, and are estimated to amount to approximately 15 percent of Mexico's working age population (Mishra 2003).

The scale and growth in remittances has attracted increased intention regarding the development impact of these flows (for example, Ratha 2005; International Monetary Fund 2005). However, identifying the effects of remittances on households is difficult, because both the decision to migrate, and the decision among migrants of how much to remit, are likely to be related to the outcomes of interest. The chapter estimates the overall impact of Mexican migration to the United States on several household outcomes, and shows that migration has a number of impacts that are distinct from the direct effects of remittances. I draw on the findings of recent research I have conducted with Nicole Hildebrandt and Hillel Rapoport on the impact of migration on child health (Hildebrandt and McKenzie forthcoming), the probability of other community members migrating and on inequality in the sending community (McKenzie and Rapoport 2004), and education (McKenzie and Rapoport 2005).

Migration is shown to improve child health outcomes, lowering infant mortality and increasing birthweights. While some of the improvement in health outcomes is likely to arise from the increase in household income after remittances, it is shown that migration has at least two additional impacts on child health. Higher opportunity costs of time and the absence of parents may make children of migrants less likely to receive some forms of health inputs. Evidence for this effect is seen in children in migrant households having a lower probability of being breastfed and of receiving their full dose of vaccines. A more positive impact is seen in terms of maternal health knowledge. Mothers in migrant families are found to have higher levels of health knowledge, and there is also evidence of knowledge spillovers to mothers in nonmigrant households.

A second role for migration, other than through the direct effect of remittances, is in the creation of networks of individuals with migration experience. Sociologists have long emphasized the role of social networks in the migration process. Friends and relatives with previous migration experience may help new immigrants in the process of crossing the border (91 percent of first-time migrants in our sample had no legal documentation), help provide shelter and assistance upon arrival, and arrange jobs for other community members. This chapter shows econometrically that a larger migration network does increase the probability of additional community members also migrating, with differential impacts across the wealth distribution. When few community members have previously migrated, the cost of migration is still relatively high, and it is the upper-middle range of the wealth distribution that benefits most from the migrant network. As more of the community migrates, however, a larger network progressively benefits poorer individuals in the community, because costs fall enough for them to overcome liquidity constraints on migration. As a consequence, the size of the migrant network affects the way remittances and migration change inequality in the sending community. There is some evidence for an inverse-U-shaped relationship between inequality and migration, with the migration of the first few community members possibly raising inequality, and then inequality falling as the migration network grows.

The third role for migration studied in this chapter is its impact on education attainment in Mexico. Education is often seen as one of the areas in which remittances can play a positive role, allowing households to pay for school fees and alleviate liquidity constraints, which prevent parents from attaining the desired level of schooling for their children. However, migration may have other, less positive, impacts on schooling. This chapter provides some preliminary evidence that children age 16 to 18 in migrant households have lower levels of schooling than children in nonmigrant households. This effect is larger for children with more educated parents, who would be expected to have the highest levels of schooling in the absence of migration. The return to education is much higher in Mexico than for Mexican immigrants in the United States, and thus children who anticipate migrating have less incentive to invest in education. In addition, if parents are absent from the household as a result of migration, their children may receive less parental inputs into education acquisition.

Taken together, these results provide strong evidence for a number of impacts of migration on households that are not the direct result of remittances. Studies that focus purely on the effects of remittances are likely to conflate remittance effects with other consequences of migration. In the conclusion, I suggest directions for future research that may help to address these issues.

The remainder of this chapter is structured as follows. The first section discusses the methodology used to identify the impact of migration; the second section describes the data used for analysis. The body of the chapter appears in the third through sixth sections, which estimate the impact of migration on child health, the ability of others to migrate, community inequality, and incentives for education. The seventh section concludes the chapter and provides suggestions for further research. Annex 4.A provides additional technical details on the econometric methods used for estimation.

Can We Identify the Impact of Migration or Remittances?

Remittances are perhaps the most tangible consequence of migration for many households. Coupled with the rapid growth in remittances over the past decade, it is no surprise that a large research interest has focused on the effects of remittances on receiving households. Two main approaches have been employed in the literature. The most basic descriptive approach asks households to identify what remittances are spent on or for what purpose they are intended.[1] However, resources are fungible, and even if the remittance itself is used for one purpose, it may free up other sources of income that may be used for other means.

Therefore, the second approach used is to examine an outcome of interest, such as poverty, education, business ownership, or child health, by comparing households who receive remittances with households that do not. One branch of literature[2] assumes that all the systematic differences between remittance-receiving and non-remittance-receiving households can be explained by a set of characteristics of the migrant, receiving household, and community, X_i, and then estimates the impact of remittances on an outcome of interest through ordinary least squares (OLS) regression of the following equation.

$$\text{Outcome}_i = \mu + \gamma^* \text{Remittances}_i + \lambda' X_i + \varepsilon_i \qquad (4.1)$$

However, if migration has other impacts on the outcome of interest in addition to its effect through remittances, then the error term in equation 4.1 contains omitted variables (these other effects of migration) that are correlated with remittances and the outcome variable. As a result, estimates of the effect of remittances will suffer from omitted variables bias. Therefore, we instead focus our attention on the overall impact of having a migrant member, given by the following.

$$\text{Outcome}_i = \alpha + \beta^*\text{Migrant}_i + \delta'X_i + \varepsilon_i \qquad (4.2)$$

where Migrant_i is a dummy variable taking the value 1 if a household has a migrant member, and 0 otherwise. The coefficient β then captures the joint impact of remittances and of other consequences of migration. One can then determine whether the sign of the coefficient differs from what would be expected from the impact of remittances alone. Because the decision to migrate may depend on unobserved characteristics of the household that also influence household outcomes, I employ the method of instrumental variables in the estimation, using historic migration networks as an instrument for current migration. This will enable us to determine the overall impact of migration on those left behind, and allow me to show that migration has some effects that are unlikely to be caused by remittances. Annex 4.A provides the technical justification for this methodology and a discussion of why such an instrument is unable to detect the causal impact of remittances as distinct from the overall impact of migration.

Data

The estimates in this chapter are based on data from the 1997 *Encuesta Nacional de Dinámica Demográfica* (ENADID) (National Survey of Demographic Dynamics) conducted by Mexico's national statistical agency, Instituto Nacional de Estadística, Geografía e Informática (INEGI) in the last quarter of 1997. The ENADID is a nationally representative demographic survey of more than 70,000 households. As detailed above, the identification strategy uses historic migration networks to help predict current migration. These historic networks are more important in rural areas, and I therefore restrict our analysis to households in municipalities with populations of less than 100,000.[3] All women ages 15 to 54 in each household are asked detailed questions about their fertility history. This gives a sample of 42,527 women ages 15 to 54 living in 29,498 households located in 612 municipalities across all 32 states that we can use to examine the impact of migration on child health. I restrict the sample to the 214 municipalities in which 50 or more households were sampled in the later sections of this chapter to measure the migration network at the community level and thereby examine its impact on inequality and on the migration of other community members.

The ENADID survey asks whether any household member has ever been to the United States in search of work. This is asked about all household members who normally live in the household, including those who are temporarily studying or working elsewhere. Households are also asked if any household members have gone to live in another country in the past five years. These questions enable us to determine whether a household has a member who has ever gone to the United States, in which case we classify them as a migrant household.[4] We also can then construct the proportion of adults age 15 and over in a community who have ever migrated, which Massey, Goldring, and Durand (1994) call the "migration prevalence ratio."

The Impact of Migration on Child Health

Child health outcomes are an important direct component of household well-being, and a key determinant of future levels of human capital. The Grossman (1972) health production function relates the health status of a given child to the medical and nutritional inputs the child receives (including prenatal and post-natal care and maternal nutrition), the disease environment, the time inputs of the parents, parental health knowledge, biological endowments, and random health shocks. Using this framework, remittances are predicted to improve child health outcomes by allowing the purchase of additional medical and nutritional inputs. Migration may potentially have additional effects on child health through changing the time inputs parents are able to provide, and perhaps through changing the health knowledge of parents as they become exposed to U.S. health practices.[5]

Hildebrandt and McKenzie (forthcoming) examine the impact of migration on child health outcomes by estimating the following version of equation 4.2 for a given child health outcome for child i in community c.

$$\text{Child health outcome}_{i,c} = \alpha + \beta^*\text{Migrant Household}_{i,c} + \delta'X_{i,c} + \lambda'Z_c + \varepsilon_{i,c}$$
$$(4.3)$$

where Migrant Household$_{i,c}$ is a dummy variable taking the value 1 if child i lives in a household with a household member who has ever migrated to the United States, and 0 otherwise; $X_{i,c}$ are a set of characteristics of child i's household, such as the age and education of the child's mother and household size.[6] Z_c are a set of community controls at the state level, which in this case are information on the infant mortality rate in 1930; the current level of doctors, nurses, hospitals, and hospital beds per 1,000 inhabitants; and state gross domestic product (GDP) per capita. As discussed above, the migration dummy variable is instrumented with the 1924 historic migration rate in the state child i is living in. Because many of the outcomes considered are binary outcomes, such as whether a child died or not, probit and IV-probit methods are used.[7]

The ENADID enables us to construct several health outcome measures. Mothers are asked questions about their fertility history, and then asked more detailed information about their last two births since January 1, 1994, including the birthweight in kilograms of the baby. The four health outcomes we consider are as follows: infant mortality, defined in the standard way as a live birth dying during the first year of life; child mortality between ages 1 and 4 inclusive; birthweight in kilograms; and low birthweight, defined according to the international standard of whether or not the birthweight was below 2.5 kilograms. Birthweight is an important early indicator of child health. Low birthweight has been linked to a higher likelihood of cognitive and neurological impairment that limits the returns to human capital investment later in life, while higher birthweight has been found to be associated with greater schooling attainment and better labor-market payoffs (Wolpin 1997; Behrman and Rosenzweig 2003).

The top panel of table 4.1 presents the estimated coefficient on being in a migrant household from equation 4.3 for each of these four health outcomes. Standard probit estimation, which treats migration as exogenous, shows a small, negative, and insignificant effect of migration on infant mortality. After instrumenting for migration, we find a strong significantly negative effect.[8] Children born in a household with a migrant member are estimated to be 3 percent less likely to die in their first year than children born in similar households without migrant members. The effect is much weaker in magnitude for child mortality, with children in migrant households having a 0.5 percent lower chance to dying when between the ages of 1 and 4. Migration is also estimated to raise birthweight by 364 grams, or 0.64 of a standard deviation, lowering the probability of being born underweight by 5.4 percent.

Both the infant mortality and birthweight results show stronger improvements in child health from migration after instrumentation. Failure to consider the selectivity of migration therefore understates the impact of migration. This suggests that, in the absence of migration, children in what are currently migrant households would have poorer health status than children in observationally similar nonmigrant households. From this we infer that on net, Mexican migrants to the United States are negatively selected in terms of the health status of their children.

The ENADID survey also provides information on several health inputs during the time of birth and during infancy. The lower half of table 4.1 presents the estimated impact of migration on health input use, based on the estimation of equation 4.3 for health inputs rather than outcomes. Children in migrant households

TABLE 4.1 The Impact of Migration on Health Outcomes and Health Inputs

	Coefficient on being in a migrant household			
Dependent variable:	OLS	2SLS	Probit	IV-probit
Health Outcomes				
Infant mortality under age 1			−0.003 (0.96)	−0.030 (3.97)**
Child mortality between ages1 and 4			−0.002 (3.08)**	−0.005 (2.70)**
Birthweight in kilograms	0.069 (4.00)**	0.364 (2.79)**		
Low birthweight			−0.021 (2.81)**	−0.054 (2.59)**
Health Inputs/Health Care				
Child was delivered by a doctor			0.065 (3.21)**	0.300 (13.26)**
Child was breastfed			−0.017 (2.51)*	−0.192 (5.56)**
Child received all vaccines			−0.000 (0.01)	−0.108 (2.58)**

Source: Hildebrandt and McKenzie 2004, tables 5,6, and 7.

Note: All regressions include characteristics of the mother (age, education), household demographic controls, and community characteristics. Probit coefficients are marginal effects. Robust t-statistics in parentheses clustered at the state level. 1924 state migration rate is used as instrument for being in a migrant household. OLS = ordinary least square; 2SLS = two-stage least squares.

* significant at 5 percent; ** significant at 1 percent.

are found to be 30 percent more likely to be delivered by a doctor, but 19 percent less likely to be breastfed and 11 percent less likely to have received all of their recommended vaccinations for tuberculosis, diphtheria, polio, and measles. It therefore seems that migrant children are receiving less preventive health care in their infancy.[9] Nevertheless, as we have seen, migrant children are still slightly less likely than nonmigrant children to die between ages 1 and 4, so the positive effects of migration on health outweigh any negative impact from less preventive care at this age.

Remittances or repatriated savings will allow migrant mothers to have the ability to buy more food, increasing the nutritional inputs. The more frequent use of doctors for child delivery is also likely to be due at least in part to a greater ability to pay for medical services as a result of remittances. However, one would expect households receiving remittances to also generally increase purchases of other health inputs, so the decline in preventive care during infancy is not likely to be due to remittances. Although we do not have direct time allocation information to allow us to verify this theory, a likely explanation is that there is a higher opportunity cost of time for migrant parents, and periods during which one or both parents are absent from the children, making it more difficult to breastfeed and take the child to health clinics.

In addition to causing a change in time inputs into health production, migration may affect child health beyond its remittance effect by improving maternal health knowledge. This may come about through exposure to different health practices and information about contraceptive practices, the importance of sanitation, and knowledge about diet and exercise. Hildebrandt and McKenzie (forthcoming) construct an index of maternal health knowledge, based on detailed questions asked in the ENADID about knowledge of contraceptive practices.[10] They show that this index is associated with mothers knowing more about the causes of diarrhea. The index directly measures fertility knowledge and is likely to be a reasonable indicator of general child health knowledge among mothers. Moreover, higher levels of this health knowledge measure are associated with lower rates of infant mortality and higher birthweights.

Table 4.2 presents the estimated impact of migration on maternal health knowledge. After instrumenting, we find a strong effect of migration: being in a migrant household is estimated to increase health knowledge by 0.65 standard deviations. Because health knowledge is likely to be gained directly by the migrant member, and then passed on in part to other household members, we would expect to see a much larger increase in maternal health knowledge if the mother herself has migrated. Columns 3 through 6 of table 4.2 show that this is the case: the gain in health knowledge is 3.8 times as large when mothers migrate as when the father migrates. Hildebrandt and McKenzie (forthcoming) show that there appears to be evidence of knowledge spillovers from migrant to nonmigrant households. A one-standard-deviation increase in the proportion of households in a community with migration experience is estimated to lead to a 0.11 standard deviation increase in health knowledge of mothers in nonmigrant households.

In addition to the health improvements one would expect from the rise in income and wealth after remittances, migration is therefore seen to have a number of additional impacts on child health. Migration is found to increase the health knowledge of mothers, with smaller spillover benefits for the health knowledge of mothers in nonmigrant households. However, migrant children are found to be less likely to be breastfed or fully vaccinated, which is likely a result of a reallocation of time inputs with migration. Although child mortality between age 1 and 4 is not negatively impacted by migration on net, these results do suggest a need for

TABLE 4.2   The Impact of Migration on Maternal Health Knowledge

Dependent variable: Maternal health knowledge index

	(1) OLS	(2) 2SLS	(3) OLS	(4) 2SLS	(5) OLS	(6) 2SLS
Migrant household	0.266 (4.01)**	1.289 (2.61)**				
Mother has migrated			0.473 (4.41)**	4.853 (2.45)*		
Father has migrated					0.238 (3.37)**	1.290 (2.51)*
Observations	12,744	12,744	10,676	10,676	12,489	12,489

Source: Hildebrandt and McKenzie 2004, table 8.
Note: Regressions are for women age 15 to 54 who gave birth between 1994 and 1997 and were the household head or spouse of the household head. All regressions also include a quadratic in mother's age, mother's years of schooling, household size, 1930 infant mortality rate, health infrastructure, and 1997 GDP per capita and a constant. Robust t-statistics in parentheses are clustered at the state level GDP = gross domestic product; OLS = ordinary least square; 2SLS = two-stage least squares.
* significant at 5 percent; ** significant at 1 percent.

further research into the long-term impacts of migration on health outcomes, as well as into investigating health policy actions that can enhance the ability of migrants to engage in preventive health care.

Impacts of the Migration Network on the Ability of Others to Migrate

International migration is costly, involving upfront monetary costs, information and search costs, opportunity costs in terms of income foregone while traveling and searching for work, and psychic costs (Massey 1988). The majority of rural Mexican migrants surveyed in our work migrate illegally on their first trip to the United States. Using the Mexican Migration Project (MMP), a survey of mostly high-migration communities, we calculate that, on average, 89 percent of first-time migrants between 1970 and 1990 were undocumented and an additional 7 percent were on tourist visas. In the 1997 ENADID survey, 91 percent of first-time migrants going to work in the United States had no legal documentation to do so. Crossing the border illegally is a risky and dangerous process, and migrants often rely on smugglers (*coyotes*) to help them cross. Orrenius (1999) reports the median cost of a coyote was $619 in 1994, having fallen over time. However, the Immigration and Naturalization Service (INS) estimates that the cost has increased substantially since then, especially following increased border enforcement after September 11, 2001, with prices reaching between $1,500 and $2,000 in 2002.[11]

Sociologists have emphasized that social networks can play an important role in lowering migration costs. Espinosa and Massey (1997) report that social networks play an important role in mitigating the hazards of crossing the border. Friends and relatives who have migrant experience often accompany new immigrants across the border or arrange coyotes. A reduction in migration costs has two main impacts on the decision to migrate (McKenzie and Rapoport 2004). The first is that it increases the ability of liquidity-constrained households to meet the costs of sending members to the United States. Second, lowering the costs of migrating increases the net benefit to households, which thereby increases the incentive to migrate. As a result, the impact of a larger migration network on the probability of migrating is predicted to vary with the level of household wealth.

We measure the size of the community migration network, with the migration prevalence ratio, defined by Massey, Goldring, and Durand (1994) as the "proportion of all members of a community age 15 and over who have ever migrated to the United States." As in most of the literature, this is a measure of relative network size.[12] Household resources are measured as the log of nondurable consumption (NDC),[13] which we denote by $lndc$. We then estimate the following regression for the probability of migrating, p.

$$p = \beta_0 + \beta_1 \times ndc + \beta_2 \times ndc^2 + \beta_3 \times \text{network} + \beta_4 \times ndc \times \text{network} + \varepsilon$$
(4.4)

We assume that the opportunity costs of migration, in terms of productive opportunities in Mexico, are increasing in wealth level, so that the richest individuals in a community are unlikely to wish to migrate. This accords with the sociological observation that the first migrants from a community are usually those with sufficient resources to afford the costs and risks of migrating, but who are not so affluent that foreign labor is unattractive (Massey, Goldring, and Durand 1994). Then we predict that $\beta_1 > 0$, $\beta_2 < 0$, $\beta_3 > 0$. When migration costs are relatively low, we further predict that $\beta_4 < 0$, so that additional reductions in migration costs increase the propensity for the poor to migrate.

The ENADID contains a wide range of community migration prevalence rates, allowing substantial variation in migration costs. At the 25th percentile only 3.8 percent of adults have ever migrated, compared with 15.9 percent of adults in the community with the median network size, and 35.6 percent of adults at the 75th percentile of network size. Data on NDC are only available for the current year. Current consumption of households that already have migrants will reflect the result of remittances and other impacts of migration. We therefore estimate equation 4.4 only for first-time migrants and estimate the probability that a male household head ages 15–49 migrated for the first-time within the last two years, which is conditional on his not having previously migrated.[14]

Columns 1 and 2 of table 4.3 present the results from estimating equation 4.4 with the full ENADID sample. The estimates presented here are from ordinary least squares (OLS) and two-stage least squares (2SLS) estimation, although IV-probit estimation gave similar results. The historic migration networks in 1924 are used as instruments for the current migration prevalence in a community. As predicted, the probability of migrating is found to first increase and then decrease with household resources, and to be higher in communities with larger networks. The interaction between network size and household resources is significant and negative, showing that a larger migration network (and hence lower migration costs) increases the probability of migrating more for the poor than the rich.

TABLE 4.3 Network Size and Probability of Migration
Probability of Household Head First Migrating in Survey Year or Year prior to Survey Year

	Full sample		Low network sample	
	(1) OLS	(2) IV-probit	(3) OLS	(4) IV-probit
Log nondurable consumption log NDC	0.3309 (3.43)**	0.3281 (3.20)**	0.0775 (1.43)	0.0833 (1.51)
Log NDC squared	−0.0194 (3.46)**	−0.0188 (3.10)**	−0.0046 (1.45)	−0.0049 (1.50)
Migration prevalence	0.7749 (4.64)**	1.2253 (2.70)**	0.3443 (0.48)	0.3057 (0.29)
Migration prevalence log NDC*	−0.0788 (4.14)**	−0.1314 (2.53)*	−0.0274 (0.32)	−0.0332 (0.28)
Observations	11,315	11,315	5,499	5,499
Communities	214	214	90	90

Source: McKenzie and Rapoport 2004, table 4.
Note: T-statistics in parentheses with standard errors clustered at the community level. For male household heads ages 15 to 49 who have not previously migrated. Instruments are the 1924 state migration rate and its interaction with log NDC. OLS = ordinary least square.
* significant at 5 percent; ** significant at 1 percent.

If migration costs are relatively high, then a small reduction in costs might actually benefit the upper-middle range of the wealth distribution more than the bottom, because the incentive effect of lower costs will induce more migration from those who can afford the costs. One should therefore expect to find β_4 to be less negative, or even positive, when equation 4.4 is only estimated for communities with small networks. Columns 3 and 4 of table 4.3 examine this hypothesis by restricting estimation to the 40 percent of ENADID communities in which 10 percent or less of the adults have ever migrated to the United States. The interaction between network size and household resources is seen to become less negative, and is insignificantly different from zero for this subsample.

Figure 4.1 then plots the estimated relationship between migration and log NDC for different deciles of the ENADID community migration prevalence distribution using the estimates in column 2 of table 4.3. When migration networks are small, the probability of migration first increases and then decreases with household resources. Increasing the network size from this low level shifts the turning point to the right, and so the upper-middle range of the consumption distribution benefits most from increasing the network. Once the network gains suf-

FIGURE 4.1   Estimated Probability of a Household Head Migrating by Household Consumption Level at Different Deciles of the Community Migration Prevalence Distribution

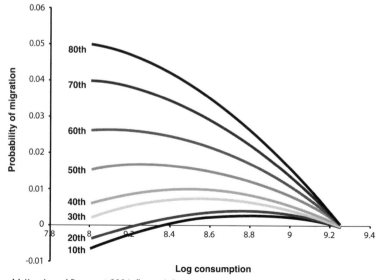

Source: McKenzie and Rapoport 2004, figure 4.6.

ficient size, the turning point begins to move left, and at high levels of migration networks, one sees a declining propensity to migrate with wealth.[15]

These results show that migration by some members of a community can have large effects on the likelihood of other members of that community migrating. This impact is not through remittances, but through migration networks that lower the costs of migrating and increase the benefits of migrating to other community members. The new wave of migrants that follows will then be likely to send remittances, help additional community members to migrate, and encourage several of the other impacts of migration studied in this chapter.

Migration and Inequality in the Sending Community

The previous section showed that the network effects of migration affect the selection of who migrates. Poor households in a community with a large migration network are much more likely to migrate, and hence to send remittances, than poor households in a community with a small migration network. As a consequence, the size of the migration network will be a key factor in determining how remittances affect inequality in a community. In particular, when migration networks are small, and migration costs high, households at the upper-middle range of the wealth distribution in a community will be most likely to send migrants, and their remittances and repatriated income may therefore increase inequality. However, as migration networks increase, increasing numbers of household in the lower part of the income distribution will also be able to send migrants, and the increased income of these households should act to lower inequality.

The relationship between the level of migration in a community and inequality within that community is examined through a regression of the Gini coefficient of NDC in community i, $Gini_i$ on the migration prevalence in that community, denoted Mig_i and other community characteristics, Z_i.

$$Gini_i = \alpha_0 + \alpha_1 \times Mig_i + \alpha_2 \times Mig_i^2 + \alpha_3 \times Z_i + u_i \qquad (4.5)$$

Table 4.4 presents the estimates of equation 4.5. The quadratic shows a positive coefficient on migration and a negative coefficient on squared migration, which suggests that migration first increases inequality and then lowers inequality at higher levels of migration. However, the coefficients are not significant, and so we drop the quadratic term from the model. For the full sample of communities, migration is estimated to lower inequality, although this effect is not significant at the 10 percent level. We next split the sample into low-migration and high-migration communities, again using a cutoff of 10 percent of adults having ever

Table 4.4   The Impact of Migration on Consumption Inequality in ENADID Communities
Dependent Variable: Gini of Nondurable Consumption

	Full sample			Low network sample		High network sample	
	(1) OLS	(2) IV-probit	(3) IV-probit	(4) OLS	(5) IV-probit	(6) OLS	(7) IV-probit
Migration prevalence	−0.013 (2.37)*	0.088 (0.82)	−0.018 (1.60)	−0.008 (0.12)	0.032 (0.17)	−0.011 (1.38)	−0.044 (1.76)
Migration prevalence squared		−0.193 (0.96)					
Proportion of heads age < 30	0.041 (1.66)	0.047 (1.93)	0.037 (1.78)	0.015 (0.37)	0.006 (0.18)	0.068 (2.51)*	0.087 (3.68)**
Proportion of heads age > 60	0.041 (2.28)*	0.048 (2.19)*	0.061 (3.58)**	0.035 (0.96)	0.046 (1.31)	0.051 (2.89)**	0.064 (4.11)**
Proportion of heads with education < 6 years	0.031 (1.46)	0.038 (1.83)	0.024 (1.44)	0.007 (0.24)	0.004 (0.20)	0.058 (2.88)**	0.068 (3.62)**
Proportion of heads with education at least 9 years	−0.005 (0.20)	−0.005 (0.21)	−0.004 (0.18)	−0.013 (0.39)	−0.009 (0.36)	0.012 (0.54)	0.009 (0.34)
Constant	0.373 (18.48)**	0.360 (18.78)**	0.372 (22.99)**	0.394 (13.27)**	0.390 (17.47)**	0.346 (19.46)**	0.347 (18.69)**

F-stat for first stage migration prevalence		35.88	71.92		12.26	16.80
F-stat for first stage migration prevalence squared		30.50				
Observations	214	214	214	90	90	124	124

Source: McKenzie and Rapoport 2004, table 7.

Notes: T-statistics in parentheses with robust standard errors. Instrument set B uses the 1924 state migration rate (and its square in column 2). The low-network sample includes municipalities with migration prevalence less than 0.10, high-network municipalities have prevalence greater than 0.10. OLS = ordinary least squares.

* significant at 5 percent; ** significant at 1 percent.

migrated to the United States. Migration is found to have a positive, but insignificant effect on inequality in low-migration communities, and a negative effect on inequality in high-migration communities, which is significant at the 10 percent level. The estimated magnitude of the impact on inequality is relatively large, with a one-standard-deviation increase in migration prevalence leading to a 0.5 standard deviation reduction in inequality.

McKenzie and Rapoport (2004) provide further supporting evidence for migration having nonlinear effects on inequality. Using the MMP, they find migration lowers inequality by more than in the ENADID. Using a small panel of communities observed in both the 1992 and 1997 ENADIDs, they find moderate support for an inverse-U-shaped relationship between migration and inequality by examining the association between changes in migration and changes in inequality over a five-year period.

Taken together with the results of the previous section, these results show that migration networks help determine the impact of remittances and migration on inequality. The migrants from communities with low networks are likely to be relatively rich, so that transfers to their families will increase inequality, at least between the poor and middle class. However, the migration networks formed within communities act, over time, to increase the set of households who can migrate, allowing poorer households to begin sending migrants. Remittances from such households will tend to lower inequality.

Migration and Incentives for Education

Empirical research on remittances and schooling has stressed the potential for remittances to raise schooling levels by increasing the ability of households to pay for schooling. Recent examples include Cox Edwards and Ureta (2003) who find that remittances lower the likelihood of children leaving school in El Salvador; Yang (2004) who finds greater child schooling in families whose migrants receive larger positive exchange rate shocks in the Philippines; and Lopez Cordoba (2004) who finds municipalities in Mexico that receive more remittances have greater literacy levels and higher school attendance among 6 to 14 year olds.

A recent, largely theoretical, body of literature on the "brain gain" has suggested that migration may have an additional positive impact on education by increasing the returns to schooling and thereby improving the incentives to acquire education (for example, Mountford 1997; Stark, Helmenstein, and Prskawetz 1997; Beine, Docquier, and Rapoport 2001). In ongoing work, McKenzie and Rapoport (2005) suggest that migration may actually have a disincentive effect on education in Mexico. The Mexican income distribution is more unequal than the U.S. income distribution, so one might actually expect higher marginal return to schooling in Mexico than in the United States. Chiquiar and Hanson (2005) provide evidence to support this, showing higher returns to education in Mexico than for Mexicans in the United States. As a result, individuals who intend to migrate may decide to accumulate less education in Mexico. This may occur as a result of direct substitution, with individuals migrating at an age at which they would otherwise be in school. However, it may also arise from individuals who plan to migrate making the decision to drop out of school now, because the effective returns to education are now lower.[16]

The effect of migration on education should then vary according to the level of education that children would undertake in the absence of migration. A child who would drop out of school after six years of primary education in the absence of the possibility to migrate should be much less affected by the lower returns to schooling when migration becomes possible than a child who would complete lower-secondary education (grades 7 to 9) and perhaps high school (grades 10 to 12) when migration is not an option. A mother's education is a strong predictor of the education of their children, and it is also highly correlated with household wealth. In the absence of migration, we would therefore expect children of more highly educated mothers to obtain more years of schooling. We therefore allow the impact of living in a migrant household on $S_{i,o}$ the years of schooling completed by child i in community c, to vary with the level of maternal education.

$$S_{i,c} = \lambda_0 + \lambda_1 \text{Mig}_{i,c} \times \lambda_2 \text{Mig}_{i,c} \times \text{MidEduc}_{i,c} + \lambda_3 \text{Mig}_{i,c} \times \text{HighEduc}_{i,c}$$
$$+ \alpha_1 \text{MidEduc}_{i,c} + \alpha_2 \text{HighEduc}_{i,c} + \phi' X_{i,c} + \gamma' Z_c + \varepsilon_{i,c} \qquad (4.6)$$

where MidEduc and HighEduc are dummy variables for child i having a mother with three to five years of schooling and six or more years of education respectively; $X_{i,c}$ are a number of child controls, such as age and age squared; and Z_c are the set of state-level controls. Thirty-four percent of children have mothers with zero to two years of education, 26 percent have mothers with three to five years of education, and 40 percent have six or more years education.

Table 4.5 presents the results of estimating equation 4.6 separately for boys ages 16 to 18 and girls ages 16 to 18. First, when we do not allow the effect of migration to vary with maternal education, columns 3 and 7 show an overall impact of migration lowering years of education completed by 1.4 years for boys and 1.7 years for girls.[17] Columns 4 and 8 allow the impact of migration to vary with maternal education. Migration is seen to have a significantly larger negative effect for children of highly educated mothers. Migration lowers completed years of education by 3.05 years for boys with mothers who have six or more years of education. This has the effect of completely erasing the boost in education that we

TABLE 4.5 Impact of Migration on Years of Schooling

	Males Ages 16 to 18				Females ages 16 to 18			
	(1) OLS	(2) OLS	(3) IV-Probit	(4) IV-Probit	(5) OLS	(6) OLS	(7) IV-Probit	(8) IV-Probit
Child is in a migrant household	-0.3965 (2.21)*	0.0261 (0.07)	-1.4017 (2.91)**	-0.9404 (2.12)*	-0.0970 (0.47)	0.5850 (2.37)*	-1.7059 (1.45)	-1.9298 (2.09)*
Migrant household* mother has 3 to 5 years schooling		-0.4151 (1.09)		-1.0820 (1.40)		-0.7663 (2.51)*		-1.0127 (0.87)
Migrant household* mother has 6 or more years schooling		-0.5498 (1.53)		-2.1113 (2.04)*		-1.1656 (3.98)**		-2.4555 (2.15)*
Mother has 3 to 5 years schooling		1.0784 (7.57)**		1.3074 (6.22)**		1.2040 (6.24)**		1.2415 (3.19)**
Mother has 6 or more years schooling		2.4809 (18.15)**		2.7563 (9.69)**		2.7650 (17.90)**		2.9581 (9.85)**
Observations	3,336	2,930	3,336	2,930	3,332	2,539	3,332	2,539

P-value for testing the impact of migration is zero by mother's education:				
Mother has 0 to 2 years of education	0.941	0.034	0.025	0.037
Mother has 3 to 5 years of education	0.040	0.001	0.516	0.011
Mother has 6 or more years of education	0.015	0.003	0.346	0.036

Source: McKenzie and Rapoport (2005), tables 4 and 5.

Notes: All regressions also contain a constant, age and age squared, and controls for population size, historic levels of inequality and schooling, and school infrastructure. T-statistics are in parentheses with standard errors clustered at the state level. Instruments are 1924 state-level migration rate and its interaction with mother's year of schooling categories. OLS = ordinary least squares.

* significant at 5 percent; ** significant at 1 percent.

would otherwise predict from having a highly educated mother and, in practice, means that on average these children only complete elementary school, instead of carrying out three years of lower-secondary education. The magnitude of the estimated effect is even worse for girls, with a reduction of more than four years of education for children of the more highly educated mothers in migrant households. However, we can not reject equality of the effect for boys and girls.

The negative impact of migration on child schooling is in stark contrast to the increase in education one would expect from remittances. Basic education is provided for free by the state in Mexico, and, coupled with government programs that target education of the poor, it is possible that liquidity constraints are not a major factor in the education decision. Several explanations for the negative impact of migration on child education are suggested. The first is that children ages 16 to 18 migrate to obtain work instead of going to school, or migrated with their adult parents and, as a result, dropped out of school. There is some evidence of this for male children. A second explanation is that the future returns to schooling are now lower for children who are likely to migrate, and so education aspirations are lower. A third explanation is that the absence of migrant parents results in less supervision of children and, perhaps, in the need for children to undertake household work in place of migrant adults. This may explain the reduction in schooling of girls, who are less likely to migrate than boys. In our ongoing work, McKenzie and Rapoport (2005) seek to disentangle these explanations further.

Conclusions and Directions for Further Research

This chapter has shown that migration has a number of impacts on households that cannot be directly attributed to remittances. As a result of migration, children are less likely to be breastfed or less likely to receive their full schedule of vaccines, but migration increases the level of health knowledge of mothers. Migration by some community members has spillover effects to other community members. The migration networks formed increase the likelihood of other community members also migrating, with different impacts across the wealth distribution depending on the size of the network. As a result, migration can cause inequality in the sending community to first increase, and then later decrease, as the network gets larger. Finally, it was shown that migration lowers the education attainment of children of more highly educated parents, which is likely to be due to the combination of parental absence arising from current migration, as well as from lower future returns to schooling for children who intend to migrate.

Estimates of the effect of remittances that compare households receiving remittances with households not receiving remittances are therefore likely to be biased because of these other impacts of migration. It appears that if one wishes to isolate the effects of remittances from other impacts of migration, one needs to think of factors that determine whether a migrant decides to remit, and how much they remit, which are not determinants of the migration decision. The historic migrant networks used in this chapter do not fit this criterion. Future research on the impact of remittances should therefore focus on trying to identify exogenous reasons why one migrant will remit more than an otherwise similar migrant. Two possible reasons may be exogenous variation in the transfer costs among migrants to send remittances,[18] and labor market shocks varying across migrants in different destinations.[19]

Annex 4.A Econometric Issues in Identifying the Impact of Migration and Remittances

Estimation of equation 4.1 or 4.2 by ordinary least squares (OLS) regression assumes that all systematic differences between remittance-receiving and non-remittance-receiving households can be explained by a set of observable characteristics of the migrant, receiving household, and community. This approach is not satisfactory, because if the two groups of households (remittance receivers and nonreceivers or migrant households and nonmigrant households) are really the same after controlling for observable differences, they should have the same migration and remittance behavior (LaLonde and Topel 1997). In particular, one is usually concerned that the fact whether a household receives remittances or sends a migrant may be correlated with unobserved variables that also affect the outcome of interest.

There are two main categories of concern: unobserved shocks and unobserved attributes of the household. As an example of the first concern, consider using equation 4.1 to estimate the impact of remittances on child health outcomes, such as weight-for-age. It may be that a household that experiences a negative health shock, such as sudden illness of a child, is likely to request remittances from relatives abroad to help pay for treatment. Because the researcher is unlikely to be able to precisely observe all such health shocks, the estimation of equation 4.1 by OLS may understate the effect of remittances.

The second concern is that households that send migrants and receive remittances differ in terms of motivation, ability, concern for their children, and other such hard-to-measure attributes. For example, consider using equation 4.2 to measure the effect of migration on child schooling. A poor household that particularly values schooling may decide to send a migrant to earn remittances to be able to pay for schooling, and also undertake a number of other actions to help their children with schooling. In such a case, estimation of equation 4.2 will overstate the impact of migration on schooling.

One solution to this problem is to employ the method of instrumental variables. The idea is to find a variable (the instrument) which helps predict either remittances or migration, but it does not otherwise have an impact on the outcome of interest. There is a sizeable body of literature that looks at the empirical determinants of remittances and migration.[20] However, most of the variables that help predict whether a household member migrates, or whether a household receives remittances, are likely to have an impact on the outcomes of interest. For example, the household head's age and education, and the income and demographic composition of a household, may help predict whether they receive remittances, but they will also affect the health and education of their children and other outcomes of interest. We follow Woodruff and Zenteno (2001), who suggest that historic migration networks (formed as a result of the pattern of development of the railroads in Mexico) may be used as a valid instrument to examine the impact of migration on microenterprises in Mexico. Historic migration networks made it easier for others in the same communities to migrate, and as a result, the state-level migration rate in 1924 helps predict whether a particular household will contain a migrant member today.

The assumption required for this approach to work is that these historic migration rates have no impact on the outcomes of interest, such as child health, inequality, and education, other than through current migration. This assumption would be violated if there were persistent community characteristics that influence migration and the outcomes of interest both historically and today. For example, in the case of child health, a concern might be that certain states have always had a bad disease environment, which led people to migrate both in the past and today, and that also affects disease outcomes. Hildebrandt and McKenzie (forthcoming) show that this does not appear likely in the case of child health, because infant mortality rates in the 1930s are statistically independent of historic migration rates. McKenzie and Rapoport (2004, 2005) likewise show their results to be robust to the inclusion of controls for historic inequality and historic schooling levels.

Historic migration rates can therefore be used as an instrumental variable in equation 4.2, allowing us to determine the impact of migration on a variety of outcomes. Can we then also use historic migration networks as an instrument in equation 4.1 to identify the causal impact of remittances on Mexican households? This requires assuming that historic migration networks affect the outcomes of interest *only through remittances*, and are therefore uncorrelated with the error term ε in equation 4.1. Because we have argued that historic migration networks help predict current migration, this amounts to assuming that the only impact of migration on the outcome of interest is through remittances. However, as this chapter has shown, this does not appear to be a tenable assumption.

Identifying the effect of remittances, as distinct from the overall impact of migration, therefore involves a second level of complexity. We must find a variable that not only helps determine why one household migrates and another with similar observable characteristics does not, but that also explains why one family with a migrant household member receives more remittances than another similar family that also has a migrant member. Variables that help predict migration, such as migrant networks or institutional arrangements such as migrant quotas, do not appear to be suitable for predicting why one migrant will send more remittances than another similar migrant. This chapter's conclusion discusses potential approaches that could be used in further research to try to separately isolate the remittance impact.

Endnotes

1. See Durand and Massey (1992) for a review of such studies in the case of Mexican migration.

2. Some examples include Adams (1991), Taylor and Wyatt (1996), and Cox-Edwards and Ureta (2003).

3. Migrant networks are also likely to be important in large cities, but in these areas the neighborhood network rather than the whole city network is likely to be most relevant. Unfortunately the surveys used here do not allow for close study of neighborhood networks.

4. We thus include return migrants and migrants with family members remaining, but we are not able to include cases in which the whole household migrates and does not return. This is an issue in almost all migration surveys, although it is less common for the whole household to migrate in rural areas. Moreover, because many of our results concern the impact of migration on remaining household members, it does not appear to pose a severe problem for our work. The survey does not reveal whether households have deceased members who were prior migrants. The effect of any such misclassification would be standard measurement error bias, which would tend to make us less likely to detect significant impacts of migration. However, it is likely that the proportion of households whose only migration experience is through a deceased member is low and hence will have little substantive impact on our results.

5. It is also possible that migration may have an impact on the disease environment. An example is the transmission of the HIV/AIDS virus by migrant workers in some regions of Africa.

6. Note that household income is not included in these characteristics. Household income is a function of migration because of the impacts of remittances and changes in household labor supply induced by migration. Including income directly would therefore remove several of the key channels through which migration affects health outcomes. Hildebrandt and McKenzie (2004) discuss in more detail identification of the channels through which migration operates.

7. Two-stage least squares (2SLS) gives very similar results for health outcomes (see Hildebrandt and McKenzie 2004).

8. The first-stage equation in all the instrumental variables specifications used in this chapter always shows the historic migration rate to be a strong instrument for current migration. See Hildebrandt and McKenzie (2004) and McKenzie and Rapoport (2004) for details.

9. Breastfeeding is associated with a number of positive health outcomes and is recommended by the World Health Organization.

10. The index is the first principal component from answers to 10 questions about knowledge of contraceptive methods. The index has mean zero and standard deviation of 1.98.

11. Source http://www.migrationint.com.au/ruralnews/guam/jul_2002-15rmn.asp. Accessed January 25, 2005.

12. See Bauer, Epstein, and Gang (2002) for a discussion of alternative measures of network size. Identification of both relative and absolute network size effects requires more instruments than we have available, and therefore we follow the existing literature in preferring relative network size.

13. This is predicted from household characteristics and asset indicators using the Mexican National Income and Expenditure Survey. See McKenzie and Rapoport (2004) for details.

14. Similar results were obtained using all first-time male migrants, rather than just heads.

15. Note that the interaction term in column 2 of table 4.3 is significant, so the turning points shown in figure 4.1 are significant.

16. An additional possible explanation that our ongoing work will investigate is that children of migrant parents may have lower schooling because of the effects of parental absence.

17. The mean effect is not significant for girls, but it is for boys.

18. Gibson, McKenzie, and Rohorua (2005) estimate the elasticity of remittances with respect to the costs of sending and find suggestive evidence for sizeable increases in remittances when costs fall.

19. McKenzie and Rapoport (2004) try using demand shocks in U.S. labor markets as instruments for migration stocks, but they find they have little predictive power. Such demand shocks would be likely to have better power at predicting remittance flows. Yang forthcoming comes closest to this approach in the Philippines, but notes that the exchange rate shocks he considers are likely to also have wealth effects that prevent them from picking up the pure remittance impact.

20. See Rapoport and Docquier (forthcoming) for an overview of motives to remit.

References

Adams, Richard H. 1991. "The Economic Uses and Impact of International Remittances in Rural Egypt." *Economic Development and Cultural Change* 39(4): 695–722.

Bauer, Thomas, Gil Epstein, and Ira N. Gang. 2002. "Herd Effects or Migration Networks? The Location Choice of Mexican Migrants in the U.S." IZA Discussion Paper, no. 551. Institute for the Study of Labor (12A) Bonn.

Behrman, Jere R., and Mark R. Rosenzweig. 2003. "Returns to Birthweight." Mimeo. University of Pennsylvania.

Beine, Michel, Frédéric Docquier, and Hillel Rapoport. 2001. "Brain Drain and Economic Growth: Theory and Evidence." *Journal of Development Economics* 64(1): 275–89.

Chiquiar, Daniel, and Gordon H. Hanson. 2005. "International Migration, Self-Selection, and the Distribution of Wages: Evidence from Mexico and the United States." *Journal of Political Economy* 113(2): 239–81.

Cox Edwards, A., and M. Ureta. 2003. "International Migration, Remittances and Schooling: Evidence from El Salvador." *Journal of Development Economics* 72(2): 429–61.

Durand, Jorge, and Douglas S. Massey. 1992. "Mexican Migration to the United States: A Critical Review." *Latin American Research Review* 27(2): 3–42.

Espinosa, Kristin, and Douglas Massey. 1997. "Undocumented Migration and the Quantity and Quality of Social Capital." *Soziale Welt* 12: 141–62.

Gibson, John, David J. McKenzie, and Hala Rohorua. 2005. "How Cost-elastic are Remittances? Evidence from Tongan Migrants in New Zealand." Mimeo. World Bank, Washington, DC.

Grossman, Michael. 1972. "On the Concept of Health Capital and the Demand for Health." *Journal of Political Economy* 80(2): 223–55.

Hildebrandt, Nicole, and David J. McKenzie. forthcoming. "The Effects of Migration on Child Health in Mexico." *Economia*.

International Money Fund (IMF). 2005. *World Economic Outlook: Globalization and External Imbalances*, April 2005. IMF: Washington, DC.

LaLonde, R., and R. Topel. 1997. "Economic Impact of International Migration and the Economic Performance of Migrants." In *Handbook of Population and Family Economics*, ed. M. Rosenzweig and O. Stark 799–850. New York: Elsevier Science.

Lopez Cordoba, Ernesto. 2004. "Globalization, Migration, and Development: The Role of Mexican Migrant Remittances." Mimeo. The Inter-American Development Bank, Washington, D.C.

Massey, Douglas S. 1988. "Economic Development and International Migration in Comparative Perspective." *Population and Development Review* 14(3): 383–413.

Massey, Douglas S., Luin Goldring, and Jorge Durand. 1994. "Continuities in Transnational Migration: An Analysis of Nineteen Mexican Communities." *American Journal of Sociology* 99(6): 1,492–533.

McKenzie, David J., and Hillel Rapoport. 2004. "Network Effects and the Dynamics of Migration and Inequality: Theory and Evidence from Mexico." Bureau for Research in Economic Analysis of Development (BREAD) Working Paper, no. 063. Cambridge, MA.

———. 2005. "Migration Networks, Migration Incentives, and Education Inequality in Rural Mexico." Paper presented at the Inter-American Development Bank Economic Integration, Remittances, and Development Conference. Washington, D.C.

Mishra, Prachi. 2003. "Effect of Emigration on Wages in Developing Countries: Evidence from Mexico." Mimeo. Department of Economics, Columbia University, New York.

Mountford, Andrew. 1997. "Can a Brain Drain be Good for Growth in the Source Country?" *Journal of Development Economics* 53(2): 287–303.

Orrenius, Pia M. 1999. "The Role of Family Networks, Coyote Prices, and the Rural Economy in Migration from Western Mexico: 1965–1994." Federal Reserve Bank of Dallas Working Paper, no. 9910.

Rapoport, Hillel, and Frédéric Docquier. forthcoming. "The Economics of Migrants' Remittances." In *Handbook of the Economics of Reciprocity, Giving and Altruism*, ed. L.A. Gerard-Varet, S.C. Kolm, and J. Mercier Ythier. Amsterdam: North-Holland.

Ratha, Dilip. 2005. "Workers' Remittances: An Important and Stable Source of External Development Finance." Chapter 1 in *Remittances: Development Impact and Future Prospects*, ed. Samuel Maimbo and Dilip Ratha, 19–51. World Bank, Washington, DC.

Stark, Oded, Christian Helmenstein, and Alexia Prskawetz. 1997. "A Brain Gain With a Brain Drain." *Economics Letters* 55(2): 227–234.

Taylor, J. Edward, and T.J. Wyatt. 1996. "The Shadow Value of Migrant Remittances, Income and Inequality in a Household-farm Economy." *Journal of Development Studies* 32(6): 899–912.

United Nations. 2002. *International Migration Report 2002*. New York: United Nations, Department of Economic and Social Affairs, Population Division.

Wolpin, Kenneth I. 1997. "Determinants and Consequences of the Mortality and Health of Infants and Children." In *Handbook of Population and Family Economics*, volume 1A, ed. M.R. Rosenzweig and O. Stark, 483–557. New York: Elsevier Science.

Woodruff, Christopher, and Rene Zenteno. 2001. "Remittances and Microenterprises in Mexico." Working Paper, University of California, San Diego (UCSD) and ITESM-Guadalajara, December.

Yang, Dean. 2004. "International Migration, Human Capital, and Entrepreneurship: Evidence from Philippine Migrants' Exchange Rate Shocks." Mimeo. Ford School of Public Policy, University of Michigan, Ann Arbor.

PART II

BRAIN DRAIN, BRAIN GAIN, BRAIN WASTE

5

INTERNATIONAL MIGRATION BY EDUCATION ATTAINMENT, 1990–2000

Frédéric Docquier and Abdeslam Marfouk

Introduction

For the last few years, the pace of international migration has accelerated. According to the United Nations (2002), the number of international migrants increased from 154 million to 175 million between 1990 and 2000. The consequences for countries of origin and destination have attracted the increased attention of policymakers, scientists, and international agencies. The phenomenon is likely to further develop in the coming decades as a part of the world globalization process. The international community must be prepared to address the challenges raised by the increasing mobility of workers. In particular, the migration of skilled workers (the so-called brain drain) is a major piece of the migration debate. The transfer[1] of human resources has undergone extensive scrutiny in developing countries but also in such industrial countries as Canada, the United Kingdom, and Germany, where an important fraction of talented natives is working abroad.

When considering the consequences for countries of origin, early literature supports the view that skilled migration is unambiguously detrimental for those left behind (Grubel and Scott 1966; Johnson 1967; Bhagwati and Hamada 1974; Kwok and Leland 1982). This is the case if the migrants' contribution to the economy is greater than their marginal product or if the education of skilled emigrants was partly funded by taxes on residents. The negative effects of the brain drain for source countries have been reformulated in an endogenous growth framework (Miyagiwa 1991; Haque and Kim 1995; Wong and Yip 1999). More recently, the effects of migration prospects on human capital formation have been the focus of several studies, which suggest that such prospects may in fact foster human capital

151

formation and growth in sending countries (Mountford 1997; Stark, Helmenstein, and Prskawetz 1998; Vidal 1998; Beine, Docquier, and Rapoport 2001). The authors argue that if the return to education is higher abroad than at home, the possibility of migration increases the expected return of human capital, thereby enhancing domestic enrollment in education.[1] More people, therefore, invest in human capital as a result of increased migration opportunities. This acquisition can contribute positively to growth and economic performance. Along with the incentive to acquire education, other channels through which the brain drain may positively affect the sending economy have also been proposed. These include a range of "feedback effects" such as remittances (Cinar and Docquier 2004), return migration after additional knowledge and skills have been acquired abroad (Stark, Helmenstein, and Prskawetz 1997; Domingues Dos Santos and Postel-Vinay 2003), and the creation of business and trade networks (Dustmann and Kirchkamp 2002; Mesnard and Ravallion 2001). A survey on the "new economics of the brain drain" can be found in Commander, Kangasniemi, and Winters (2004) or Docquier and Rapoport (2004).

Understanding and measuring all the mechanisms at work require reliable data and empirical analysis. Regarding the size and the education structure of international migration, there is a fair amount of evidence suggesting that the brain drain is now much more extensive than it was two or three decades ago. For example, Haque and Jahangir (1999) indicate that the number of highly skilled emigrants from Africa increased from 1,800 a year on average during 1960–75 to 4,400 during 1975–84 and 23,000 during 1984–87. These trends were confirmed in the 1990s in the face of the increasingly "quality-selective" immigration policies introduced in many Organisation for Economic Co-operation and Development (OECD) countries. Since 1984, Australia's immigration policy has officially privileged skilled workers, with candidates being selected according to their prospective "contribution to the Australian economy." In November 1991, the New Zealand immigration policy shifted from a traditional "source-country preference" toward a "points-system" selection, similar to that in Australia (Statistics New Zealand 2004). The Canadian immigration policy follows similar lines, resulting in an increased share of highly educated people among the selected immigrants. For example, in 1997, 50,000 professional specialists and entrepreneurs immigrated to Canada with 75,000 additional family members, representing 58 percent of total immigration. In the United States, since the Immigration Act of 1990 (followed by the American Competitiveness and Work Force Improvement Act of 1998), emphasis has been put on the selection of highly skilled workers. This is accomplished through a system of quotas favoring candidates with academic degrees or specific professional skills. For the latter category, the annual number of visas issued for highly skilled professionals (H-1B visas) increased from 110,200 in 1992 to 355,600 in 2000. The totality of this increase is the result of immigration from developing countries, and about half of these workers now come from India.

In European Union (EU) countries, immigration policies are less clear and still oriented toward traditional targets such as asylum seekers and applicants requesting family reunion. However, there is some evidence suggesting that EU countries are also leaning toward becoming quality selective. As reported in Lowell (2002a), "European Commission President Prodi has called for up to 1.7 million immigrants to fill an EU-wide labor shortage through a system similar to the US green cards for qualified immigrants." A growing number of EU countries (including France, Ireland, and the United Kingdom) have recently introduced programs aiming at attracting a qualified labor force (especially in the field of information, communication, and technology, ICT) through the creation of labor-shortage occupation lists (see Lowell 2002b). In February 2000, German Chancellor Schröder announced plans to recruit additional specialists in the field of information technology. Green cards came into force in August 2001, giving German ICT firms the opportunity to hire up to 20,000 non-EU ICT specialists for a maximum of five years. More recently, the German Sübmuth Commission recommended the introduction of a coherent flexible migration policy that allows for temporary and permanent labor migrants (see Bauer and Kunze 2004). In 2002, the French Ministry of Labor established a system to induce highly skilled workers from outside the EU to live and work in France. Given the apparent demographic problems and aging populations, the intensity of the brain drain could continue to increase during the next decades.[2]

Until recently, despite numerous case studies and anecdotal evidence, there has been no systematic empirical assessment of the brain-drain magnitude. Many institutions consider the lack of harmonized international data on migration by country of origin and education level as the major problem for monitoring the scope and impact of brain drain in developing areas.[3] In the absence of such empirical data, the debate has remained almost exclusively theoretical. In their influential contribution, Carrington and Detragiache (1998, 1999) provided estimates of the emigration rates of tertiary educated workers for 61 developing countries. These estimates are based on three main statistical sources: U.S. Census data on the skill structure of immigration, OECD data on immigration per country of origin, and Barro and Lee (2000) data describing the skill structure in sending countries. The estimates rely on a set of assumptions. First, for non-U.S. countries, they use OECD migration statistics, which report limited information on the origin of immigrants.[4] Second, they transpose the skill structure of U.S. immigrants on the OECD total immigration stock. For example, migrants from Morocco to France are assumed to be distributed across education categories in the same way as migrants from Morocco to the United States. This assumption is particularly tentative for countries that do not send many migrants to the United States. Relying on OECD statistics produced an average underestimation of 8.9 percent in skilled-worker migration rates in 2000 (this is the major source of bias, especially for small countries). Imposing the U.S. education structure on other OECD countries produced an average overestimation of 6.3 percent in skilled-worker migration rates in 2000 (the bias is obviously strong in countries sending a minor percentage of their emigrants to the United States). On average, we demonstrate that Carrington and Detragiache's (1998, 1999) method underestimated the emigration rates of skilled workers by 2.6 percent in 2000. While it seems rather small, the overall bias is heterogeneously distributed across countries. It ranges from about +51.5 percent for São Tomé and Principe to −51.2 percent for Mauritius.[5] Adams (2003) used the same methodology to update the emigration rates of 24 labor-exporting countries in 2000. Beine, Docquier, and Rapoport (2003) used Carrington and Detragiache's data to predict the growth impact of the brain drain. Yet, given the assumptions, the evidence concerning the consequences of skilled migration for developing countries remains not only limited but also largely inconclusive.

The purpose of this chapter is to build an exhaustive international database on international migration by education attainment. This data set describes the loss of skilled workers (in absolute and relative terms) for all developing and developed countries. The majority of highly skilled workers go to industrial countries. We focus on the south-north and north-north brain drain. We are aware that a brain drain is evident outside the OECD area—migration of skilled workers to the six member states of the Gulf Cooperation Council (Bahrain, Kuwait, Oman, Qatar, Saudi Arabia, and the United Arab Emirates) and also to South Africa, Malaysia, Hong Kong (China), Singapore, and Taiwan (China). At this stage, however, we do not take these flows into account. According to the United Nations (2002), migration to developed countries represented 53 percent of world migration in 1990 and 60 percent in 2000. Highly skilled migration is even more concentrated. Given census data collected from various non-OECD countries, we estimate that about 90 percent of these highly skilled migrants live in 1 of the 30 member states of the OECD.

We use data on the immigration structure by education attainment and country of birth from all OECD receiving countries. Census and register data are available in nearly all OECD countries. This chapter clearly builds on Release 1.0 (Docquier and Marfouk 2004), which was the first attempt to evaluate migration stocks and rates by education attainment on an exhaustive scale.[6] In comparison to Release 1.0 (which built on survey data for 12 European countries), we significantly extend the quality of the data. Special attention has been paid to the homogeneity and the comparability of the data (definition of immigration, comparability between immigration and human capital indicators, treatment of the dependent territories, homogeneity of the data sources). Consequently, we characterize (on a very homogeneous basis) the country of origin and education attainment of more than 98 percent of the OECD stock of working-age adults in 2000. Focusing on tertiary educated migrants (defined as working-age migrants with more than a secondary school diploma), our calculations reveal that the stock of educated immigrants has increased by about 800,000 a year between 1990 and 2000 (the total stock of migrants has increased by about 1.7 million a year). Our country measures can be used to examine the changes in the international distribution of migration rates, to test for the (push-and-pull) determinants per skill group, or to evaluate the macroeconomic consequences of migration on source and destination countries.

The remainder of this chapter is organized as follows. The second section describes the methodology. Results for 1990 and 2000 are presented in the third section. The fourth section focuses on OECD countries and provides the net gains and losses of skilled workers (in percentage of the working-age population). The fifth section concludes this chapter. Country classifications, and comparisons with previous studies are given in annex 5.A.

Definition, Principles, and Data Sources

This section describes the methodology and data sources used to compute emigration stocks and rates by education attainment and origin country in 1990 and 2000. In what follows, the term "country" usually designates independent states while "dependent territory" refers to other entities attached to a particular independent state. Our 2000 data set distinguishes 192 independent territories (Vatican City and the 191 UN member states, including Timor-Leste, which became independent in 2002) and 39 dependent territories. Stocks are provided for both types of territories while rates are only provided for independent countries as well as three dependent territories, which are treated as economies—Hong Kong (China), Macao SAR, and Taiwan (China)—and one occupied territory (Palestine). Because most of the Korean migrants to the United States did not accurately report their origin, we cannot distinguish between the Republic of Korea and Democratic People's Republic of Korea (estimates are provided for Korea as a whole). We distinguish 174 countries in 1990, before the secession of the Soviet bloc, the former Yugoslavia, the former Czechoslovakia, the independence of Eritrea and Timor-Leste, and the German and the Republic of Yemen reunifications.[7]

For economic and statistical reasons, working on stocks is more attractive than working on flows. Stock variables are more appropriate to analyze the endogeneity and the dynamics of migration movements (the equilibrium values are often expressed in terms of stocks). Regarding statistics, it has long been recognized that migration flow data are less reliable than stock data, because of the impossibility of evaluating emigration and return migration movements.

We count as migrants all working-age (25 and over) foreign-born individuals living in an OECD country.[8] Skilled migrants are those who have at least tertiary education attainment wherever they completed their schooling. Our methodology proceeds in two steps. We first compute emigration stocks by education attainment from all countries of the world. Then, we evaluate these numbers in percentage of the total labor force born in the sending country (including the migrants themselves). This definition of skilled migrants deserves two main comments.

First, the set of receiving countries is restricted to OECD nations. Compared with existing works (such as *Trends in International Migration*, OECD 2002), our database reveals many insights about the structure of south-north and north-north migration. Generally speaking, the skill level of immigrants in non-OECD countries is expected to be very low, except in a few countries such as South Africa (1.3 million immigrants in 2000), the six member states of the Gulf Cooperation Council (9.6 million immigrants in Saudi Arabia, the United Arab Emirates, Kuwait, Bahrain, Oman, and Qatar), and some Eastern Asian countries (4 million immigrants in Hong Kong (China) and Singapore only). According to their census and survey data, about 17.5 percent of adult immigrants have tertiary education in these countries (17 percent in Bahrain, 17.2 percent in Saudi Arabia, 14 percent in Kuwait, 18.7 percent in South Africa). Considering that children constitute 25 percent of the immigration stock, we estimate the number of educated workers at 1.9 million in these countries. The number of educated immigrants in the rest of the world lies between 1 and 4 million (if the average proportion of educated immigrants among adults lies between 2.5 and 10 percent). This implies that, focusing on OECD countries, we should capture a large fraction of the worldwide educated migration (about 90 percent). Nevertheless, we are aware that by disregarding non-OECD immigration countries, we probably underestimate the brain drain for a dozen developing countries (such as the Arab Republic of Egypt, Sudan, Jordan, the Republic of Yemen, Pakistan, or Bangladesh in the neighborhood of the Gulf states, and Swaziland, Namibia, Zimbabwe, and other countries that send emigrants to South Africa, and so on). Incorporating data collected from selected non-OECD countries could refine the data set.

Second, we have no systematic information on the age of entry. It is therefore impossible to distinguish between immigrants who were educated at the time of their arrival and those who acquired education after they settled in the receiving country; for example, Mexican-born individuals who arrived in the United States at age 5 or 10 and graduated from U.S. higher-education institutions are counted as highly skilled immigrants. Hence, our definition of the brain drain is partly determined by data availability. Existing data do not allow us to systematically eliminate foreign-born individuals who arrived with completed schooling or after a given age threshold. In the United States, the proportion of foreign-born individuals who arrived before age 10 represents 10 percent of the immigration stock (16 percent for those who arrived before age 16). This average proportion amounts to 13 percent among skilled immigrants (20.4 for age 16). Important differences are observed across countries. The share is important for high-income and Central American countries (about 20 percent). It is quite low for Asian and African countries (about 9 percent). Having no systematic data for the other receiving countries, we cannot control for familial immigration. Our database includes these individuals who arrived at young age. Our choice is also motivated by several reasons: (a) our numbers are comparable to traditional statistics on international migration, which include all migrants whatever their age of entry; (b) it is impossible to quantify the share of these young immigrants who were partly educated in their birth country and/or who arrived with foreign fellowships; and (c) young immigrants who spent part of their primary or secondary schooling in the origin country or who got foreign schooling fellowships induced a fiscal loss for their origin country.

Emigration Stocks

It is well documented that statistics provided by origin countries do not provide a realistic picture of emigration. When available, they are incomplete and imprecise.[9] While detailed immigration data are not easy to collect on an homogeneous basis, information on emigration can only be captured by aggregating consistent immigration data collected in receiving countries. Information about the origin and skill of natives and immigrants is available from national population censuses and registers. More specifically, country i's census usually identifies individuals on the basis of age, country of birth j, and skill level s. Our method consists of collecting census or register data from a large set of receiving countries, with the highest level of detail on birth countries and (at least) three levels of education attainment: $s=h$ for high-skilled, $s=m$ for medium-skilled, $s=l$ for low-skilled and $s=u$ for the unknowns. Let $M_{t,s}^{i,j}$ denote the stock of working-age individuals born in j, of skill s, living in country i, at time t.

Low-skilled workers are those with primary education (or with 0 to 8 years of schooling completed); medium-skilled workers are those with secondary education (9 to 12 years of schooling); high-skilled workers are those with tertiary education (13 years and above). The unknowns are either the result of the fact that some immigrants did not declare their education attainment or the result of the absence of data on education in some receiving countries. Education categories are built on the basis of country-specific information and are compatible with human capital indicators available for all sending countries. A mapping between the country education classification is sometimes required to harmonize the data.[10] Some statistics offices have difficulties determining the education level of their immigrants.[11] By focusing on census and register data, our methodology does not capture illegal immigration for which systematic statistics by education level and country of origin are not available.[12] According to the U.S. Immigration and Naturalization Services, the illegal population residing in the United States amounted to 3.5 million in January 1990 and 7.0 million in January 2000. It is even possible to identify the main countries of origin (in 2000, 68.7 percent were from Mexico, 2.7 percent from El Salvador, 2.1 percent from Guatemala, 2.0 percent from Colombia and Honduras, and so on).[13] However, there is no accurate data about the education structure of these illegal migrants. For the other member states of the OECD, data on illegal immigration are less reliable or do not exist. By disregarding illegal migrants, we probably overestimate the average level of education of the immigrant population (it can be reasonably assumed that most illegal immigrants are uneducated). Nevertheless, this limit should not significantly distort our estimates of the migration rate of highly skilled workers.

As far as possible, we turn our attention to the homogeneity and the comparability of the data. This provides a few methodological choices:

- To allow comparisons between 1990 and 2000, we consider the same 30 receiving countries in 1990 and 2000. Consequently, the former Czechoslovakia, Hungary, the Republic of Korea and Democratic People's Republic of Korea, Poland, Mexico, and Turkey are considered as receiving countries in 1990 despite the fact that they were not members of the OECD.
- Migration is defined on the basis of the country of birth rather than citizenship. While citizenship characterizes the foreign population, the concept of foreign-born individuals better captures the decision to emigrate.[14] Usually, the number of foreign-born individuals is much higher than the number of foreign citizens (twice as large in countries such as Hungary, the Netherlands, and Sweden).[15] Furthermore, the concept of country of birth is time-invariant (contrary to citizenship, which changes with naturalization) and independent of the changes in policies regarding naturalization. The OECD statistics report that 14.4 million foreign-born individuals were naturalized between 1991 and 2000. Countries with a particularly high number of acquisitions of citizenship are the United States (5.6 million), Germany (2.2 million), Canada (1.6 million), and France (1.1 million). Despite the fact that they are partially reported

in traditional statistics (OECD 2002), the number of foreign-born individuals can be obtained for a majority of OECD countries. In a limited number of cases, the national census only gives immigrants' citizenship (Germany, Italy, Greece, Japan, and the Republic of Korea and the Democratic People's Republic of Korea). As indicated in table 5.2, 88.3 percent of working-age immigrants can be characterized in terms of country of birth in 2000 (11.7 percent in terms of citizenship). Contrary to common belief, data availability is not significantly different in 1990, even among European states. We obtain information about country of birth for 88 percent of working-age immigrants in 1990 (12 percent in terms of citizenship).

- It is worth noting that the concept of foreign born is not fully homogeneous across OECD countries. As in many OECD countries, our main criterion relies on country of birth and citizenship at birth: we define foreign born as an individual born abroad with foreign citizenship at birth. For example, the U.S Census Bureau considers as natives children who are born in the United States (as well as in Puerto Rico or U.S. dependent territories, such as the U.S. Virgin Islands and Guam), or who are born abroad from a U.S. citizen.[16] Other residents are considered foreign born. France and Denmark use a similar concept. Statistics Netherlands defines first-generation immigrants as people who are born abroad and have at least one parent who is also born abroad (Alders 2001). However, in a few countries (for example, Australia, New Zealand, and Belgium), the foreign-born concept used by the Statistics Institute essentially means "overseas born," that is, an individual simply born abroad. While it is impossible to use a fully comparable concept of immigration, we have tried to maximize the homogeneity of our data sources. It is worth noting that our definition clearly excludes the second generation of immigrants. A couple of countries offer a more detailed picture of immigration, distinguishing the foreign born from those with foreign backgrounds (basically immigrants' descendants born locally from one of two foreign-born parents).[17]

- As discussed above, emigration rates are provided for 195 territories in 2000 (191 UN member states, Vatican City, Palestine, Hong Kong (China), Taiwan (China), and Macao SAR minus the Democratic People's Republic of Korea). The world configuration has changed between 1990 and 2000. The former Czechoslovakia divided and became the Czech Republic and the Slovak Republic; the former Soviet Union collapsed, leading to the formation of 15 countries (7 on the European continent and 8 on the Asian continent); the former Yugoslavia broke into 5 countries; Eritrea and Timor-Leste emerged as independent countries in 1993 and 2002. East and West Germany and the Democratic Republic and the Republic of Yemen were each unified. Consequently, for this study, we distinguished 174 countries in 1990 (the former Soviet Union replaces 15 countries, the former Yugoslavia replaces 5 countries, and the former Czechoslovakia replaces 2 countries). For homogeneity reasons, we aggregated East and West Germany as well as the Democratic Republic and the Republic of Yemen in 1990. In 1990, the former Soviet Union totally belonged to the European area.[18]

- A related issue concerns the dependent territories. Each dependent territory is linked to a nation. Individuals born in these territories have the unrestricted right to move to and to live in the nation. We naturally consider them as natives of the sovereign nation. Once the category of foreign born is chosen, it means that these individuals should not be considered as immigrants if they move to the sovereign state (internal migration). They should only be considered as immigrants if they move to another independent state (external migration). This criterion is especially important for U.S. dependent territories (Puerto Rico, Guam, and so on), U.K. overseas territories (Bermuda, Anguilla, and so on), French dependent territories (Guadalupe, Reunion, and so on), Denmark (Greenland and the Faroe Islands, and so on), or around Australia and New Zealand (Cook Islands, Niue, Tokelau, and so on). For example, in accordance with the U.S. Census Bureau definition, we consider that the 1 million Puerto Ricans living in the United States are U.S. natives but not immigrants. This considerably reduces the total stock of Puerto Rican emigrants. We have computed on the same basis the emigration stock for the other dependent territories— except for Taiwan (China), Hong Kong (China), and Macao SAR—which are assimilated to independent countries. Then, given the small numbers obtained, we have eliminated the Northern Mariana Islands and Western Sahara (a disputed rather than dependent territory) and have summed up Jersey and Guernsey (forming the Channel Islands).

- Because the second step of our analysis consists of comparing the numbers of emigrants and residents by education attainment, we have to consider homogeneous groups. Working with the working-age population (age 25 and over) maximizes the comparability of the immigration population with data on education attainment in source countries. It also excludes a large number of students who temporarily emigrate to complete their education. We cannot control for graduate students age 25 and over completing their schooling.[19] As shown in table 5.1, this age group is slightly different in a limited number of countries.

Building an aggregate measure of emigration per education attainment requires a rule for sharing the unknown values. At the OECD level, the number of migrants whose education attainment is not described amounts to 1.287 million, that is, 2.2 percent of the total stock. Two reasonable rules could be considered:

either unknown values can be distributed in the same way as the known values, or they can be assimilated as unskilled. We combine both rules depending on the information available in the receiving country. For receiving countries where information about immigrants' education is available, we assimilate the unknowns to unskilled workers.[20] For example, Australian immigrants who did not mention their education attainment are considered unskilled. In receiving countries where no information about skill is available, we transpose the skill distribution observed in the rest of the OECD area or in the neighboring region. For example, if we have no information about the skill structure of immigrants to Iceland, Algerian emigrants to Iceland are assumed to be distributed the same way as Algerian emigrants to all other Scandinavian countries. The assumptions will be discussed below.

Formally, the stocks of emigrants of skill s from country j at time t ($M_{t,s}^j$) are obtained as follows:

$$M_{t,h}^j = \sum_i M_{t,h}^{i,j} + \sum_i M_{t,u}^{i,j}{}'\gamma_t^{i}{}' \frac{\sum_i M_{t,h}^{i,j}}{\sum_i [M_{t,l}^{i,j} + M_{t,m}^{i,j} + M_{t,h}^{i,j}]}$$

$$M_{t,m}^j = \sum_i M_{t,h}^{i,j} + \sum_i M_{t,u}^{i,j}{}'\gamma_t^{i}{}' \frac{\sum_i M_{t,m}^{i,j}}{\sum_i [M_{t,l}^{i,j} + M_{t,m}^{i,j} + M_{t,h}^{i,j}]} \qquad (5.1)$$

$$M_{t,h}^j = \sum_i M_{t,h}^{i,j} + \sum_i M_{t,u}^{i,j}{}'\gamma_t^{i}{}' \frac{\sum_i M_{t,l}^{i,j}}{\sum_i [M_{t,l}^{i,j} + M_{t,m}^{i,j} + M_{t,h}^{i,j}]} + \sum_i M_{t,u}^{i,j}(1 - \gamma_t^i)$$

where γ_t^i is a (time- and country-dependent) binary variable equal to 1 if there is no data on the immigrants' skill in country i, and equal to 0 otherwise.

Table 5.1 describes the data sources. In 2000, we use census, microcensus, and register data for 29 countries. European Council data are used in the case of Greece. Information on the country of birth is available for the majority of countries, representing 88.3 percent of the OECD immigration stock. Information on citizenship is used for the remaining countries (Germany, Italy, Greece, Japan, and the Republic of Korea and the Democratic People's Republic of Korea). The education structure can be obtained in 24 countries and can be estimated in 3 additional countries (Belgium, Greece, and Portugal) on the basis of the European

TABLE 5.1   Data Sources

Country (age group)	1990 (+) Origin	1990 (+) Education	2000 (+) Origin	2000 (+) Education
Australia (25+)	Census (#)	Census (#)	Census (#)	Census (#)
Austria (25+)	Census	Census	Census	Census
Belgium (25+)	Census	Census	Improved EC (**)	LFS
Canada (25+)	Census (#)	Census (#)	Census (#)	Census (#)
Czech Republic (25+)	Census (#)	—	Census (#)	Census (#)
Denmark (25+)	Register	Register	Register	Register
Finland (25+)	Register	Register	Register	Register
France (25+)	Census (#)	Census (#)	Census (#)	Census (#)
Germany (25–65)	Microcensuz* (Cit)	Microcensuz* (Cit)	Microcensuz* (Cit)	Microcensuz* (Cit)
Greece (25+)	EC (Cit)	LFS (Cit.)	EC (Cit)	LFS (Cit.)
Hungary (All;25+)	EC (Cit)	—	Census	Census
Iceland (All)	Register	—	Register	—
Ireland (25+)	Census	Census	Census	Census
Italy (25+)	EC (Cit)	—	Census (Cit)	Census (Cit)
Japan (All/25+)	Register (Cit)	—	Census (Cit)	—
Korea, Rep of (All)	Register (Cit)	—	Register (Cit)	—
Luxembourg (25+)	Census (#)	Census (#)	Census (#)	Census (#)
Mexico (25+)	Ipums (+) 10%	Ipums (+) 10%	Ipums (+) 10.6%	Ipums (+) 10.6%
Netherlands (All)	Census*	Census*	Census*	Census*
New Zealand (15+)	Census	Census	Census	Census
Norway (25+)	Register	Register	Register	Register

Poland (13+)	Census (#)	—	Census (#)	Census (#)
Portugal (25+)	Census	LFS	Census	LFS
Slovak Republic (25+)	See Czech Republic	See Czech Republic	Census (#)	Census (#)
Spain (25+)	Census	Census	Census	Census
Sweden (25+)	Census	Census	Census	Census
Switzerland (18+)	Census (#)	Census (#)	Census (#)	Census (#)
Turkey (15+)	Census (#)	Census (#)	Census (#)	Census (#)
United Kingdom (15+)	Census*	Census*	Census*	Census*
United States (25+)	Ipums (+) 5%	Ipums(+) 5%	Census 100%*	Census 100%*

Source: Various statistical sources and agencies.

Notes: EC = European Council (register data); LFS = Labor Force Survey; (*) = limited level of detail. (**) European Council data corrected by the country-specific "foreign born/foreign citizen" ratio in Census 1991. (+) Year around 1990 and 2000 (for example, the Australian censuses refer to 1991 and 2001) (#) Data available in Release 1.0. See Ruggles et al. (2004) on the United States and Sobek et al. (2002) on the Mexican sample.

TABLE 5.2 International Mobility by Education Attainment—An Overview

	1990	% of stock (*)	2000	% of stock (*)
Total stock of migrants in OECD countries	41.845	100.0%	59.022	100.0%
Information about country of origin	41.845	100.0%	59.022	100.0%
including information about country of birth	36.812	88.0%	52.145	88.3%
including information about citizenship	5.033	12.0%	6.878	11.7%
Information about educational attainment	38.169	91.2%	57.900	98.1%
including "education not described"	1.576	3.8%	1.287	2.2%
including Labor Force Survey data	0.283	0.7%	1.181	2.0%
Migrants with tertiary education	12.462	29.8%	20.403	34.6%
including skilled migrants to the United States (*)	6.203	49.8%	10.354	50.7%
including skilled migrants to Canada (*)	1.879	15.1%	2.742	13.4%
including skilled migrants to Australia (*)	1.110	8.9%	1.540	7.5%
including skilled migrants to the United Kingdom (*)	0.570	4.6%	1.257	6.2%
including skilled migrants to Germany (*)	0.556	4.5%	0.996	4.9%
including skilled migrants to France (*)	0.300	2.4%	0.615	3.0%
Migrants with secondary education	10.579	25.3%	17.107	29.0%
Migrants with less than secondary education	18.804	44.9%	21.512	36.4%
World total labor force (independent territories only)	2568.229	% of labor force	3187.233	% of labor force
World labor force with tertiary education	234.692	9.1%	360.614	11.3%
World labor force with secondary education	755.104	29.4%	945.844	29.7%
World labor force with less than secondary education	1578.433	61.5%	1880.775	59.0%
World average emigration rate - tertiary education	5.0%		5.4%	—
World average emigration rate - secondary education	1.4%		1.8%	—
World average emigration rate - less than secondary education	1.2%		1.1%	—

		% of all groups		% of all groups
OECD total labor force	657.718		750.089	
OECD labor force with tertiary education	144.050	21.9%	207.352	27.6%
OECD emigrants with tertiary education	6.094	26.7%	8.533	30.2%
OECD average emigration rate - tertiary education	4.1%	—	4.0%	—
Non-OECD total labor force	1910.511	% of all groups	2437.144	% of all groups
Non-OECD labor force with tertiary education	90.642	4.7%	153.262	6.3%
Non-OECD emigrants with tertiary education	6.367	33.5%	11.870	38.6%
Non-OECD average emigration rate - tertiary education	6.6%	—	7.2%	—

Source: Various statistical sources and agencies.

Note: (*) Percentage of the stock of skilled immigrants only.

—not available.

Labor Force Survey. As shown in table 5.2, data built on the Labor Force Survey represent only 2 percent of the OECD migration stock in 2000 (0.7 percent in 1990). In the three remaining countries, the education structure is extrapolated on the basis of the Scandinavian countries (for Iceland) or the rest of the OECD (for Japan and the Republic of Korea and the Democratic People's Republic of Korea). In 1990, European Council data were used for Hungary and Italy. These data are based on the concept of citizenship. Compared with 2000, education attainment was not available in Italy, the Czech Republic, and Hungary. The Italian education structure is based on the rest of the EU-15. For the other two countries, we use proportions computed from the rest of Europe. Information from the Belgian 1991 Census is available and provides complete data by country of birth and education attainment.

Emigration Rates

In the spirit of Carrington and Detragiache (1998) and Adams (2003), our second step consists of comparing the emigration stocks with the total number of people born in the source country and belonging to the same education category. Calculating the brain drain as a proportion of the total educated labor force is a better strategy to evaluate the pressure imposed on the local labor market. The pressure exerted by 1,037,000 Indian skilled emigrants (4.3 percent of the educated total labor force) is less important than the pressure exerted by 16,000 skilled emigrants from Grenada (85 percent of the educated labor force).

Denoting $N_{t,s}^j$ as the stock of individuals age 25 or over, of skill s, living in country j, at time t, we define the emigration rates by the following.

$$m_{t,s}^j = \frac{M_{t,s}^j}{N_{t,s}^j + M_{t,s}^j} \tag{5.2}$$

In particular, $m_{t,s}^j$ provides some information about the intensity of the brain drain in the source country j. It measures the fraction of skilled agents born in country j and living in other OECD countries.[21]

This step requires using data on the size and the skill structure of the working-age population in the countries of origin. Population data by age are provided by the United Nations.[22] We focus on the population age 25 and older. Data are missing for a couple of countries but can be estimated using the Central Intelligence Agency *World Factbook* Web site.[23] Population data are split across education groups using international human capital indicators. Several sources based on attainment and/or enrollment variables can be found in the literature. These data sets suffer from two important limits. First, data sets published in the 1990s reveal a number of suspicious features and inconsistencies.[24] Second, given the variety of education systems around the world, they are subject to serious comparability problems. Three major competing data sets are available: Barro and Lee (2000), Cohen and Soto (2001), and De la Fuente and Domenech (2002). The first two sets depict the education structure in both developed and developing countries. The latter data set focuses only on 21 OECD countries (De la Fuente and Domenech 2002). Statistical comparisons between these sets reveal that the highest signal/noise ratio is obtained in De la Fuente and Domenech. These tests are conducted in OECD countries. Regarding developing countries, Cohen and Soto's set (2001) outperforms Barro and Lee's set (2000) in growth regressions. However, Cohen and Soto's data for Africa clearly underestimate official statistics. According to the South African 1996 census, the share of educated individuals amounts to 7.2 percent. Cohen and Soto report 3 percent (Barro and Lee report 6.9 percent). The Kenyan 1999 Census reports the share of educated individuals at 2 percent, while Cohen and Soto report 0.9 percent (1.2 percent for Barro and Lee).

Generally speaking, the Cohen and Soto data set predicts extremely low levels of human capital for African countries[25] (the share with tertiary education is lower than 1 percent in a large number of African countries) and a few other non-OECD countries.[26] The Barro and Lee estimates seem closer to the African official statistics. As the brain drain is particularly important in African countries, Barro and Lee's indicators are preferable. Consequently, data for $N_{t,s}^j$ are taken from De la Fuente and Domenech (2002) for OECD countries and from Barro and Lee (2000) for non-OECD countries. For countries where Barro and Lee measures are missing (about 70 countries in 2000), we transpose the skill-sharing level of the neighboring country with the closest human development index regarding education. This method gives good approximations of the brain drain rate, which are broadly consistent with anecdotal evidence.

The Database 1990–2000

World Migration—An Overview

Table 5.2 depicts the major trends regarding the international mobility of the working-age population. The number of working-age individuals born in one country and living in another country increased from 42 million in 1990 to 59 million in 2000, that is, by 1.7 million a year. Regarding the education structure of migrants, skilled workers are much more concerned with international migration. At the world level in 2000, highly skilled immigrants represented 34.6 percent of the OECD immigration stock, while only 11.3 percent of the world labor force had tertiary education. Between 1990 and 2000, the percentage of skilled workers among immigrants increased by 4.8 percentage points (from 29.8 percent to 34.6 percent). In 2000, the number of migrants with tertiary education living in the OECD countries amounted to about 20.4 million.

The share of migrants who completed their secondary school degree increased from 25.3 to 29.0 percent. Consequently, low-skilled migration becomes increasingly less important in relative terms (44.9 percent in 1990 and 36.4 percent in 2000). In absolute terms, the size of all groups has increased. More than 85 percent of OECD skilled immigrants live in one of the six largest immigration countries. About half of these immigrants are living in the United States; 13.4 percent live in Canada, 7.5 percent in Australia, 6.2 percent in the United Kingdom, 4.9 percent in Germany, and 3 percent in France. Contrary to other major receiving countries, the proportions of high-skilled migrants have decreased in Canada and Australia between 1990 and 2000.

Such a change in the education structure of migration can be related to the global change observed in the world labor force structure. The world potential labor force (defined as the population age 25 and more, including retirees) has increased from 2.6 billion to 3.2 billion between 1990 and 2000. Over this period, the share of workers with tertiary education increased by 1.8 percentage points and the share of low-skilled workers has decreased by 2.5 points. Comparing immigrants with the rest of the population, the world average emigration rate increased from 5.0 to 5.4 percent among the highly skilled and from 1.4 to 1.8 percent for the medium skilled. A slight decrease (from 1.2 to 1.1 percent) was observed for low-skilled workers.

These global trends hide important differences across countries and country groups. Table 5.2 distinguishes emigrants from OECD and non-OECD countries. Between 1990 and 2000, the number of highly skilled emigrants from OECD countries increased less than the number of working-age highly skilled residents. The average emigration rate of OECD highly skilled workers decreased from 4.1 to 4.0 percent. Regarding non-OECD countries, the number of highly skilled emigrants increased more than the number of highly skilled residents. The skilled migration rate increased from 6.6 to 7.2 percent in non-OECD countries.

Clearly, the international mobility of skilled workers is a crucial issue for middle- and low-income countries, mainly because their share of tertiary educated workers remains low compared with high-income countries. Antecol, Cobb-Clark, and Trejo (2003) also confirm these results by comparing the stock of immigrants who arrived after 1985 in the United States, Canada, and Australia. They show that low-income countries have been strongly affected by the recent brain drain. In all OECD areas, the percentage of skilled immigrants coming from low-income countries (such as India, China, Vietnam, Pakistan, and Indonesia) increased between 1990 and 2000, especially in North America.

Stylized Facts by Country Group

Let us now focus on more detailed figures by country group. Table 5.3 provides basic indicators of migration and education attainment by country group in 2000 (the definition of these groups is provided in annex 5.A):

- Countries are classified by country size on the basis of total population data (more than 25 million for large countries, between 10 and 25 million for upper-middle countries, between 2.5 and 10 million for lower-middle countries, and less than 2.5 million for small countries).
- They are classified by income group: we use World Bank classifications distinguishing high-income, upper-middle income, lower-middle income, and low-income countries.
- They are classified by geographic area: we distinguish four American areas (North America, the Caribbean, Central America, and South America), four European areas (Northern Europe, Western Europe, Eastern Europe, and Southern Europe), five African areas (Northern Africa, Central Africa, Western Africa, Eastern Africa, and Southern Africa), four Asian areas (Western Asia, South-Central Asia, South-Eastern Asia, and Eastern Asia) and four areas in Oceania (Australia and New Zealand, Melanesia, Micronesia, and Polynesia).
- Some groups of political interest are also provided: Middle East and North African countries (MENA), economies in transition, the EU-15 members, Sub-Saharan African countries, Islamic countries (members of the Organization of Islamic Countries, OIC), Arab countries (members of the Arab League), the least developed countries (UN definition), landlocked developing countries (UN definition), and small island developing countries (UN definition).

For these groups, we compute their share in the total OECD immigration stock (total and skilled migrants), their average emigration rate (total and skilled migrants), and the share of skilled workers among emigrants (a measure of selection) and residents.

Regarding size groups, the share in the OECD stock is obviously increasing with the country size. It is noteworthy that the share of lower-middle-size countries exceeds the share of upper-middle-size countries. In relative terms, we obtain a decreasing relationship between emigration rates and country population sizes. The average rate in small countries is seven times larger than the average rate in

TABLE 5.3   Data by Country Group in 2000

	Share in the OECD stock (*)		Rate of emigration		Share of skilled workers	
	Total	Skilled	Total	Skilled	Among residents	Among migrants
By country size						
Large countries (Pop>25 million)	60.6%	63.9%	1.3%	4.1%	11.3%	36.4%
Upper-middle (25>Pop>10)	15.8%	15.2%	3.1%	8.8%	11.0%	33.2%
Lower-middle (10>Pop>2.5)	16.4%	15.7%	5.8%	13.5%	13.0%	33.1%
Small countries (Pop<2.5)	3.7%	3.7%	10.3%	27.5%	10.5%	34.7%
By income group						
High-income countries	30.4%	33.7%	2.8%	3.5%	30.7%	38.3%
Upper-middle income countries	24.3%	17.7%	4.2%	7.9%	13.0%	25.2%
Lower-middle income countries	26.6%	27.2%	3.2%	7.6%	14.2%	35.4%
Low-income countries	15.1%	19.8%	0.5%	6.1%	3.5%	45.1%
By group of particular interest						
Middle East and Northern Africa	6.5%	6.0%	2.8%	8.9%	9.4%	32.0%
Economies in transition	12.3%	10.8%	2.7%	4.8%	17.1%	30.3%
European Union (EU-15)	23.0%	21.6%	4.8%	8.1%	18.6%	32.5%
Sub-Saharan Africa	3.8%	4.7%	0.9%	12.9%	2.8%	42.6%
Islamic countries	14.4%	11.9%	1.6%	7.1%	5.9%	28.7%
Arab countries	5.5%	4.2%	2.6%	7.8%	8.5%	26.4%
UN least developed countries	4.2%	4.2%	1.0%	13.2%	2.3%	34.0%
UN landlocked developing countries	2.1%	2.3%	1.0%	5.0%	6.8%	37.1%
UN small island developing states	6.8%	7.4%	13.8%	42.4%	8.2%	37.6%
By region						
America	26.3%	22.6%	3.3%	3.3%	29.6%	29.7%
North America	2.8%	4.6%	0.8%	0.9%	51.3%	57.9%

Caribbean	5.1%	5.7%	15.3%	42.8%	9.3%	38.6%
Central America	13.7%	6.6%	11.9%	16.9%	11.1%	16.6%
South America	4.7%	5.6%	1.6%	5.1%	12.3%	41.2%
Europe	35.7%	32.8%	4.1%	7.0%	17.9%	31.7%
Eastern Europe	7.9%	7.8%	2.2%	4.3%	17.4%	34.2%
Northern Europe	7.9%	9.9%	6.8%	13.7%	19.9%	43.2%
Southern Europe	12.4%	6.5%	6.6%	10.7%	10.8%	18.2%
Western Europe	7.5%	8.6%	3.3%	5.4%	23.4%	39.3%
Africa	7.6%	6.8%	1.5%	10.4%	4.0%	30.9%
Eastern Africa	1.4%	1.7%	1.0%	18.6%	1.8%	40.8%
Central Africa	0.5%	0.5%	1.0%	16.1%	1.6%	30.9%
Northern Africa	3.9%	2.2%	2.9%	7.3%	7.5%	19.6%
Southern Africa	0.5%	0.8%	1.0%	6.8%	8.7%	62.1%
Western Africa	1.3%	1.6%	1.0%	14.8%	2.4%	42.0%
Asia	25.5%	34.5%	0.8%	5.5%	6.3%	46.8%
Eastern Asia	7.1%	11.3%	0.5%	3.9%	6.3%	55.5%
South-Central Asia	6.0%	9.2%	0.5%	5.3%	5.0%	52.5%
South-Eastern Asia	7.0%	10.5%	1.6%	9.8%	7.9%	51.4%
Western Asia	5.3%	3.5%	3.5%	6.9%	11.4%	22.9%
Oceania	1.4%	1.8%	4.3%	6.8%	27.8%	45.0%
Australia and New Zealand	1.0%	1.4%	3.7%	5.4%	32.7%	49.2%
Melanesia	0.2%	0.3%	4.5%	44.0%	2.7%	45.0%
Micronesia	0.0%	0.0%	7.2%	32.3%	7.1%	43.6%
Polynesia	0.2%	0.1%	48.7%	75.2%	7.1%	22.7%

Source: Various statistical sources and agencies.

Note: (*) Contrary to country groups, the total OECD stock includes the unknowns and the dependent territories. The sum of regional shares is slightly lower than 100 percent.

large countries. From the last two columns, these differences cannot be attributed to the education structure of residents or to a stronger selection in migration flows. Smaller countries simply tend to be more open to migration. Hence, differences in skilled migration are more or less proportional to differences in total migration rates. This explains why small island developing countries exhibit particularly high migration rates while landlocked countries exhibit lower rates.

As for income groups, their share in the OECD stock is variable. Nevertheless, the highest average rates are clearly observed in middle-income countries. High-income countries (less incentives to emigrate) and low-income countries (where liquidity constraints are likely to be more binding) exhibit the lowest rates. As reported in Schiff (1996), liquidity constraints in poor and unequal societies explain the increasing relationship between income and migration at low-income levels. Papers by Freeman (1993), Faini and Venturini (1993), Funkhouser (1995), and World Bank (1994) have shown that emigrants essentially do not come from the low-income group. This inverted-U-shaped relationship between skilled migration and income is rather stable even if, between 1990 and 2000, the situation clearly improved in lower-middle-income countries and deteriorated in low-income countries. Nevertheless, the reality is more complex than this global picture shows. Sub-Saharan African countries and the least developed countries exhibit a high rate of skilled migration (13 percent). The latter groups exclude large low-income countries (such as India, China, and Indonesia) with low emigration rates. While our indicators suggest that country size and gross domestic product (GDP) per capita are potential determinants of emigration, formal tests are required to assess their real contribution, as well as the relative effect of selection policies; networks; and economic, cultural, historical, or political determinants of emigration. Whether these push-and-pull factors play differently across skill groups is a crucial issue.

Regarding the regional distribution of skilled migration, the most affected continent is Africa (10.4 percent on average). The lowest-skilled migration rates are observed in America (3.3 percent) and Asia (5.5 percent). Oceania and Europe exhibit an intermediate rate of about 7 percent (note that European data include migration between EU countries). Data by detailed area exhibit stronger disparities. The most affected regions are the Caribbean and areas in the Pacific Oceania, which are groupings of small islands. Other remarkable areas are Eastern, Middle, and Western Africa and Central America. The difference between skilled and total emigration rates is especially strong in Africa. This is essentially the result of the low level of education in that part of the world.

Finally, data by area of particular interest shed light on the situation of particular developing zones. Islamic and Arab countries are not strongly affected by the brain drain. We note that Arab countries (a subset of Islamic countries) are more affected by the brain drain than Islamic countries as a whole. On the contrary, Sub-Saharan African countries are strongly affected. The MENA zone exhibits an 8.9 percent rate. On average, landlocked nations are less affected by the brain drain.

Remarkable Country Facts

The distribution of emigration rates is strongly heterogenous within groups. For example, the disparities between the Caribbean countries and the United States are tremendously high in America; large differences are observed between high-income countries such as Malta, Ireland, Hong Kong (China), Australia, or Japan.

Table 5.4 depicts the situation of the 30 most affected countries in 2000 regarding skilled migration. The brain-drain intensity differs if it is measured in absolute or relative terms. In absolute terms (number of educated emigrants), the largest countries are obviously strongly affected by the brain drain. The stock of skilled emigrants is high in the Philippines (1.136 million), India (1.037 million), Mexico (0.922 million), China (0.816 million), and Vietnam (0.506 million), as well as in developed countries, such as the United Kingdom and Germany, the Republic of Korea and the Democratic People's Republic of Korea (mainly the Republic of Korea), Canada, and Italy.

In relative terms (in proportion of the educated labor force), small countries are the most affected. The emigration rate exceeds 80 percent in nations such as Guyana, Jamaica, Haiti, Grenada, and St. Vincent and the Grenadines. One could argue that the distance from the United States is a key element explaining the high emigration rates from these countries. Nevertheless, we believe that the reality is much more complex. Migration decisions of skilled workers are likely to be less dependent on distances. It also appears that some African countries exhibit high rates of skilled migration. The rate of skilled migration exceeds 50 percent in five African countries (67.5 percent in Cape Verde, 63.3 percent in The Gambia, 55.9 percent in the Seychelles, 56.2 percent in Mauritius, and 52.5 percent in Sierra Leone). Excluding small countries (population below 5 million), column 5 stresses the importance of the brain drain in Africa and Central America. On the western and eastern coasts of Africa, tremendous rates of emigration are found in nations such as Ghana, Mozambique, Sierra Leone, Kenya, Uganda, Angola, and Somalia. In Asia, the countries most affected by migration are the Lao People's Democratic Republic, Sri Lanka, Hong Kong (China), Vietnam, Afghanistan, and Cambodia. Regarding Europe, emigration rates are particularly strong in Portugal, the Slovak Republic, and the United Kingdom. The last column in table 5.3 reveals that countries from the former Soviet Union and the Gulf States exhibit small rates of migration. This is also the case of OECD countries, such as Japan, France, Sweden, Australia, and the United States. Finally, it is worth noting that developing countries with large stocks of skilled emigrants may exhibit low rates of emigration. This is the case in India (4.3 percent), China (3.8 percent), Indonesia (2.1 percent), and Brazil (2.2 percent).

Many economists have demonstrated that immigrants are not randomly selected. An interesting selection indicator is given by the proportion of skilled emigrants in the total emigration stock. Table 5.4 gives the 30 highest and lowest selection rates among emigrants. The highest selection rates are observed in Asian countries where the rate of brain drain is rather low. Interestingly, Qatar, Oman, the United Arab Emirates, Bahrain, and Kuwait exhibit drastic selection rates despite a low brain drain. Other high-education countries are affected—Taiwan (China), Japan, Hong Kong (China), Canada, and Israel—as well as a few African countries—including Nigeria, Swaziland, South Africa, and Zambia. At the other extremity of the distribution, selection rates are low in traditional unskilled emigration countries such as Turkey, Mali, Portugal, Algeria, Morocco, Tunisia, and Mauritania. Several OECD countries also exhibit low selection rates (such as Portugal, Mexico, Italy, the Slovak Republic, and Spain). The selection is rather low in a few poor countries characterized by an important brain drain (for example, Senegal, The Gambia, Samoa, Suriname, and Mozambique).

Gains and Losses in OECD Countries

Our data set produces information about the gains and losses of skilled workers in OECD countries. The issue of gains and losses has attracted considerable attention in the recent years given the efforts to turn the brain drain into a net brain gain. There are many examples of countries that explicitly replace their personnel loss with highly skilled foreigners attracted from less developed countries. Akbar and Devoretz (1993) provide an interesting discussion of the Canadian immigration policy in the nineties.

Tables 5.5 and 5.6 draw a picture of the net impact of the international mobility of skilled workers in 1990 and 2000. The first three columns of tables 5.5.A and 5.6.A shed light on the relative contribution of immigrants on the working-age population.

It appears that immigrants represent about 25 percent of the labor force in three countries (Australia, Luxembourg, and Switzerland). Other countries such as New Zealand and Canada are also strongly affected. Conversely, migration has a minor effect in Mexico, Turkey, Greece, Japan, the Republic of Korea and the Democratic People's Republic of Korea, and Italy. Columns 4 through 6 of tables 5.5.A and 5.6.A describe the education structure of immigrants. Immigrants are particularly well educated in Canada, Australia, New Zealand, the United States, and the United Kingdom. On the contrary, the proportion of tertiary educated

TABLE 5.4   Top-30 Skilled Emigration Countries, 2000

All countries	Highest emigration stocks	All countries	Highest emigration rates, %	All countries	Highest selection rates, %
United Kingdom	1 441 307	Guyana	89.0	Taiwan (China)	78.0
Philippines	1 126 260	Grenada	85.1	Qatar	69.6
India	1 037 626	Jamaica	85.1	Kuwait	67.8
Mexico	922 964	St. Vincent and the Grenadines	84.5	United Arab Emirates	67.3
Germany	848 414	Haiti	83.6	Philippines	67.1
China	816 824	Trinidad and Tobago	79.3	Nigeria	65.0
Rep. of Korea	652 894	St. Kitts and Nevis	78.5	Saudi Arabia	64.6
Canada	516 471	Samoa	76.4	Japan	63.8
Vietnam	506 449	Tonga	75.2	Oman	62.7
Poland	449 059	St. Lucia	71.1	South Africa	62.6
United States	431 330	Cape Verde	67.5	Hong Kong (China)	61.9
Italy	408 287	Antigua and Barbuda	66.8	Mongolia	61.1
Cuba	332 673	Belize	65.5	India	60.5
France	312 494	Dominica	64.2	Canada	60.1
Iran	308 754	Barbados	63.5	Venezuela, R. B.	60.1
Jamaica	291 166	Gambia, The	63.3	Uzbekistan	59.5
Hong Kong (China)	290 482	Fiji	62.2	Brunei	59.3
Russia	289 090	Bahamas, The	61.3	Malaysia	59.2
Taiwan (China)	275 251	Malta	57.6	Egypt, Arab Rep. of	58.9
Japan	268 925	Mauritius	56.2	Iran, Islamic Rep. of	58.5
Netherlands	256 762	Seychelles	55.9	Liberia	58.5

TABLE 5.4 Top-30 Skilled Emigration Countries, 2000 *(continued)*

All countries		Countries with population above 5 million		Countries with population above 5 million	
Ukraine	246 218	Sierra Leone	52.5	Panama	57.7
Colombia	233 536	Suriname	47.9	Israel	57.6
Pakistan	222 372	Ghana	46.9	Singapore	57.1
Ireland	209 156	Mozambique	45.1	Myanmar	56.1
Romania	176 393	Liberia	45.0	Swaziland	56.1
Turkey	174 043	Marshall Islands	39.4	Jordan	55.6
Brazil	168 308	Lebanon	38.6	United States	55.4
South Africa	168 083	Kenya	38.4	China, Macao SAR	55.2
Peru	163 750	Micronesia, Federated States of	37.8	Palestine	55.0

All countries	Lowest selection rates	Countries with population above 5 million	Highest emigration rates, %	Countries with population above 5 million	Lowest emigration rates, %
Serbia and Montenegro	20.7%	Haiti	83.6	Egypt, Arab Rep. of	4.6
Liechtenstein	20.7%	Ghana	46.9	Sweden	4.3
Croatia	20.5%	Mozambique	45.1	Bangladesh	4.3
Gambia, The	20.4%	Kenya	38.4	Spain	4.3
Slovak Republic	20.0%	Lao PDR	37.4	India	4.3
FYR Macedonia	19.6%	Uganda	35.6	Myanmar	4.0
El Salvador	19.1%	Angola	33.0	Paraguay	3.9
Guatemala	19.0%	Somalia	32.7	China	3.8
Albania	18.4%	El Salvador	31.0	Ukraine	3.5
São Tomé and Principe	18.4%	Sri Lanka	29.7	France	3.4

Country	%	Country		Country	
Suriname	18.4%	Nicaragua	29.6	Venezuela, R. B.	3.4
Mozambique	17.7%	Hong Kong (China)	28.8	Belarus	3.2
Italy	17.3%	Cuba	28.7	Australia	2.7
Bosnia and Herzegovina	17.0%	Papua New Guinea	28.5	Burkina Faso	2.6
Angola	16.9%	Vietnam	27.1	Argentina	2.5
Senegal	16.7%	Rwanda	26.0	Chad	2.4
Bulgaria	16.4%	Honduras	24.4	Thailand	2.4
San Marino	16.0%	Guatemala	24.2	Libya	2.4
Cape Verde	15.2%	Afghanistan	23.3	Brazil	2.2
Tunisia	14.9%	Dominican Republic	21.6	Indonesia	2.1
Mexico	14.4%	Portugal	19.5	Azerbaijan	2.0
Guinea-Bissau	14.2%	Malawi	18.7	Georgia	1.6
Algeria	14.1%	Cambodia	18.3	Russian Federation	1.5
Tuvalu	13.8%	Senegal	17.7	Japan	1.2
Comoros	13.4%	Cameroon	17.2	Kazakhstan	1.2
Morocco	12.9%	Morocco	17.0	Saudi Arabia	0.9
Equatorial Guinea	12.4%	Zambia	16.8	Uzbekistan	0.7
Portugal	12.0%	Slovakia	16.7	Swaziland	0.5
Mali	10.9%	United Kingdom	16.7	United States	0.5
Turkey	8.8%	Mexico	15.3	Tajikistan	0.4

Source: Various statistical sources and agencies.

TABLE 5.5.A   Net Brain Gain in OECD Countries in 1990

	Working-age immigrants (total)	Working-age natives (total)	Proportion of immigrants among residents	Working-age immigrants (primary)	Working-age immigrants (secondary)	Working-age immigrants (tertiary)
Australia	3,284,279	10,453,000	23.9%	1,266,265	908,267	1,109,747
Austria	324,201	5,209,000	5.9%	188,518	108,421	27,262
Belgium	748,543	6,767,000	10.0%	138,461	134,603	94,044
Canada	3,709,285	17,907,000	17.2%	1,392,305	437,485	1,879,495
Czech Republic (**)	–	–	–	–	–	–
Denmark	93,934	3,500,000	2.6%	17,392	20,688	11,375
Finland	34,305	3,373,000	1.0%	22,028	8,248	4,029
France	3,480,664	36,731,000	8.7%	2,910,066	208,570	300,122
Germany	3,262,057	55,795,000	5.5%	1,558,529	481,882	555,735
Greece	112,805	6,663,000	1.7%	38,806	45,427	28,572
Hungary	211,715	6,789,000	3.0%	125,550	31,155	32,317
Iceland	10,565	149,000	6.6%	2,776	3,963	2,239
Ireland	130,940	1,953,000	6.3%	21,905	67,050	34,750
Italy	533,312	38,897,000	1.4%	316,260	78,479	81,407
Japan	1,075,317	82,019,000	1.3%	421,394	279,169	330,355
Korea, Rep of (*)	49,500	33,328,000	0.1%	19,398	12,851	15,207
Luxembourg	83,398	260,000	24.3%	54,739	5,547	10,659
Mexico	363,626	32,797,000	1.1%	180,163	60,163	123,300
Netherlands	961,662	9,883,000	8.9%	570,278	141,513	146,792
New Zealand	456,792	2,016,000	18.5%	121,641	113,169	194,937
Norway	136,241	2,784,000	4.7%	3,108	61,303	33,464

Poland	661,517	23,222,000	2.8%	392,288	97,345	100,977
Portugal	170,390	6,304,000	2.6%	11,897	8,899	14,579
Slovak Republic (**)	196,205	9,703,000	2.0%	116,352	28,872	29,949
Spain	645,977	25,036,000	3.3%	477,484	220,448	148,044
Sweden	617,449	5,852,000	9.5%	189,190	240,585	138,034
Switzerland	1,463,670	4,724,000	23.7%	83,430	1,050,239	197,141
Turkey	596,045	24,830,000	2.3%	429,419	100,100	48,972
United Kingdom	2,778,527	37,978,000	6.8%	1,892,892	315,482	570,153
United States	15,472,972	162,796,000	8.7%	3,957,187	5,312,740	6,203,045
EU-15	14,178	244,201	5.5%	8,408	2,086	2,166
Scandinavian countries	892	15,658	5.4%	234	335	189
OECD (in millions)	41.866	657.718	6.0%	16.920	10.583	12.467

Source: Various statistical sources and agencies.

TABLE 5.5.B   Net Brain Gain in OECD Countries in 1990

	Proportion of tertiary among immigrants (PI)	Proportion of tertiary among residents (PR)	Ratio immigrants / residents (PI/PR)	Working-age expatriates (tertiary)	Net brain gain (immigrants - expatriates)	Net brain gain in % of working-age residents
Australia	33.8%	31.1%	1.087	69,529	1,040,218	10.0%
Austria	8.4%	11.2%	0.748	113,432	-86,170	-1.7%
Belgium	12.6%	20.8%	0.605	67,627	26,417	0.4%
Canada	50.7%	43.8%	1.156	396,162	1,483,333	8.3%
Czech Republic (**)	—	—	—	—	—	—
Denmark	12.1%	19.3%	0.627	51,906	-40,531	-1.2%
Finland	11.7%	20.2%	0.581	53,939	-49,910	-1.5%
France	8.6%	21.9%	0.393	225,415	74,707	0.2%
Germany	17.0%	21.8%	0.781	735,191	-179,456	-0.3%
Greece	25.3%	10.9%	2.330	119,572	-91,000	-1.4%
Hungary	15.3%	10.1%	1.511	115,707	-83,390	-1.2%
Iceland	21.2%	11.0%	1.927	5,435	-3,196	-2.1%
Ireland	26.5%	13.9%	1.905	150,929	-116,179	-5.9%
Italy	15.3%	6.3%	2.423	309,014	-227,607	-0.6%
Japan	30.7%	21.2%	1.447	230,540	99,815	0.1%
Korea, Rep of (*)	30.7%	13.4%	2.293	464,228	-449,020	-1.3%
Luxembourg	12.8%	20.8%	0.616	5,303	5,356	2.1%
Mexico	33.9%	9.2%	3.686	359,933	-236,633	-0.7%
Netherlands	15.3%	15.7%	0.975	207,656	-60,864	-0.6%
New Zealand	42.7%	23.3%	1.832	90,464	104,473	5.2%
Norway	24.6%	15.7%	1.564	34,601	-1,137	0.0%

Poland	15.3%	7.9%	1.932	308,051	−207,074	−0.9%
Portugal	8.6%	6.5%	1.316	78,035	−63,456	−1.0%
Slovak Republic (**)	15.3%	9.9%	1.541	95,253	−65,304	−0.7%
Spain	17.5%	9.5%	1.846	94,122	53,923	0.2%
Sweden	22.4%	20.5%	1.088	49,455	88,579	1.5%
Switzerland	13.5%	17.2%	0.781	67,307	129,834	2.7%
Turkey	8.2%	5.0%	1.643	112,739	−63,767	−0.3%
United Kingdom	20.5%	13.9%	1.473	1,156,056	−585,903	−1.5%
United States	40.1%	39.2%	1.023	326,472	5,876,573	3.6%
EU-15	17.1%	15.5%	1.103	3,418	−1,252	−0.5%
Scandinavian countries	24.9%	19.2%	1.296	195	−6	0.0%
OECD (in millions)	31.2%	21.9%	1.424	6.094	6.373	1.0%

Source: Various statistical sources and agencies.

Note: (*) The number of expatriates includes Democratic People's Republic of Korea; the number of immigrants includes Republic of Korea only.

(**) Results for Ex-Czechoslovakia are provided at the Slovak Republic line.

– not available

TABLE 5.6.A Net Brain Gain in OECD Countries in 2000

	Working-age immigrants (total)	Working-age natives (total)	Proportion of immigrants among residents	Working-age immigrants (primary)	Working-age immigrants (secondary)	Working-age immigrants (tertiary)
Australia	4,075,721	12,521,000	24.6%	1,293,435	1,242,616	1,539,670
Austria	816,001	5,802,000	12.3%	387,425	325,337	103,239
Belgium	867,620	7,233,000	10.7%	485,386	195,983	186,186
Canada	4,661,330	20,805,000	18.3%	1,378,260	540,980	2,742,090
Czech Republic	410,249	7,017,000	5.5%	155,660	191,239	59,631
Denmark	169,664	3,748,000	4.3%	37,734	53,611	31,873
Finland	90,511	3,580,000	2.5%	44,051	24,945	21,515
France	3,755,514	40,418,000	8.5%	2,802,954	337,962	614,598
Germany	4,746,000	60,269,000	7.3%	2,545,000	578,000	996,000
Greece	106,041	7,750,000	1.3%	35,484	43,160	23,810
Hungary	251,715	6,836,000	3.6%	109,307	87,908	54,502
Iceland	16,927	174,000	8.9%	3,851	7,016	4,512
Ireland	281,232	2,309,000	10.9%	23,495	127,146	115,721
Italy	923,788	42,627,000	2.1%	488,538	292,781	142,469
Japan	951,302	92,337,000	1.0%	325,594	275,692	328,870
Korea, Rep of (*)	150,812	42,289,000	0.4%	51,617	43,706	52,137
Luxembourg	114,625	303,000	27.4%	37,780	36,644	29,321
Mexico	417,371	45,226,000	0.9%	139,186	119,414	141,912
Netherlands	1,320,320	11,109,000	10.6%	715,337	351,331	253,651
New Zealand	603,606	2,400,000	20.1%	93,909	182,109	232,296
Norway	204,182	3,051,000	6.3%	5,693	112,202	64,239

Poland	741,517	24,675,000	2.9%	441,529	187,418	103,496
Portugal	207,476	6,889,000	2.9%	122,236	43,137	29,816
Slovak Rep	426,072	3,416,000	11.1%	321,721	17,134	41,989
Spain	1,370,657	28,839,000	4.5%	440,493	700,005	230,159
Sweden	805,143	6,219,000	11.5%	201,319	335,463	220,731
Switzerland	1,704,948	5,200,000	24.7%	119,714	970,084	286,682
Turkey	826,110	33,130,000	2.4%	449,020	232,450	141,034
United Kingdom	3,639,907	40,353,000	8.3%	1,334,821	1,048,194	1,256,892
United States	24,366,085	183,564,000	11.7%	5,608,020	8,403,780	10,354,285
EU-15	19,214	267,448	6.7%	9,702	4,494	4,256
Scandinavian countries	1,286	16,772	7.1%	293	533	343
OECD (in millions)	59.022	750.089	7.3%	20.199	17.107	20.403

Source: Various statistical sources and agencies.

TABLE 5.6.B Net brain gain in OECD countries in 2000

	Proportion of tertiary among immigrants (PI)	Proportion of tertiary among residents (PR)	Immigrants / residents (PI/PR)	Ratio working-age expatriates (tertiary)	Net brain gain (immigrants - expatriates)	Net brain gain in % of working-age residents
Australia	37.8%	34.0%	1.112	116,723	1,422,947	11.4%
Austria	12.7%	14.4%	0.878	130,487	−27,248	−0.5%
Belgium	21.5%	27.5%	0.782	102,187	83,999	1.2%
Canada	58.8%	51.5%	1.143	516,471	2,225,619	10.7%
Czech Republic	14.5%	10.8%	1.346	88,112	−28,481	0.4%
Denmark	18.8%	21.9%	0.858	68,643	−36,770	−1.0%
Finland	23.8%	26.3%	0.905	76,132	−54,617	−1.5%
France	16.4%	21.9%	0.747	312,494	302,104	0.7%
Germany	21.0%	25.5%	0.823	848,414	147,586	0.2%
Greece	22.5%	15.2%	1.481	159,895	−136,085	−1.8%
Hungary	21.7%	12.0%	1.804	124,426	−69,923	−1.0%
Iceland	26.7%	15.5%	1.720	6,598	−2,086	−1.2%
Ireland	41.1%	21.7%	1.900	209,156	−93,435	−4.0%
Italy	15.4%	8.7%	1.781	408,287	−265,818	−0.6%
Japan	34.6%	24.6%	1.404	268,925	59,946	0.1%
Korea, Rep of (*)	34.6%	25.8%	1.340	652,894	−600,757	−1.4%
Luxembourg	25.6%	27.5%	0.932	7,281	22,040	7.3%
Mexico	34.0%	11.3%	3.009	922,964	−781,052	−1.7%
Netherlands	19.2%	21.9%	0.879	256,762	−3,111	0.0%
New Zealand	38.5%	25.9%	1.489	161,740	70,556	2.9%
Norway	31.5%	21.8%	1.447	46,286	17,953	0.6%

Poland	14.0%	11.1%	1.257	449,059	−345,563	−1.4%
Portugal	14.4%	8.8%	1.630	147,438	−117,622	−1.7%
Slovak Rep	9.9%	11.6%	0.850	79,451	−37,462	−1.1%
Spain	16.8%	12.2%	1.372	159,889	70,271	0.2%
Sweden	27.4%	27.5%	0.997	77,703	143,029	2.3%
Switzerland	16.8%	17.2%	0.975	88,051	198,631	3.8%
Turkey	17.1%	8.5%	2.008	174,043	−33,009	−0.1%
United Kingdom	34.5%	17.8%	1.938	1,441,307	−184,415	−0.5%
United States	42.5%	51.3%	0.828	431,330	9,922,955	5.4%
EU-15	23.1%	18.6%	1.240	4,406	−150	−0.1%
Scandinavian countries	29.3%	24.8%	1.182	275	68	0.4%
OECD (in millions)	35.4%	27.6%	1.279	8.533	11.870	1.6%

Source: Various statistical sources and agencies.

Note: (*) The number of emigrants includes Democratic People's Republic of Korea; the number of immigrants includes Republic of Korea only.

workers is rather low in the Slovak Republic, the Czech Republic, Austria, and Spain. The skill structure of immigrants can be compared with the structure of the native population. On average, columns 2 and 3 of tables 5.5.B and 5.6.B show that OECD immigrants are more skilled than individuals in the OECD who are native born. This is especially true when the education of the native population is low (for example, in Mexico, the Republic of Korea and the Democratic People's Republic of Korea, Greece, Turkey, Italy, and Ireland). This is also true in countries where the immigration policy relies on a "points system" (such as in Australia, Canada, and New Zealand) and in the United Kingdom. In highly educated countries, such as the United States, France, Belgium, and Austria, immigrants are less educated than natives.

Finally, columns 4 through 6 of tables 5.5.B and 5.6.B offer a measure of the net brain gain. The net brain gain is defined as the net immigration of skilled workers, expressed in percentage of the working-age resident population. Of course, such an indicator suffers from serious shortcomings: given the variety of education systems, emigrants' and immigrants' education levels are subject to serious comparability problems. Additionally, immigrants take time to assimilate into the labor market and suffer from discrimination. Nevertheless, our indicator provides new insights about who wins and who loses from skilled migration. Because $M_{t,h}^{i,j}$ denotes the stock of working-age skilled individuals born in country j and living in country i at time t, the net brain gain in country i can be evaluated as follows.

$$NBG_t^i = \frac{\sum_j M_{t,h}^{i,j} - \sum_k M_{t,h}^{k,i}}{\sum_s N_{t,s}^i} \quad (5.3)$$

The first term in the numerator is the number of skilled emigrants from country i (column 4 of tables 5.5.B and 5.6.B). The second term is the number of skilled immigrants (column 6 of tables 5.5.A and 5.6.A). Expressing the difference between these two terms in proportion to the resident labor force (column 2 of tables 5.5.A and 5.6.A), we obtain the net brain gain (column 6 of tables 5.5.B and 5.6.B). Countries exhibiting a positive (respectively, a negative) amount are net gainers (respectively, net losers). On the whole, OECD countries benefit from the international mobility of skilled workers. The net gain amounts to 1.6 percent in 2000, compared with 1.0 percent in 1990. The net brain gain has globally improved in all OECD countries. Hence, the 1990 balanced situation in Scandinavian countries turned into a net brain gain in 2000. The EU-15 deficit turned into a quasi-balanced situation. The main winners of this brain gain are Australia,

Canada, and Luxembourg (the latter country experienced a strong improvement between 1990 and 2000), followed by the United States, Switzerland, and New Zealand. Conversely, Ireland, Greece, and Portugal experienced a brain loss of 2 percent.

Conclusion

Because of the poor quality of international data, assessing the economic impact of international migration is a challenging issue. This chapter provides a new data set for skilled emigration rates describing the loss of skilled workers in both developing and developed countries.

In absolute terms, we show that the largest stocks of educated emigrants are from Europe (specifically the United Kingdom, Germany, and Italy); Southern and Eastern Asia (including the Philippines, India, China, the Republic of Korea and the Democratic People's Republic of Korea, and Vietnam); and, to a lesser extent, Central America and Mexico. These emigrants are concentrated in a few destination countries: about 50 percent of skilled migrants live in the United States; this percentage increases to 70 percent if two other immigration countries (Canada and Australia) are included and to 85 percent if the three largest EU countries (the United Kingdom, Germany, and France) are included.

In proportion to the educated labor force in the origin countries, the highest rates are observed in Central America and Africa (in Middle, Western, and Eastern Africa), as well as in the Caribbean and the Pacific area. The emigration rate exceeds 80 percent in nations such as Guyana, Jamaica, Haiti, and Grenada. High rates are observed in a few islands in Oceania. The emigration rate exceeds 50 percent in five African countries (Cape Verde, The Gambia, Mauritius, the Seychelles, and Sierra Leone). Conversely, the brain drain is rather low in the former Soviet Union; the Gulf States; and large countries such as India, China, Indonesia, Brazil, and most of the OECD countries. Calculations made by area of particular interest shed light on the situation in important developing zones. Islamic and Arab countries are not strongly affected by the brain drain, in contrast with Sub-Saharan African countries and, to a lesser extent, the MENA countries.

Regarding selection (that is, the proportion of skilled emigrants in the total emigration stock), the highest selection rates are observed in the Gulf countries where the rate of brain drain is rather low (such as in Qatar, Oman, the United Arab Emirates, Bahrain, and Kuwait), in some high-income countries (for example, Taiwan (China), Japan, Hong Kong (China), Canada, and Israel), and in a few of African countries (including Nigeria, Swaziland, South Africa, and Zambia). Conversely, selection rates are low in traditional unskilled emigration countries (such as Turkey, Mali, Portugal, Algeria, Morocco, Tunisia, and Mauritania), in selected OECD countries (including Portugal, Mexico, Italy, the Slovak Republic, and Spain), and in a few countries that are characterized by high emigration rates (for example, Senegal, The Gambia, Samoa, Suriname, and Mozambique).

By increasing the number of observations and improving their degree of reliability, our method provides useful material for the empirical analysis of the causes and consequences of the brain drain. Our data set is obviously evolutionary and could be refined in several ways. Nevertheless, we believe that the current version delivers new information that is rich enough to assess the changes in the international distribution of migration rates, to test for the (push-and-pull) determinants per skill group, and to evaluate the macroeconomic consequences of migration on source and destination countries.

Annex 5.A

This annex provides definitions of the country sets distinguished in the tables, and a comparison with previous works.

Data

We distinguish America (including the United States, Canada, and Mexico), Europe (including the EU-15, Switzerland, the Czech and Slovak Republics, Hungary, Poland, Norway, and Iceland), and the rest of the Organisation for Economic Co-operation and Development (OECD) countries (including Australia, New Zealand, Japan, the Republic of Korea and the Democratic People's Republic of Korea, and Turkey).

Country Groups

By region. AMERICA: North America (Canada, the United States), the Caribbean (Antigua and Barbuda, The Bahamas, Barbados, Cuba, Dominica, the Dominican Republic, Grenada, Haiti, Jamaica, St. Kitts and Nevis, St. Lucia, St. Vincent and the Grenadines, Trinidad and Tobago), Central America (Belize, Costa Rica, El Salvador, Guatemala, Honduras, Mexico, Nicaragua, Panama), South America (Argentina, Bolivia, Brazil, Chile, Colombia, Ecuador, Guyana, Paraguay, Peru, Suriname, Uruguay, República Bolivariana de Venezuela).

EUROPE: Eastern Europe (Belarus, Bulgaria, the Czech Republic, Hungary, Moldova, Poland, Romania, the Russian Federation, the Slovak Republic, Ukraine), Northern Europe (Denmark, Estonia, Finland, Iceland, Ireland, Latvia, Lithuania, Norway, Sweden, the United Kingdom), Southern Europe (Albania,

Andorra, Bosnia and Herzegovina, Croatia, the former Yogoslav Republic of Macedonia, Greece, Holy See (Vatican City), Italy, Malta, Portugal, San Marino, Serbia and Montenegro, Slovenia, Spain), Western Europe (Austria, Belgium, France, Germany, Liechtenstein, Luxembourg, Monaco, the Netherlands, Switzerland).

AFRICA: Eastern Africa (Burundi, the Comoros, Djibouti, Eritrea, Ethiopia, Kenya, Madagascar, Malawi, Mauritius, Mozambique, Rwanda, the Seychelles, Somalia, Tanzania, Uganda, Zambia, Zimbabwe), Middle Africa (Angola, Cameroon, the Central African Republic, Chad, the Democratic Republic of Congo, Equatorial Guinea, Gabon, the Republic of Congo, São Tomé and Principe), Northern Africa (Algeria, the Arab Republic of Egypt, Libya, Morocco, Sudan, Tunisia), Southern Africa (Botswana, Lesotho, Namibia, South Africa, Swaziland), Western Africa (Benin, Burkina Faso, Cape Verde, Côte d'Ivoire, The Gambia, Ghana, Guinea, Guinea-Bissau, Liberia, Mali, Mauritania, Niger, Nigeria, Senegal, Sierra Leone, Togo).

ASIA: Eastern Asia (China, Hong Kong (China), Macao SAR, Japan, Mongolia, the Republic of Korea and the Democratic People's Republic of Korea, Taiwan (China)), South-Central Asia (Afghanistan, Bangladesh, Bhutan, India, Islamic Republic of Iran, Kazakhstan, Kyrgyz Republic, Maldives, Nepal, Pakistan, Sri Lanka, Tajikistan, Turkmenistan, Uzbekistan), South-Eastern Asia (Brunei Darussalam, Cambodia, Indonesia, the Lao People's Democratic Republic, Malaysia, Myanmar, the Philippines, Singapore, Timor-Leste, Thailand, Vietnam), Western Asia (Armenia, Azerbaijan, Bahrain, Cyprus, Georgia, Iraq, Israel, Jordan, Kuwait, Lebanon, Occupied Palestinian Territory, Oman, Qatar, Saudi Arabia, the Republic of Yemen, the Syrian Arab Republic, Turkey, the United Arab Emirates).

OCEANIA: Australia and New Zealand (Australia, New Zealand), Melanesia (Fiji, Papua New Guinea, the Solomon Islands, Vanuatu), Micronesia (Kiribati, the Marshall Islands, the Federated States of Micronesia, Nauru, Palau), Polynesia (Samoa, Tonga, Tuvalu).

By income group. HIGH INCOME: Andorra, Australia, Austria, The Bahamas, Belgium, Brunei Darussalam, Canada, Cyprus, Denmark, Finland, France, Germany, Greece, Hong Kong (China), Iceland, Ireland, Israel, Italy, Japan, Kuwait, Liechtenstein, Luxembourg, Macao SAR, Malta, Monaco, the Netherlands, New Zealand, Norway, Portugal, Qatar, San Marino, Singapore, Slovenia, Spain, Sweden, Switzerland, Taiwan (China), the United Arab Emirates, the United Kingdom, the United States.

UPPER-MIDDLE INCOME: Antigua and Barbuda, Argentina, Bahrain, Barbados, Brazil, Botswana, Chile, Croatia, the Czech Republic, Estonia, Gabon, Grenada, Hungary, Lebanon, Libya, Malaysia, Mauritius, Mexico, Oman, Palau, Panama, Poland, República Bolivariana de Venezuela, the Republic of Korea and the Democratic People's Republic of Korea, St. Kitts and Nevis, St. Lucia, Saudi Arabia, the Seychelles, the Slovak Republic, Trinidad and Tobago, Turkey, Uruguay. LOWER-MIDDLE INCOME: Albania, Algeria, Belarus, Belize, Bolivia, Bosnia and Herzegovina, Bulgaria, Cambodia, Cape Verde, Colombia, Costa Rica, Cuba, Djibouti, Dominica, the Dominican Republic, Ecuador, Egypt, El Salvador, Equatorial Guinea, Fiji, FYR Macedonia, Georgia, Guatemala, Guyana, Iraq, Islamic Republic of Iran, Jamaica, Jordan, Kazakhstan, Kiribati, Latvia, Lithuania, Maldives, the Marshall Islands, the Federated States of Micronesia, Morocco, Namibia, Papua New Guinea, Paraguay, Peru, the Philippines, Romania, Russia, St. Vincent and the Grenadines, Samoa, Serbia and Montenegro, South Africa, Sri Lanka, Suriname, Swaziland, the Syrian Arab Republic, Thailand, Tonga, Tunisia, Ukraine, Uzbekistan, Vanuatu.

LOW INCOME: Afghanistan, Angola, Armenia, Azerbaijan, Bangladesh, Benin, Bhutan, Burkina Faso, Myanmar, Burundi, Cameroon, the Central African Republic, Chad, China, the Comoros, the Democratic Republic of Congo, Côte d'Ivoire, Eritrea, Ethiopia, The Gambia, Ghana, Guinea, Guinea-Bissau, Haiti, Honduras, India, Indonesia, Kenya, Kyrgyzstan, Lao PDR, Lesotho, Liberia, Madagascar, Malawi, Mali, Mauritania, Moldova, Mongolia, Mozambique, Nepal, Nicaragua, Niger, Nigeria, Pakistan, the Republic of Congo, the Republic of Yemen, Rwanda, São Tomé and Principe, Senegal, Sierra Leone, the Solomon Islands, Somalia, Sudan, Tajikistan, Tanzania, Togo, Turkmenistan, Uganda, Vietnam, Zambia, Zimbabwe.

By size. LARGE (above 25 million): China, India, the United States, Indonesia, Brazil, Russia, Pakistan, Bangladesh, Japan, Nigeria, Mexico, Germany, Vietnam, the Philippines, the Republic of Korea and the Democratic People's Republic of Korea, Turkey, Egypt, Islamic Republic of Iran, Ethiopia, Thailand, France, the United Kingdom, Italy, Ukraine, the Democratic Republic of Congo, Myanmar, South Africa, Colombia, Spain, Poland, Argentina, Tanzania, Sudan, Canada, Kenya, Algeria, Morocco, Peru.

UPPER MIDDLE (from 10 to 25 million): Uzbekistan, República Bolivariana de Venezuela, Nepal, Uganda, Iraq, Malaysia, Taiwan (China), Romania, Saudi Arabia, Afghanistan, Ghana, Australia, Sri Lanka, the Republic of Yemen, Mozambique, the Syrian Arab Republic, Madagascar, the Netherlands, Côte d'Ivoire, Kazakhstan, Chile, Cameroon, Cambodia, Zimbabwe, Ecuador, Angola, Mali, Burkina Faso, Guatemala, Malawi, Cuba, Greece, Niger, Serbia and Montenegro, Zambia, the Czech Republic, Belgium, Belarus, Portugal, Hungary.

LOWER MIDDLE (from 2.5 to 10 million): Tunisia, Senegal, Sweden, Somalia, the Dominican Republic, Bolivia, Azerbaijan, Guinea, Austria, Bulgaria, Haiti, Chad, Rwanda, Switzerland, Swaziland, Hong Kong (China), Honduras, Burundi,

Benin, El Salvador, Tajikistan, Israel, Paraguay, the Slovak Republic, Papua New Guinea, Denmark, Lao PDR, Georgia, Libya, Finland, Nicaragua, Jordan, Kyrgyz Republic, Turkmenistan, Togo, Norway, Croatia, Sierra Leone, Moldova, Singapore, Bosnia and Herzegovina, Costa Rica, Ireland, New Zealand, the Central African Republic, Eritrea, Lithuania, Lebanon, the Republic of Congo, Uruguay, Palestine, Albania, Armenia, Panama, Liberia, the United Arab Emirates, Mauritania, Oman, Jamaica,

SMALL (lower than 2.5 million): Mongolia, Latvia, Kuwait, Bhutan, FYR Macedonia, Slovenia, Namibia, Lesotho, Botswana, Guinea-Bissau, Estonia, The Gambia, Trinidad and Tobago, Gabon, Mauritius, Fiji, Cyprus, Guyana, the Comoros, Timor-Leste, Bahrain, Djibouti, Qatar, Equatorial Guinea, Macao SAR, Cape Verde, the Solomon Islands, Luxembourg, Suriname, Malta, Brunei Darussalam, The Bahamas, Maldives, Iceland, Barbados, Belize, Vanuatu, Samoa, São Tomé and Principe, St. Lucia, St. Vincent, the Federated States of Micronesia, Tonga, Kiribati, Grenada, the Seychelles, Andorra, Dominica, Antigua and Barbuda, the Marshall Islands, St. Kitts and Nevis, Liechtenstein, Monaco, San Marino, Palau, Nauru, Tuvalu, Holy See (Vatican City).

By group of particular interest. MIDDLE EAST AND NORTHERN AFRICA (MENA): Algeria, Bahrain, Cyprus, Djibouti, Egypt, Iraq, Islamic Republic of Iran, Israel, Jordan, Kuwait, Lebanon, Libya, Morocco, Palestine, Oman, Qatar, the Republic of Yemen, Saudi Arabia, the Syrian Arab Republic, Tunisia, the United Arab Emirates.

ECONOMIES IN TRANSITION: Belarus, Bulgaria, the Czech Republic, FYR Macedonia, Hungary, Moldova, Poland, Romania, Russia, the Slovak Republic, Ukraine, Estonia, Latvia, Lithuania, Albania, Bosnia and Herzegovina, Croatia, Serbia and Montenegro, Slovenia, Kazakhstan, Kyrgyz Republic, Tajikistan, Turkmenistan, Uzbekistan, Armenia, Azerbaijan, Georgia.

EU-15: Denmark, Finland, Ireland, Sweden, the United Kingdom, Greece, Italy, Portugal, Spain, Austria, Belgium, France, Germany, Luxembourg, the Netherlands.

SUB-SAHARAN AFRICA: Burundi, the Comoros, Djibouti, Eritrea, Ethiopia, Kenya, Madagascar, Malawi, Mauritius, Mozambique, Rwanda, the Seychelles, Somalia, Tanzania, Uganda, Zambia, Zimbabwe, Angola, Cameroon, the Central African Republic, Chad, the Democratic Republic of Congo, Equatorial Guinea, Gabon, the Republic of Congo, São Tomé and Principe, Botswana, Lesotho, Namibia, South Africa, Swaziland, Benin, Burkina Faso, Cape Verde, Côte d'Ivoire, The Gambia, Ghana, Guinea, Guinea-Bissau, Liberia, Mali, Mauritania, Niger, Nigeria, Senegal, Sierra Leone, Togo.

ISLAMIC COUNTRIES: Afghanistan, Albania, Algeria, Azerbaijan, Bahrain, Bangladesh, Benin, Brunei Darussalam, Burkina Faso, Cameroon, Chad, the

Comoros, Côte d'Ivoire, Djibouti, Egypt, Gabon, The Gambia, Guinea, Guinea-Bissau, Guyana, Indonesia, Iraq, Islamic Republic of Iran, Libya, Jordan, Kazakhstan, Kuwait, Kyrgyzstan, Lebanon, Malaysia, Maldives, Mali, Mauritania, Morocco, Mozambique, Niger, Nigeria, Palestine, Oman, Pakistan, Qatar, the Republic of Yemen, Saudi Arabia, Senegal, Sierra Leone, Somalia, Sudan, Suriname, the Syrian Arab Republic, Tajikistan, Togo, Tunisia, Turkey, Turkmenistan, Uganda, the United Arab Emirates, Uzbekistan.

ARAB COUNTRIES: Algeria, Bahrain, the Comoros, Djibouti, Egypt, Iraq, Libya, Jordan, Kuwait, Lebanon, Mauritania, Morocco, Palestine, Oman, Qatar, the Republic of Yemen, Saudi Arabia, Somalia, Sudan, the Syrian Arab Republic, Tunisia, the United Arab Emirates.

UN LEAST DEVELOPED COUNTRIES: Afghanistan, Angola, Bangladesh, Benin, Bhutan, Burkina Faso, Burundi, Cambodia, Cape Verde, the Central African Republic, Chad, the Comoros, the Democratic Republic of Congo, Djibouti, Equatorial Guinea, Eritrea, Ethiopia, The Gambia, Guinea, Guinea-Bissau, Haiti, Kiribati, Lao PDR, Lesotho, Liberia, Madagascar, Malawi, Maldives, Mali, Mauritania, Mozambique, Myanmar, Nepal, Niger, the Republic of Yemen, Rwanda, Samoa, São Tomé and Principe, Senegal, Sierra Leone, the Solomon Islands, Somalia, Sudan, Tanzania, Timor-Leste, Togo, Tuvalu, Uganda, Vanuatu, Zambia.

UN LANDLOCKED DEVELOPING COUNTRIES: Afghanistan, Armenia, Azerbaijan, Bhutan, Bolivia, Botswana, Burkina Faso, Burundi, the Central African Republic, Chad, Ethiopia, FYR Macedonia, Kazakhstan, Kyrgyz Republic, Lao PDR, Lesotho, Malawi, Mali, Moldova, Mongolia, Nepal, Niger, Paraguay, Rwanda, Swaziland, Tajikistan, Turkmenistan, Uganda, Uzbekistan, Zambia, Zimbabwe.

UN SMALL ISLANDS DEVELOPING STATES: Antigua and Barbuda, The Bahamas, Barbados, Belize, Cape Verde, the Comoros, Cuba, Dominica, the Dominican Republic, Fiji, Grenada, Guinea-Bissau, Guyana, Haiti, Jamaica, Kiribati, Maldives, the Marshall Islands, Mauritius, the Federated States of Micronesia, Nauru, Palau, Papua New Guinea, St. Kitts and Nevis, St. Lucia, St Vincent, Samoa, São Tomé and Principe, the Seychelles, Singapore, the Solomon Islands, Suriname, Timor-Leste, Tonga, Trinidad and Tobago, Tuvalu, Vanuatu.

Comparison with Previous Studies

Comparison with Carrington and Detragiache (1998)

Carrington and Detragiache's 1998 study clearly initiated new debates on the magnitude and distribution of the brain drain. Our data set refines their method by incorporating additional statistical sources. By collecting census, register, and survey data from all OECD countries, we eliminate two sources of bias:

- Relying on OECD statistics on immigration brings up several problems. First, in 1990, these data only provided information on the country of origin for the top-10 or top-5 sending countries. Hence, small sending countries are usually not identified, at least in the majority of receiving countries. Second, immigration in EU countries is based on the concept of citizenship rather than on country of birth. Third, immigration data are missing for a few OECD countries (Greece, Iceland, Mexico, Poland, the Slovak Republic, and Turkey). Finally, the OECD provides data on the total immigration stock rather than on the adult immigration stock (which can be compared with the labor force in sending countries). Compared with national censuses, we estimate that relying on OECD statistics implies an average underestimation in skilled workers migration rates by 8.9 percent in 2000. This is the major source of bias, especially for small countries that usually are not identified as important sending countries.
- Imposing the U.S. education structure on other OECD countries induces an average overestimation in skilled workers migration rates by 6.3 percent in 2000. The bias is obviously strong in countries sending a minor part of their emigrants to the United States.

On average, Carrington and Detragiache's method underestimates the emigration rates of skilled workers by 2.6 percent in 2000. This average bias seems rather small but hides a strong heterogeneity. This appears on figure 5.A.1, which gives skilled migration rates evaluated under three measurement methods: (a) a method fully based on census and administrative data (our method); (b) a method based on OECD statistics and U.S. education attainment data (Carrington and Detragiache 1998); and (c) an intermediate method based on census and administrative data and U.S. education attainment data. The observations calculated with our method are ranked in a decreasing order. In comparison with the census method, the second method clearly underestimates the brain drain for a majority of countries. On the contrary, the third method overestimates the brain drain.

The two sources of bias cancel each other in a couple of cases. However, the brain drain is particularly overestimated in countries such as São Tomé and Principe, Algeria, Tunisia, Morocco, Turkey, Suriname, and Algeria. By transposing the education structure observed in the United States, Carrington and Detragiache (1998) and Adams (2003) obtain high emigration rates of tertiary educated workers for these countries (between 35 and 45 percent for North Africa and Turkey). Taking into account the low level of education observed among emigrants to

Europe (where the majority of these migrants live), we obtain much lower-skilled emigration rates (between 5 and 20 percent). On the contrary, the brain drain is largely underestimated in Sub-Saharan Africa (Kenya, The Gambia, the Seychelles, Mauritius) and in small countries sending a small number of emigrants to the OECD area (Malta, Cyprus, and so on).

Comparison with Release 1.0 (Docquier and Marfouk 2004)

Figure 5.A.2 compares the skilled migration rates evaluated in "Measuring the International Mobility of Skilled Workers—Release 1.0" with those evaluated in Release 1.1. It appears that there were no systematic biases in the previous release: a simple regression gives Release 1.1 = 0.0081 + 0.9866' Release 1.0, R^2 = 0.8701. Nevertheless, replacing survey data with census data obtained from European countries strongly improves our measure for about 20 sending countries.

Acknowledgments

We are grateful to the statisticians from the Statistics Offices of OECD countries that sent us the data and helped us interpret them. We would particularly like to

FIGURE 5.A.1 Emigration Rates under 3 Measurement Methods, 2000

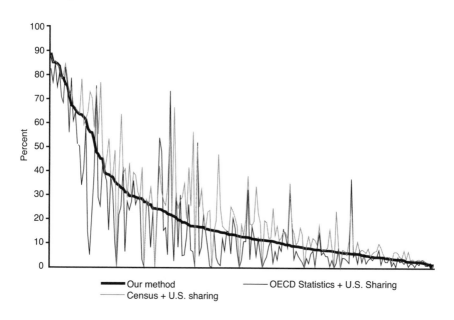

FIGURE 5.A.2   Comparison between Release 1.1 and Release 1.0

thank the members of Statistics Canada, the U.S. Bureau of Census, Statistics New Zealand and the New Zealand Department of Labour, (INSEE)-France (Lille center), Statistik Austria, the Hungarian Central Statistical Office, the Polish Central Statistical Office, the Australian Bureau of Statistics, Statistics Denmark, Statistics Finland, Statistics Norway, Statistics Sweden, the Czech Statistica Office, the Statistical Office of the Slovak Republic, the Spanish Instituto Nacional de Estadistica, the U.K. Office for National Statistics, the Turkish State Institute of Statistics, the Central Statistical Office Ireland, Statec Luxemburg, the Swiss Federal Statistical Office, the Italian Instituto Nazionale di Statistica, and the German Federal Statistical Office.

Special thanks to Steven Ruggles and the other Integrated Public Use Microdata Series (IPUMS) members for their comments on U.S. and Mexican data (http://www.ipums.umn.edu/); to the Institute for the Study of Labor (IZA) Data Service Center (IZA-Bonn); to Maarten Alders (Netherlands Statistics); to Peter O'Brien (Statistics New Zealand); to Marc Debuisson (Belgian 1991 Census); to John Ede (Hungarian Central Statistical Office); and to Daniel Cohen, Marcelo Soto, Angel De la Fuente, and Rafael Domenech for providing the human capital indicators.

Regarding non-OECD countries, we thank the Statistical Offices of South Africa, Botswana, Macao SAR, Mauritius, Slovenia, and Armenia. All of their comments on data and assumptions were very helpful.

Endnotes

1. See the International Organization for Migration on Africa (IOM 2003). The United Nations Development Programme (United Nations 2001) notes that, under the new U.S. legislation, about 100,000 software professionals are expected to leave India each year, over the next three years. The emigration of those professionals costs $2 billion a year for India.

2. The IOM (2003) reports that "prospects of working abroad have increased the expected return to additional years of education and led many people to invest in more schooling, especially in occupations in high demand overseas."

3. See IOM (2003) and World Bank (2003) on the perspectives of brain drain in the twenty-first century.

4. This was the position of the United Nations Economic Commission for Africa (UNECA), the IOM, and the International Development Research Centre at the regional conference on Africa, held in Addis Ababa in 2000.

5. OECD statistics suffer from various limitations (see OECD 2002). For example, they only provide information on the country of origin for the main sending countries. Other sending countries are considered as residual in the entry "other countries." African migration is particularly mismeasured. In addition, OECD data are not avalaible for Greece, Iceland, Mexico, Poland, the Slovak Republic, and Turkey in 2000.

6. A brief comparion is provided in appendix 6.3 of Docquier and Marfouk 2004.

7. Since then, a similar study by Dumont and Lemaître (2004) came out in October 2004. The main differences are as follows: (a) the data sources are somewhat different; (b) the definition of immigrant differs for some countries (for example, French citizens born in Algeria are counted as immigrants (the so-called "Pieds noirs"), while we use data on foreign born (people born abroad with foreign citizenship at birth) published by the French Statistic Institute; (c) we consider the population age 25 and over, while they consider the population age 15 and over; (d) we provide skilled emigration rates for 195 countries in 2000 and 174 countries in 1990, while they provide rates for 102 observations in 2000 (94 in a variant); (5) they aggregate dependent territories and their sovereign state, while we treat dependent territories as separate areas.

8. Note that we report 1990 estimates for a few countries that became independent after January 1, 1990 (for example, Namibia, the Marshall Islands, Micronesia, and Palau).

9. Our working-age concept includes retirees.

10. Bhorat, Meyer, and Mlatsheni (2002) compare South African emigration data with immigration numbers collected in five important receiving countries (Australia, Canada, New Zealand, the United Kingdom, and the United States). They show that the emigration sum was approximately three times larger than South African official statistics.

11. For example, Australian data mix information about the highest degree and the number of years of schooling.

12. Using registration data from Finnish schools and universities, Statistics Finland has problems with degrees obtained abroad. In New Zealand, there was a major change in the classification of postschool qualifications between 1991 and 1996.

13. Hatton and Williamson (2002) estimate that illegal immigrants residing in OECD countries represent 10 to 15 percent of the total stock.

14. See http://uscis.gov/graphics/shared/aboutus/statistics/III Report 1211.pdf.

15. In some receiving countries, such as Germany, immigrants' children (that is, the second generation) usually keep their foreign citizenship.

16. Conversely, in other OECD countries with a restricted access to nationality (such as Japan, Korea, and Switzerland), the foreign population is important (about 20 percent in Switzerland).

17. See Malone and others (2003) for more details.

18. Data by foreign background are provided in the Netherlands, France, and Scandinavian countries. See Alders (2001) for the Netherlands or Ostby (2002) for Norway.

19. Note that aggregating appropriated stock data would allow computation of emigration rates for the former Yugoslavia, the former Soviet Union, and the former Czechoslovakia in 2000.

20. Carrington and Detragiache (1998) used data from the Institute of International Education to estimate the number of graduate students completing their schooling in the United States. We consider that some of these students age 25 and over receive grants and can be considered as workers (researchers).

21. Country-specific data by occupation reveal that the occupational structure of those with unknown education is similar to the structure of low-skilled workers (and strongly different from that of high-skilled workers). See Debuisson and others (2004) on Belgium data.

22. For some countries, immigrants often travel back and forth between their new and old countries (for example, Mexico). These immigrants are likely to be counted as still being residents in their home country. For that reason, Carrington and Detragiache (1998) provide an upper bound ($m=M/N$) and a lower bound ($m=M/(N+M)$). Because the upper bound is not interpretable for a large number of countries (higher than one), we only report the lower bound.

23. See http://esa.un.org/unpp.

24. See http://www.cia.gov/cia/publications/factbook.

25. This partly explains why human capital did not prove to be significant or distort the "good sign" in growth regressions.

26. For this reason, Cohen and Soto (2001) exclude African countries from their growth regressions.

27. In Cyprus, the 2001 census gives share of population with tertiary education at 22 percent to be compared with 4.6 percent in Cohen and Soto (and 17.1 percent in Barro and Lee).

References

Adams, R. 2003. "International Migration, Remittances and the Brain Drain: A Study of 24 Labor-Exporting Countries." World Bank Policy Research Working Paper, no. 3069. World Bank, Washington, DC.

Akbar, S., and D. J. Devoretz. 1993. "Canada's Demand for the Third World Highly Trained Immigrants." *World Development* 21(1): 1976–86.

Alders, M. 2001. "Classification of the Population with Foreign Background in the Netherlands, Statistics Netherlands." Paper for the conference The Measure and Mismeasure of Populations. The statistical use of ethnic and racial categories in multicultural societies. Centre for Educational Research and Innovation-Institut national d'études démographiques (CERI-INED), Paris, December 17–18.

Antecol, H., D. Cobb-Clark, and S. Trejo. 2003. "Immigration Policy and the Skills of Immigrants to Australia, Canada and the United States." *Journal of Human Resources* 38(1): 198–218.

Barro, R.J., and J.W. Lee. 2000. "International Data on Educational Attainment: Updates and Implications." CID Working Papers, no. 42. Center for International Development, Harvard University.

Bauer, T.K., and A. Kunze. 2004. "The Demand for High-Skilled Workers and Immigration Policy." *Brussels Economic Review* 47(1): 58–76, Special issue on skilled migration.

Bhagwati, J.N., and K. Hamada. 1974. "The Brain Drain, International Integration of Markets for Professionals and Unemployment: A Theoretical Analysis." *Journal of Development Economics* 1(1): 19–42.

Beine, M., F. Docquier, and H. Rapoport. 2001. "Brain Drain and Economic Growth: Theory and Evidence." *Journal of Development Economics* 64(1): 275–89.

———. 2003. "Brain Drain and Growth in LDCs: Winners and Losers." IZA Discussion Paper. Institute for the Study of Labor, Bonn.

Bhorat, H., J-B. Meyer, and C. Mlatsheni. 2002. "Skilled Labor Migration from Developing Countries: Study on South and Southern Africa." ILO International Migration Papers. International Labor Office, Geneva.

Carrington, W.J., and E. Detragiache. 1998. "How Big is the Brain Drain?" IMF Working Paper WP/98/102. International Monetary Fund, Washington, DC.

———. 1999. "How Extensive is the Brain Drain?" *Finance and Development* 36(2): 46–49.

Cinar, D., and F. Docquier. 2004. "Brain Drain and Remittances: Consequences for the Source Countries." *Brussels Economic Review* 47(1): 103–18, Special issue on skilled migration.

Commander, S., M. Kangasniemi, and L.A. Winters. 2004. "The Brain Drain: A Review of Theory and Facts." *Brussels Economic Review* 47(1): 29–44, Special issue on skilled migration.

Cohen, D., and M. Soto. 2001. "Growth and Human Capital: Good Data, Good Results." CEPR Discussion Paper, no. 3025. Center for Economic Policy Research, London.

Debuisson, M., F. Docquier, A. Noury, and M. Nantcho. 2004. "Immigration and Aging in the Belgian Regions." *Brussels Economic Review* 47(1): 138–58, Special issue on skilled migration.

De la Fuente, A., and R. Domenech. 2002. "Human Capital in Growth Regressions: How Much Difference Does Data Quality Make? An Update and Further Results." CEPR Discussion Paper, no. 3587. Center for Economic Policy Research, London.

Docquier, F., and A. Marfouk. 2004. "Measuring the International Mobility of Skilled Workers—Release 1.0." Policy Research Working Paper, no. 3382. World Bank, Washington, DC.

Docquier, F., and H. Rapoport. 2004. "Skilled Migration—The Perspective of Sending Countries." Policy Research Working Paper, no. 3381. World Bank, Washington, DC.

Domingues Dos Santos, M., and F. Postel-Vinay. 2003. "Migration as a Source of Growth: The Perspective of a Developing Country." *Journal of Population Economics* 16(1): 161–75.

Dumont, J.C., and Lemaître G. 2004. "Counting Immigrants and Expatriates in OECD Countries: A New Perspective." Mimeo. Organisation for Economic Co-operation and Development.

Dustmann, C., and O. Kirchkamp. 2002. "The Optimal Migration Duration and Activity Choice after Remigration." *Journal of Development Economics* 67(2): 351–72.

Faini, R., and A. Venturini. 1993. "Italian Migrations: The Pre-War Period." In *International Migration and World Development*, ed. Hatton and J. Williamson, 1850–939. London: Routledge.

Freeman, R.B. 1993. "Immigration from Poor to Wealthy Countries. Experience to the United States." *European Economic Review* 37(2–3): 443–51.

Funkhouser, E. 1995. "Remittances from International Migration: A Comparison of El Salvador and Nicaragua." *Review of Economics and Statistics* 77(1): 137–46.

Grubel, H.G., and A. Scott. 1966. "The International Flow of Human Capital." *American Economic Review* 56(1/2): 268–74.

Haque, N.U., and A. Jahangir. 1999. "The Quality of Governance: Second-Generation Civil Reform in Africa." *Journal of African Economies* 8: 65–106.

Haque, N.U., and S.-J. Kim. 1995. "'Human Capital Flight': Impact of Migration on Income and Growth." IMF Staff Papers 42(3): 577–607. International Monetary Fund, Washington, DC.

Hatton, T.J., and J.G. Williamson. 2002. "What Fundamentals Drive World Migration?" NBER Working Paper, no. 9159. National Bureau of Economic Research, Washington, DC.

International Organization for Migration (IOM). 2003. *World Migration 2003—Managing Migration.* Geneva: IOM.

Johnson, H. 1967. "Some Economic Aspects of the Brain Drain." *Pakistan Development Review* 7(3): 379–411.

Kwok, V., and H. Leland. 1982. "An Economic Model of the Brain Drain." *American Economic Review* 72(1): 91–100.

Lowell, L.B. 2002a. "Policy Responses to the International Mobility of Skilled Labour." ILO International Migration Papers, no. 45. International Labour Office, Geneva.

———2002b. "Some Developmental Effects of the International Migration of Highly Skilled Persons." ILO International Migration Papers, no. 46. International Labour Office, Geneva.

Malone, N., K. F. Baluja, J. M. Costanzo, and Davis, C. J. 2003. "The Foreign-Born Population: 2000." Census 2000 brief, C2KBR-34. U.S. Census Bureau, Washington, DC.

Mesnard, A., and M. Ravallion. 2001. "Wealth Distribution and Self-Employment in a Developing Country." CEPR Discussion Paper, DP3026. Center for Economic Policy Research, London.

Miyagiwa, K. 1991. "Scale Economies in Education and the Brain Drain Problem." *International Economic Review* 32(3): 743–59.

Mountford, A. 1997. "Can a Brain Drain be Good for Growth in the Source Economy?" *Journal of Development Economics* 53(2): 287–303.

Organisation for Economic Co-operation and Development (OECD). 2002. *Trends in International Migration.* Paris: OECD Editions.

Ostby, L. 2002. "The Demographic Characteristics of Immigrant Population in Norway." 2002/22. Statistics Norway, Oslo.

Ruggles, S., M. Sobek, T. Alexander, C.A. Fitch, R. Goeken, P.K. Hall, M. King, and C. Ronnander. 2004. Integrated Public Use Microdata Series: Version 3.0. Minneapolis, MN: Minnesota Population Center.

Schiff, M. 1996. "South-North Migration and Trade—A Survey." World Bank Research and Policy Report, no. 1696. World Bank, Washington, DC.

Sobek, M., S. Ruggles, R. McCaa, M. King, and D. Levison. 2002. Integrated Public Use Microdata Series-International: Preliminary Version 1.0. Minneapolis: Minnesota Population Center, University of Minnesota.

Stark, O., C. Helmenstein, and A. Prskawetz. 1997. "A Brain Gain with a Brain Drain." *Economics Letters* 55(2): 227–34.

———. 1998. "Human Capital Depletion, Human Capital Formation, and Migration: A Blessing or a 'Curse'?" *Economics Letters* 60(3): 363–67.

Statistics New Zealand. 2004. "Degrees of Difference: The Employment of University-Qualified Immigrants in New Zealand." Statistics New Zealand, Wellington.

United Nations. 2001. "Human Development Report 2001." New York, Oxford: Oxford University Press.

———. 2002. "International Migration Report 2002." New York: United Nations.

Vidal, J.-P. 1998. "The Effect of Emigration on Human Capital Formation." *Journal of Population Economics* 11(4): 589–600.

Wong, K.-Y., and C.K. Yip. 1999. "Education, Economic Growth, and Brain Drain." *Journal of Economic Dynamics and Control* 23(5–6): 699–726.

World Bank. 1994. "Kingdom of Morocco—Poverty, Adjustment and Growth." Report 11918-MOR. World Bank, Washington, DC.

———. 2003. *World Development Indicators.* Washington, DC: World Bank.

6

BRAIN GAIN: CLAIMS ABOUT ITS SIZE AND IMPACT ON WELFARE AND GROWTH ARE GREATLY EXAGGERATED

Maurice Schiff

Introduction

The negative impact of the brain drain on the development of source countries has generally been accepted as received wisdom. However, a recent body of literature on the new brain drain has challenged this view. The major claims of the new literature and this chapter's main findings are described below.

Claims of the New Brain-Drain Literature

The traditional brain-drain literature has viewed the exodus of human capital as a curse for developing countries, and has considered policies to counter this exodus or reduce its negative impact on the emigration countries, including the taxation of migrants' income abroad (Bhagwati 1976; Hamada and Bhagwati 1976; Bhagwati and Wilson 1989).[1,2] That literature has recognized that the brain drain does confer certain benefits, including increased trade, remittances, knowledge, foreign direct investment (FDI)—attributed in part to a diaspora effect (Lucas 2005)—as well as the skills acquired by return migrants in the destination country.[3]

An early version of the chapter was presented at the Royal Economic Society (RES) Meetings, March 21–23, 2005. A second version was prepared during my stay at ECLAC (CEPAL) as Visiting Scholar in April 2005. The chapter represents the author's view and not necessarily those of the World Bank, its Executive Directors, or the governments they represent.

A benefit not considered in the traditional brain-drain literature is the brain-drain-induced "brain gain," a central feature of the new brain-drain literature. Because a brain drain implies that a share of skilled individuals will migrate and earn a higher wage abroad, the new brain-drain literature posits that

- The brain drain raises the expected return on education;
- This induces additional investment in education (a brain gain);
- This may result in a beneficial brain drain or net brain gain, that is, a brain gain that is larger than the brain drain; and
- A net brain gain raises welfare and growth.

These results are said to hold independently of other potential effects of the brain drain on the level of education, whether through remittances or through the skills return migrants might have acquired in the destination countries.

Seminal papers in the new brain-drain literature include Mountford (1997); Stark, Helmenstein, and Prskawetz (1997, 1998); Vidal (1998); Beine, Docquier, and Rapoport (2001, 2003); Stark and Wang (2002); Stark (2004); Stark and others (2004).[4] Their work has led to a reconsideration of the impact of the brain drain on the number of skilled individuals and on economic welfare and growth in the source country.

Most studies in that body of literature are theoretical, although empirical results are slowly emerging thanks to the work of Carrington and Detragiache (1998, 1999), Adams (2003), Docquier and Marfouk (2004, and chapter 5 in this volume), and Dumont and Lemaitre (2005). These studies have estimated the stock of skilled migrants from developing countries who are living in Organisation for Economic Co-operation and Development (OECD) countries.[5]

The number of skilled migrants—and their share in total migration—has risen dramatically in recent decades. Docquier and Rapoport (2004) report that the number of migrants residing in OECD countries increased by 50 percent between 1990 and 2000, with the increase in the number of skilled migrants equal to 2.5 times that of unskilled ones (70 percent versus 28 percent).

A case in point is the flight of human capital in the health sector, with the more extreme cases of emigration taking place in Sub-Saharan Africa and the Caribbean. For instance, Stalker (1994) reports that Jamaica has had to train five doctors to retain one, a brain drain of 80 percent.

The necessity to assess the validity of the claims of the new brain-drain literature has increased with the growing flight of skilled workers from developing countries and with the recent tilt toward skilled labor immigration policies by host countries. This chapter provides such an assessment, based on a more detailed analysis of the relationship between the brain drain and brain gain.

The remainder of the chapter is organized as follows. Based on partial equilibrium analysis, the first section shows why the brain gain is likely to be smaller than it appears from the new brain-drain literature. The second section shows this from a general equilibrium perspective, while the third section examines the impact of the brain gain on welfare and growth also from a general equilibrium perspective. The latter concept has not been incorporated in the new brain-drain literature, although it is central to the analysis of the brain-gain size and its impact on welfare and growth.

The fourth section provides a dynamic analysis of the new brain-drain literature's claim regarding the net brain gain. Specifically, it examines whether a net brain gain—or beneficial brain drain—can possibly hold in the steady state and how it evolves in the transition period. Such analysis is crucial for understanding the impact of the brain drain on development and growth. The analysis in the section "Partial Equilibrium and Exogenous Domestic Wage Rate" is based on partial equilibrium and an exogenous domestic wage rate, while a partial and general equilibrium analysis with an endogenous wage rate is provided in the section "Partial and General Equilibrium with Endogenous Skilled Wage Rate." The fifth section describes the limited empirical evidence on this issue and the final section concludes this chapter.

Main Findings

This chapter examines some of the assumptions underlying the findings of the new brain-drain literature. It concludes that the impact of the brain drain on welfare and growth is likely to be significantly smaller, and the likelihood of a negative impact on welfare and growth significantly greater, than reported in that literature. This is based on the findings that (a) the brain gain is smaller than has been indicated in the new brain-drain literature, (b) the brain gain implies a smaller human capital gain, and (c) various negative effects of the brain gain on other sources of externalities, such as human capital, welfare, and growth, have not been taken into account. These findings are derived from both partial and general equilibrium analyses.

Arguments for a smaller brain gain, resulting in a smaller net brain gain (brain gain minus brain drain) or net brain loss, and implying a smaller or negative impact on welfare and growth, include the following:

- Abilities are heterogeneous and high-ability individuals—those who acquired skills when migration was not an option and the returns to education were lower—will emigrate, resulting in a lower average ability level for the educated people remaining in the source country.

- Unskilled individuals migrate as well and benefit from it, implying that the brain drain has a smaller impact on the return to education.
- The education benefit is subject to a high degree of uncertainty (for example, with respect to education success, future employment abroad, host countries' future migration policies, and whether the individual will be among the few who migrate) and so is the cost of education (for example, because of changes in the opportunity cost of time during the study period caused, say, by income or health problems in the student's family).
- Additional resources spent on education imply greater public and private expenditures and—because students do not work full time or at all—fewer taxes and less household income, resulting in a reduction in other public and private expenditures, which also generate externalities, such as expenditures on health and public infrastructure, with a smaller and possibly negative impact on welfare and growth.

An analysis of the dynamics of the brain drain shows that the net brain gain is equal to zero in the steady state. In other words, a "beneficial brain drain" cannot occur in the steady state. Moreover, a net brain loss is likely to hold during the transition.

Contributors to the early brain-drain literature viewed the brain drain as entailing a loss for the developing source countries. The arguments presented in this chapter imply that these early views were probably close to the mark.

Smaller Brain Gain: Partial Equilibrium

The next two sections argue that the brain gain is smaller than is claimed by the new brain-drain literature. This section presents arguments based on partial equilibrium analysis. General equilibrium considerations are examined in the following section.

Graphic Analysis

Before turning to these arguments, it seems useful to provide a simple graphic representation of the central issue examined in this chapter. Figure 6.1 reflects a static partial equilibrium view of the issue. On the vertical axis, the brain drain (BD), the brain gain (BG), and the net brain gain ($NBG = BG - BD$) as a proportion of the skilled labor force are presented. These are shown as functions of the skilled-migration probability p (that is, the share of the brain drain in the skilled labor force).

FIGURE 6.1   Brain Grain, Brain Drain, and Net Brain Gain
(*NBG* = *BG–BD*)

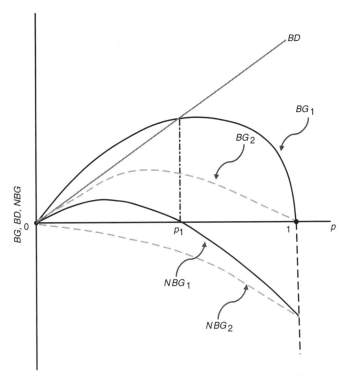

Note: Horizontal axis: *p* = migration probability; Vertical axis: share of migrants in skilled population.

BD is defined in the same way on both the horizontal and vertical axes, and it is therefore drawn as a 45-degree line rising from zero at $p = 0$ to the entire skilled labor force at $p = 1$. The brain gain $BG = 0$ for $p = 0$ (the no-migration situation) and $p = 1$ (all newly educated individuals migrate), and positive for $0 < p < 1$.

Figure 6.1 presents two alternative brain gain curves, $BG = BG_1$ and $BG = BG_2$. In the case of BG_1—the type of brain gain assumed in the new brain-drain literature—the net brain gain NBG_1 is positive for $p < p_1$ and negative for $p > p_1$. Thus, a brain drain would result in a net increase in education for low migration probabilities (for a small brain drain relative to the skilled labor force).

This chapter argues that the actual brain gain is closer to BG_2 than to BG_1 (or is actually equal to BG_2) with a negative net brain gain ($NBG_2 < 0$) or a net brain loss for any $p > 0$. Note also that *NBG* is negative for large values of *p*, irrespective of whether BG is equal to BG_1 or BG_2. This is one result on which the new brain-drain literature and this chapter agree.

Heterogeneity

Individual heterogeneity. Assume, for simplicity, that ability—or talent—is distributed uniformly and that an individual's ability affects the benefit of education but not its cost, which is a constant C. This is shown in figure 6.2, which draws on Commander, Kangasniemi, and Winters (2004). Ability is measured on the horizontal axis and declines from right to left, with the highest ability equal to A_{MAX}. The benefit and cost of education are measured on the vertical axis.

Figure 6.2 also shows three parallel lines declining from right to left, which depict the benefit of education under different circumstances. The lower line shows the benefit of education obtained in the absence of migration, that is, the domestic wage. The top line shows the benefit of education obtained by migrants in the destination country, that is, the foreign wage. The middle line shows the

FIGURE 6.2   Endogenous Migration Probability

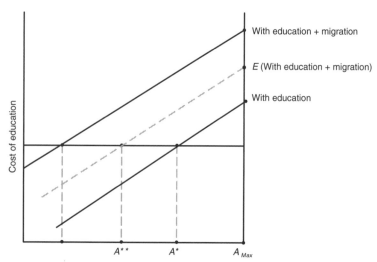

Note: Horizontal axis: ability, increasing from left to right; Vertical axis: benefit from education as a function of ability. The lower line is the skilled domestic wage (the return to education in the no-migration case); The top line is the skilled foreign wage (the return to education under migration); The middle line is the expected wage (weighted average of foreign wage (with weight p) and domestic wage (with $1 - p$)).

expected benefit of education, which is equal to a weighted average of the foreign and domestic wages. The weights are p for the foreign wage and $(1-p)$ for the domestic wage, where p is the migration probability (share of migrants in the skilled population).

In the absence of migration, the equilibrium is at A^*. Under migration, equilibrium is at A^{**}, with a brain gain equal to $(A^{**} - A^*)$. However, one cannot simply compare $(A^{**} - A^*)$ and $(A^* - A_{MAX})$, because the two groups have different ability levels. Recalling that the distribution of abilities is uniform, individuals who acquired education in the absence of migration have an average ability level $A_{NM} = (A^* + A_{MAX})/2$, which is greater than the average ability level $A_M = (A^{**} + A^*)/2$ of those who acquired education after migration became possible. Because $A_M < A_{NM}$, it is not necessarily the case that a net brain gain takes place when the share of the brain gain (relative to the total number of educated individuals) $BGS = (A^{**} - A^*)/(A^{**} - A_{MAX})$ is larger than the migration probability p.

In the absence of migration, the source country can draw on benefits from its most able individuals (with ability between A_{MAX} and A^*). Recalling that the new brain-drain literature assumes that skilled migrants are selected randomly among all skilled individuals with probability p, a share p of migrants originates from both the more able group (between A_{MAX} and A^*) and the less able group (between A^* and A^{**}).

Consequently, the skilled individuals remaining in the source country consist of a share $(1 - p)$ of nonmigrants from both the more able and the less able groups, with an average ability of $A_{MIG} = (A_{MAX} + A^{**})/2$, compared with the higher average ability $A_{NM} = (A^* + A_{MAX})/2$ of those who were educated in the absence of migration.

So, when $BGS = p$, that is, when the number of skilled individuals in the source country is the same, irrespective of whether migration takes place, migration results in a lower ability level in the source country by an amount equal to $A_{NM} - A_{MIG} = (A^* - A^{**})/2$ and thus in a lower effective human capital stock.

Thus, a brain drain results in a negative net effective brain gain—that is, a net effective brain loss—when the number of skilled individuals remains unchanged after migration takes place, that is, when $BGS = p$, and results in a greater loss when $BGS < p$. A necessary, but not sufficient, condition for a net effective brain gain is $BGS > p$. In fact, a net effective brain loss may also occur in the case of $BGS > p$.[6]

The following arguments strongly suggest that, even in the case of a homogeneous population with identical abilities, the net brain gain is likely to be negative. However, even if one assumes that the net brain gain is equal to zero, the reduction in the average ability level (a net effective brain loss) associated with migration under heterogeneity is likely to have negative implications for welfare and growth.[7]

Group heterogeneity. Heterogeneity may occur across groups rather than across individuals. This situation is depicted in figure 6.3, which shows three groups with different ability levels. In the absence of migration, two groups acquire education and the lowest-ability group does not. After migration takes place, the expected return to education rises, although not sufficiently for the low-ability group, which does not acquire education in this case either. Thus, the brain drain does not result in a brain gain ($A^{**} = A^*$), and the source country loses some of its most able individuals.[8] Alternatively, if the low-ability group acquires education, we obtain the same result as for individual heterogeneity (see previous section, *Individual heterogeneity*).

Unskilled Migration

Most analyses in the new brain-drain literature examine the incentives to acquire education in the absence of migration and compare them with the incentives prevailing in the case of skilled worker migration. However, the reality is that out-migration of unskilled workers is substantial in most source countries, and their expected wage is higher under migration, just as is true for skilled workers.[9]

FIGURE 6.3   Group Heterogeneity

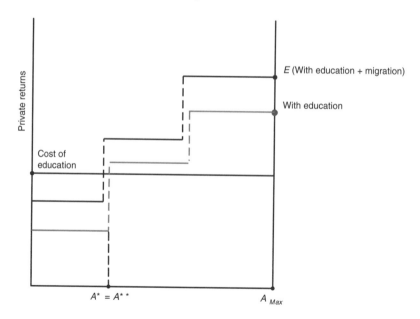

Denote the migration probability of skilled (unskilled) labor by p (q), skilled (unskilled) variables by subscript S (U), and destination country variables by $*$. In the absence of migration ($p = q = 0$), the education benefit or skill premium is as follows:

$$B_1 = W_S - W_U \tag{6.1}$$

With a brain drain ($p > 0, q = 0$), the expected benefit of education is as follows:

$$B_2 = (pW_S^* + (1 - p)W_S) - W_U = (W_S - W_U) + p(W_S^* - W_S) \tag{6.2}$$

That is, B_2 is equal to the domestic skill premium (as in equation 6.1) plus the expected skilled labor migration premium.

With migration by both skilled and unskilled labor ($p, q > 0$), the expected benefit of education is as follows:

$$\begin{aligned} B_3 &= (pW_S^* + (1 - p)W_S) - (qW_U^* + (1 - q)W_U) \\ &= (W_S - W_U) + p(W_S^* - W_S) - q(W_U^* - W_U) \end{aligned} \tag{6.3}$$

Thus, B_3 is equal to the domestic skill premium plus the expected skilled labor migration premium minus the expected unskilled labor migration premium. Equations 6.1 and 6.2 show that a brain drain raises the expected return to education by the expected migration benefit:

$$\Delta B_S \equiv B_2 - B_1 = p(W_S^* - W_S) > 0 \tag{6.4}$$

This implies a brain gain, a basic finding of the new brain-drain literature.

Equations 6.2 and 6.3 show that when both skilled and unskilled labor can migrate, the expected return to education falls compared with the case in which only the skilled can migrate, with the change equal to the following:

$$\Delta B_U \equiv B_3 - B_2 = -q(W_U^* - W_U) < 0 \tag{6.5}$$

The net benefit of education in this case is as follows:

$$\Delta B_E \equiv \Delta B_S + \Delta B_U = p(W_S^* - W_S) - q(W_U^* - W_U) \tag{6.6}$$

Thus, the impact of a brain drain on the return to education is smaller under the assumption that unskilled workers can migrate as well. This implies a smaller brain gain.[10]

Brain Waste

Foreign workers are often hired to do jobs for which they are overqualified. Examples of Caribbean doctors or Eastern European scientists working as taxi drivers in some large U.S. city are well known. Similarly, Moroccan doctors in France are typically working in less-skilled positions (for example, as interns) with significantly lower salaries.

Mattoo, Neagu, and Özden (2005) and Özden (2005, chapter 7) refer to this phenomenon as a "brain waste" in their recent study of U.S. immigration. They find that the *extent* of the brain waste—that is, the difference in the skill content of a migrant's job versus that of a native of the destination country with similar education and experience—varies according to origin country characteristics and U.S. immigration policies.

Using the same notation as in the section above ("Unskilled Migration"), the expected benefit of education B_4 under skilled migration and brain waste (BW) conditions is as follows:

$$B_4 = W_S - W_U \text{ for } W_{BW}^* < W_S \text{ (no migration)} \qquad (6.7a)$$

and

$$\begin{aligned} B_4 &= (pW_{BW}^* + (1-p)W_S) - W_U \\ &= (W_S - W_U) + p(W_{BW}^* - W_S) \text{ for } W_{BW}^* > W_S \end{aligned} \qquad (6.7b)$$

In equation 6.7a, there is no brain drain or brain gain. In equation 6.7b where $W_{BW}^* > W_S$ and a brain drain takes place, the difference in benefits without brain waste (B_2 in equation 6.2) and with brain waste (B_4 in equation 6.7b) is as follows:

$$\Delta B_{BW} \equiv B_4 - B_2 = p(W_{BW}^* - W_S^*) < 0, \partial W_{BW}^* / \partial BW < 0 \qquad (6.8)$$

The income loss reduces the impact of the brain drain on the benefit of education, implying a smaller brain gain. As seen in equation 6.8, the income loss depends on the wage gap between skilled and brain-waste jobs in the destination countries.

Negative Brain Gain

Assume that below a critical level of education, some destination countries only hire unskilled workers, irrespective of their qualifications, but nevertheless attract both unskilled and skilled migrants because $W_U^* > W_S > W_U$. This should reduce the incentive to acquire education in source countries and result in a negative brain gain. Note that this case constitutes an extreme version of the brain-waste case examined in the preceding section ("Brain Waste").

The expected wage rate for unskilled labor is $E_U(W) = pW_U^* + (1 - p)W_U$ and that for skilled labor is $E_S(W) = pW_U^* + (1 - p)W_S$. The return to education in that case is $(1 - p)(W_S - W_U) < (W_S - W_U)$, which is the return to education in the absence of migration. In other words, the migration option lowers the return to education, resulting in a negative net brain gain or net brain loss.

McKenzie (chapter 4 in this volume) presents evidence of such an effect in the case of rural Mexico, with migration having a negative impact on education levels, in general, and more so for children with more educated parents.[11,12]

This type of outcome might also prevail under less extreme forms of brain waste. For instance, with the high demand for Filipino nurses, some medical doctors have gone back to school to become nurses, and some students have changed their study plans from medicine to nursing.

Risk Aversion

Risk aversion is likely to greatly reduce the brain-drain-induced brain gain. The new brain-drain literature (for example, Beine, Docquier, and Rapoport 2001, 2003) claims that a net brain gain is more likely for low values of the migration probability p. As noted earlier, $E(W) = pW_S^* + (1 - p)W_S$ and $Var(W) = X^*$ $(W_S^* - W_S)^2$, where $X = (1 - p)^2 + p^2$ and $\partial X/\partial p = 4p - 2$. Thus, $\partial X/\partial p > (<) 0$ for $p > (<) 0.5$. This implies that, for $p < 0.5$, X increases as p falls and so does $Var(W)$. Hence, low values for p are associated with a high value for $Var(W)$, implying a smaller brain gain, with a smaller likelihood of a positive net brain gain. For high values of p, the new brain-drain literature and this chapter agree that the net brain drain is negative, even in the absence of risk aversion.

There are many other sources of uncertainty associated with the fact that studies take time to complete and the future is unknown. Sources of uncertainty include success in school and the future level of host countries' skilled wages, the exchange rate, skilled wages at home, host countries' immigration policies, the probability of obtaining a job abroad, the allowed length of stay in the host country, and the value of the student's time for the family during the entire period of studies. That value rises when family income falls (because of crop failure, lower crop prices, illness, or unemployment), which may force some students to abandon their studies and lose their investment. These further reduce the likelihood of a positive net brain gain.

Smaller Brain Gain: General Equilibrium Effects

Spending additional resources on education means that fewer resources are available for other activities. Education is typically provided publicly and is heavily subsidized, although an important part of the costs is borne by the students or their families, the main cost being the opportunity cost of the students' time.

In the case of tertiary education, a report by the World Bank (2000) states that "with developing country systems heavily dominated by public universities that tend to have low tuition fees, the costs fall predominantly on the state." The report estimates the cost of a student's tertiary education for 1995 and finds that the worldwide average amounts to 77 percent of gross national product (GNP) per capita.

Lucas (2004) updated the figures for the year 2000 and, based on both sources, finds that 24 out of 90 countries had higher costs than the world average (Lucas 2004, table 4.7). For Sub-Saharan African countries, the cost relative to GNP was more than 500 percent of the world average. Implications for the brain gain and human capital are examined below.

Public Expenditures and Tax Revenues

Assuming that education is provided publicly,[13] an increase in education will require additional funds. Moreover, time spent acquiring additional education means less work and lower tax revenues. Fiscally responsible authorities can respond to this situation by (a) a tax increase, (b) a reduction in education subsidies, or (c) a reduction in other public expenditures.[14]

A reduction in disposable income associated with the tax increase will reduce the demand for education and result in a smaller brain gain.[15] Similarly, a reduction in education subsidies will raise the cost of education and will also result in a smaller brain gain.

The third option entails a reduction in noneducation public expenditures. To check the likelihood of a substitution between the two categories of public expenditures, I estimated a relationship between public education expenditures ($\log E$) and other capital expenditures ($\log K$), both measured as a share of GDP, as well as a number of control variables. The sample covered more than 70 developing countries, with an average of 7 observations per country and a total of more than 600 observations. A negative and significant relationship between $\log K$ and $\log E$ was obtained with a coefficient of -0.47, significant at the 1 percent level. This indicates that a 1 percent increase in the share of GDP devoted to education results in close to 0.5 percent reduction in the share of other capital expenditures.[16]

This is unlikely to affect the extent of the brain gain, although it might affect welfare and growth (see the section "General Equilibrium Effects"), as well as the extent of the human capital gain. The latter is examined below.

A Brain Gain That Results in a Smaller Human Capital Gain

As discussed in the previous section, an increase in public education expenditures is associated with a reduction in other public expenditures. Among those that might be curtailed are investments in the country health care infrastructure, maintenance, and the provision of health care services. This would have an adverse impact on the population's health status, and more so for poorer families that have little or no access to private health care.

Moreover, because individuals who are studying do not contribute to family income, expenditures will have to be reduced, especially in poorer families. If expenditures on health care are reduced, household health is likely to be adversely affected. And if food expenditures are reduced, the nutrition and health status of the family is likely to suffer as well.

In his American Economic Association Presidential address entitled "Investment in Human Capital," Schultz (1961) notes that, when adults have a meager diet and cannot work more than a few hours a day, food should be treated not just as consumption but as a productive input that raises the level of human capital.[17]

Furthermore, purchases of household appliances may have to be postponed, and such purchases may cause additional harmful effects. For instance, postponing the purchase of a refrigerator might not necessarily affect nutrient intake, but it would most likely have adverse effects on nutritional status and health (Schiff and Valdés 1990a, 1990b).[18]

Because human capital depends on education as well as on health (Schultz 1961), the impact of the brain drain on human capital is likely to be smaller than its impact on the brain gain. An educated workforce that is unable to work on a regular basis because of illness is unlikely to be productive. In fact, reduced spending on health by individual families and the public sector might have devastating effects on the populations' health status and might lower the stock of human capital.[19] Thus, human capital gain might even decline. Whether the human capital gain is positive or negative, it is most likely to be smaller than the brain gain.

Smaller Impact on Welfare and Growth

Based on the analysis in the previous sections, this section examines the impact of the brain gain on welfare and growth and compares it with claims made in the new brain-drain literature.

Brain-Gain Size

The previous section provided a number of arguments based on both partial and general equilibrium analytical frameworks, supporting the assertion of a significantly smaller brain gain and, by implication, a significantly smaller net brain gain than would appear from the existing body of literature. The obvious implication is that the impact of brain gain on welfare and growth would also be significantly smaller.

General Equilibrium Effects

Romer's (1986) seminal paper on endogenous growth posited that, because of positive externalities, returns to physical capital were increasing and that policies affecting the stock of physical capital could permanently change the economy's growth rate. Lucas (1988) also provided a model of endogenous growth but emphasized the role of human capital. I assume in this section that both human and physical capital affect the economy's growth rate through contemporaneous externalities, intergenerational externalities (see Beine, Docquier, and Rapoport 2003), or both.

The section "Public Expenditures and Tax Revenues" listed three ways to deal with the higher public expenditures and lower tax revenues associated with a brain gain, namely higher taxes, lower education subsidies, or a reduction in other public expenditures. The first two lower the demand for education. The third one either lowers the level of human capital if, say, health care expenditures are reduced, or lowers other public expenditures that are likely to generate positive externalities.

The new brain-drain literature assumes that education is the only sector that generates positive externalities. In fact, positive externalities are also generated by a number of other public (and private) sector activities as well. These activities include health care provision, investment in research and development, and the provision of other public goods when the presence of large externalities (and the temptation to freeload) explains why these activities are provided publicly rather than privately.

In such a case, a government would maximize welfare through a tax and expenditure policy that results in the equalization of the per-currency-unit social marginal present value across all activities, whether private or public, consumption or investment, and pecuniary or not. Internalizing all the externalities associated with education, without taking into account the reduction in other expenditures and the consequent loss of other positive externalities, reduces the impact of the brain gain on welfare and growth and may result in a welfare loss and a lower growth rate.

The full effect of an increase in the brain drain would have to include the loss because of the brain drain itself. In other words, there are now two negative effects (the brain drain and the impact of the reduction in other expenditures) and a positive one (the brain gain). Thus, the likelihood of a beneficial brain drain seems much diminished.

Dynamic Implications of Endogenous Migration Probability and Domestic Wages

Two assumptions prevalent in the new brain-drain literature seem questionable. The first assumption is that the source country determines the migration probability (that is, the share of migrants in the skilled population). The second assumption is that the migration probability is exogenous. Another assumption in the new brain-drain literature is that the domestic (source-country) skilled wage rate is exogenous. This need not be the case, and the case of endogenous wages is considered as well. The analysis in the following section ("Partial Equilibrium and Exogenous Domestic Wage Rate") is based on partial equilibrium and an exogenous domestic wage rate, while a general equilibrium analysis with an endogenous wage rate is assumed in the section titled "Partial and General Equilibrium with Endogenous Skilled Wage Rate."

Partial Equilibrium and Exogenous Domestic Wage Rate

In this section, I argue that the migration probability is endogenous and examine the dynamics of the brain drain and the brain gain.

Who determines the brain drain?   The first assumption described above relates to the source country's ability to determine the probability or rate of migration. This assumption is found in most studies in the new brain-drain literature. For instance, Stark and Wang (2002) examine the role of a migration policy implemented by source-country governments.

In fact, although trade and capital flows have been greatly liberalized, destination countries continue to impose strict barriers on immigration. Exceptions include a few repressive regimes—for example, Cuba, Myanmar, and the Democratic People's Republic of Korea—that deny their citizens the right to migrate. The number of such regimes has greatly diminished in recent years, mainly because of the collapse of the Soviet bloc.

Thus, except for a few countries, migration controls are firmly in the hands of destination countries' authorities. This is particularly true for the more skilled migrants who have less to gain by migrating illegally.

Migration probability and evolution of the brain drain and brain gain. The second assumption in the new brain-drain literature is that the probability of migration is exogenously given and is unaffected by individuals' education decisions. However, I am not aware of any destination country immigration policy that stipulates that a specific percentage of a source country's skilled individuals is allowed entry. Rather, destination countries tend to use numeric quotas to restrict entry. In that case, the migration probability is endogenous, and its value depends on the size S of the skilled population. These quotas are (almost) always filled. Denote the quota by BD (the brain drain).

The models in the new brain-drain literature typically start from a situation of zero migration and compare it with that of positive migration. The starting migration probability $p_0 = BD/S_0$, where BD is the brain drain that is determined by the destination country (that is, the quota of skilled immigrants) and S_0 is the skilled population in period $t = 0$ before migration takes place.

Models in the new brain-drain literature assume that the migration probability p is a constant that is determined exogenously. If so, those who are considering at $t = 0$ whether to acquire additional education take the migration probability at $t = 1$ (when they graduate) as being the probability they observe at $t = 0$ when they must make the education decision. That probability is p_0. In other words, $p_1^e = p_0$, where p_1^e is the probability expected to prevail at $t = 1$.[20] The fact that $p_1^e = p_0 = BD/S_0$ is now positive raises the expected return on education and results in a brain gain BG_1. Thus, BG_1 is a function of $p_1^e = p_0$, that is, $BG_1 = BG(p_0)$. More generally:

$$BG_t = BG(p_{t-1}), BG' > 0, BG'' < 0 \qquad (6.9)$$

We start, at $t = 0$, from a steady-state situation in which the number of individuals acquiring education before migration becomes an option is equal to the number of retirees (per period of time). With migration, the benefit of education increases, and new individuals decide to acquire education (the brain gain). Then, $S_1 = S_0 + \Delta S_1 = S_0 + (BG_1 - BD)$. More generally:

$$S_t = S_{t-1} + \Delta S_t = S_{t-1} + (BG_t - BD) = S_0 + \sum_{i=1}^{t}(BG_i - BD) \qquad (6.10)$$

Note that with the brain drain BD determined by the host-country quota, the only variable is the brain gain BG.

No beneficial brain drain in the steady state. The initial stock of educated people is S_0. The increase in the stock between periods 0 and 1 is $\Delta S_1 = BG_1 - BD$, which is either positive or negative. Assume that in the first transition path, $BG_1 - BD > 0$. In that case, the number of skilled people increases to $S_1 > S_0$ and the migration probability decreases to $p_1 = BD/S_1 < p_0 = BD/S_0$. From equation 6.9, $BG_2 < BG_1$ and $\Delta S_2 < \Delta S_1$. Over time, the stock S_t increases at a decreasing rate until period j where $\Delta S_j = 0$, with a steady-state stock $S_t = S^P$ for all $t \geq j$.

In the second transition path, $\Delta S_1 = BG_1 - BD < 0$. Then, $S_1 < S_0, BG_2 > BG_1,$ $|\Delta S_2| < |\Delta S_1|$, and S_t falls at a decreasing rate. This process continues until period k where $\Delta S_k = 0$. The steady-state stock is $S_t = S^N$ for all $t \geq k$.

The first (second) transition path results in a steady-state stock S^P (S^N) that is larger (smaller) than the initial one. Thus, $S^P > S_0 > S^N$.

The previous sections provided a number of arguments showing that the brain gain is smaller than argued in the new brain-drain literature and that the net brain gain is likely to be negative during the transition period. If this is true, migration leads to a decline in the stock of educated people or a smaller stock in steady state.

In the steady state, we have the following:

$$\Delta S_j = \Delta S_k = BG - BD = 0 \qquad (6.11)$$

where BG is the value of BG_t that solves equation 6.11.

Thus, the $NBG \_ BG - BD = 0$ in the steady state, irrespective of the transition path. In other words, the brain gain is not large enough to result in a net brain gain—or beneficial brain drain—in the long run. This result is the result of the assumption that the initial (premigration) situation is characterized by a steady state with a constant number of educated people.

Alternatively, assume that the initial, premigration, situation is characterized by a net increase in the number of educated people equal to E. Then, the steady-state solution under migration is $E + BG - BD = 0$, implying that $NBG \_ BG - BD = -E < 0$. In other words, in that case, the steady state is characterized by a net brain loss.

These results hold under other expectation formation rules as well, including perfect foresight, rational expectations (see endnote 20), and adaptive expectations.[21] The new brain-drain literature claims that a brain drain results in a net brain gain under certain conditions. The analysis in this section shows that this result cannot hold in the long run.

Finally, a number of arguments have been presented in this chapter to show that the brain gain is smaller than can be inferred from the new brain-drain literature, and that the net brain gain is likely to be negative. That would imply a smaller stock of educated people in the steady state than in the premigration equilibrium.

Partial and General Equilibrium with Endogenous
Skilled Wage Rate

Under a partial equilibrium analysis, an endogenous domestic wage implies that the source country's skilled wage rate W_S changes with the supply of educated people. In fact, W_S falls (rises) for $NBG > (<) 0$ in period $t = 1$ (when migration starts). The positive (negative) NBG falls (increases) faster because two forces are at play rather than one: the reduction (increase) in the migration probability, and the fall (rise) in W_S. This results in a faster rate of convergence to the (unchanged) steady state.

One might expect the same result to hold in general equilibrium, although this is not necessarily the case. For instance, assume a 2×2 Heckscher-Ohlin model with a Hicks-neutral technological advantage in the developed host countries (resulting in higher wages than in the developing source countries), and with skilled and unskilled labor inputs.[22] In such a setting, a small economy's input and output prices are determined by world prices, domestic trade policy, and the technology gap. In that case, a positive (negative) NBG results in a reallocation of resources toward (away from) the skill-intensive activity and has no impact on input prices.

If the reallocation continues indefinitely, specialization will ensue, with all resources allocated to the skill-intensive sector for $NBG > 0$ and to the unskilled-labor-intensive sector for $NBG < 0$. However, we have seen that the NBG converges to zero as the economy approaches the steady state. If the steady state is reached before specialization takes place, the analysis with an exogenous domestic wage carries through.

Conversely, if specialization is reached before the steady state, the domestic wage rate W_S falls (rises) as the number of skilled individuals increases (falls), and we are back to the partial equilibrium solution. The same outcome is obtained for other partial and equilibrium models, such as imperfect competition models with product differentiation.

Empirical Evidence

This chapter has argued that the NBG is closer to NBG_2 (see figure 6.1) than to NBG_1. In fact, NBG_1 is quite similar to the function shown in figure 6 in Beine, Docquier, and Rapoport (2003), and reproduced here as figure 6.4. The vertical axis measures the effect on the annual growth rate rather than the effect on NBG. Despite the fact that figure 6.4 depicts an estimated relationship, while figure 6.1 does not, they tell a similar story—namely, that a beneficial brain drain is more likely at low migration rates. As Beine, Docquier, and Rapoport (2003, 35) state,

FIGURE 6.4   Brain Drain and LDC's Growth (with 2nd Order Polynominal Trend)

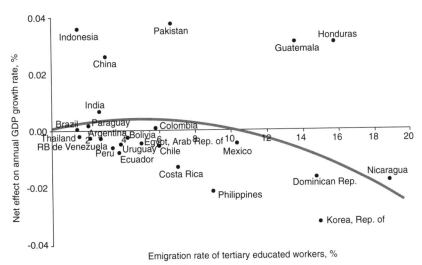

Source: Beine, Docquier, and Rapoport (2003).

". . . most countries combining low levels of human capital and low emigration rates of their highly-educated are positively affected by the brain drain."

Conversely, and as shown in figures 6.1 and 6.4, high migration rates (larger than p_1) inevitably result in a lower *NBG* and rate of growth. Consequently, countries in Sub-Saharan Africa, the Caribbean, and others that are suffering from massive outflows of medical personnel and other skilled workers cannot hope for much help from the brain-gain effect, irrespective of whether $NBG = NBG_1$ or $NBG = NBG_2$.

Three studies have examined the impact of the brain drain on education levels or growth. As mentioned above, Beine, Docquier, and Rapoport (2003) obtain a beneficial brain drain for countries with low levels of human capital and skilled migration rates. Conversely, Faini (2005) finds little indication of a positive impact of the brain drain on growth in source countries, while Lucas (2005)—using two alternative definitions for the education variable—obtains a negative impact of the brain drain on education (see table 6.1).

Thus far, empirical analysis consists of three studies generating three different sets of results with respect to the impact of the brain drain: a positive impact on the level of education (Beine, Docquier, and Rapoport 2003) for small brain-drain rates, a negative impact on the level of education (Lucas 2005), and no impact on growth (Faini 2005). These results should be considered as preliminary, and

TABLE 6.1 Impact of the Brain Drain on Education

	Log increment of tertiary education at home 1995-2000 (change in stocks)		Log tertiary enrollment
	ALL	Low Income	
Ln brain drain	−0.366 (3.53)	−0.331 (2.21)	−0.256 (2.32)
Ln income	0.567 (9.11)	1.400 (9.48)	0.691 (9.31)
Ln population	0.887 (14.95)	0.797 (8.74)	−0.112 (2.18)
Number of observations	91	39	55
R-square	.90	.91	.69

Source: Table reproduced from Lucas 2005.
Note: OLS; SE Robust; t-stats in parentheses; intercepts included, not shown. Brain Drain: OECD 2003. Tertiary Enrollment: UNESCO (several years).

additional conceptual and empirical work is needed before any conclusion can be reached.

Conclusion

Based on static analysis, this chapter has demonstrated that the size of the brain gain and its impact on welfare and growth are significantly smaller than found in the new brain-drain literature and may even be negative. Arguments include the following:

- Abilities are heterogeneous and high-ability individuals—those who acquired skills when migration was not an option and the returns to education were lower—will also emigrate, resulting in a lower average ability level for the educated people remaining in the source country.
- Unskilled individuals migrate, and benefit from migration, implying that the brain drain has a smaller impact on the return to education.
- The education benefit is subject to a high degree of uncertainty (for example, with respect to education success, future employment abroad, host countries' future migration policies, and whether the individual will be among the few who migrate), and so is the cost of education (for example, because of changes in the opportunity cost of time during the study period caused, say, by income or health problems in the student's family).

- Brain waste that, in extreme form, results in a negative brain gain.
- Additional resources spent on education imply greater public and private expenditures and—because students do not work full time or at all—fewer taxes and less household income, resulting in a reduction in other externality-generating public and private expenditures, such as expenditures on health and public infrastructure, further resulting in a smaller and possibly negative impact on welfare and growth.

An analysis of the dynamics of the brain drain shows that the net brain gain is equal to zero in the steady state. In other words, a so-called beneficial brain drain cannot occur in the steady state. Moreover, a net brain loss is likely to hold during the transition.

Dynamic aspects of the brain-drain-induced brain gain are also examined in this chapter. It is shown that the brain drain is equal to the brain gain in steady state, so that a beneficial brain drain cannot take place in the long run. Moreover, the net brain gain is likely to be negative during the transition period, so that the new steady state is characterized by a lower level of the education stock.

Contributors to the early brain-drain literature viewed the brain drain as entailing a loss for the developing source countries. The arguments presented in this chapter imply that these contributors were close to the mark.

The new brain-drain literature and this chapter are in agreement on one point, namely that the net brain gain is negative for larger migration probabilities and certainly for the most severe brain-drain cases. In other words, the new brain-drain literature offers no solution to the most severe brain-drain problems. This includes the exodus of health care providers from Sub-Saharan Africa—the world's poorest region—and the Caribbean.

Consequently, policies to slow down or stop the exodus of skilled labor are urgently needed. This issue is beyond the scope of this chapter, although it might be worth examining the possibility of (a) host countries supporting—both financially and with expertise—education in source countries in the areas in which they expect to need skilled labor in the future, and (b) instituting programs of temporary migration (possibly with migrant circulation). This solution should benefit both source and host countries.

Endnotes

1. This remains the view of the majority of analysts working on this issue (see Solimano 2001).

2. On a nationalist view of the brain drain in this literature, see Patinkin (1968). On an internationalist view, see Johnson (1968) and Bhagwati and Wilson (1989).

3. See also Özden (chapter 7 in this volume) and Javorcik, Özden, and Spatareanu (2004). They show that a larger stock of immigrants from a given source country to the United States results in greater U.S. outward FDI to that country, with the effect essentially caused by skilled immigrants.

4. Commander, Kangasniemi, and Winters (2004) provide a survey of the brain-drain literature.

5. Carrington and Detragiache's seminal work used the 1990 U.S. census data to estimate the brain drain for a number of developing countries in 1990. Docquier and Marfouk (chapter 5 in this volume; see also the early version in 2004) improved the measurement of the brain drain by expanding data sources to all OECD countries, estimating the brain drain for a much larger number of developing countries, and doing so for 2000 as well as for 1990. They also provide estimates of the brain drain among developed countries. An analysis of regional differences in the brain drain is provided by Docquier, Lohest, and Marfouk (2005).

6. In an interesting paper, Fan and Stark (2005) present a model in which decision making takes place in three stages or less, and which generates equilibrium unemployment of skilled workers. The model assumes heterogeneity with respect to education ability. However, given that ability in the job market tends to be positively related to education ability, incorporating this feature would affect the results.

7. In fact, the impact of migration on welfare and growth is likely to be significantly greater than might be inferred from the analysis above. The section titled "Individual Heterogeneity" assumed, for simplicity, a uniform distribution of ability or talent. As Haque (2005) notes, there is evidence that the distribution of talent in developing countries is highly skewed (Power Law distribution), with a large number of individuals at most talent levels and a relatively small number of highly talented individuals. Thanks to recent advances in information and communication technology, there has been a dramatic acceleration in the globalization of knowledge. The highly talented individuals in developing countries tend to belong to the global knowledge community, cognizant of the latest advances in their field or contributing to them. Such individuals tend to generate large positive externalities by imparting frontier knowledge to their colleagues, assistants, and students, thereby enabling those who benefit from that knowledge to further diffuse it. For instance, surgeons who are pioneers tend to form medical centers with teams of doctors working with them. Highly talented individuals also tend to contribute disproportionately to the political debate, public services, and institutional development. Haque (2005) provides an analysis that shows that, given that the cost of migration is lower and good jobs are more readily available for highly talented individuals, they are the most likely to migrate, and their departure is likely to have an enormous impact on their country of origin, which goes far beyond their tiny share in the skilled population.

8. Stark, Helmenstein, and Prskawetz (1997) include two groups in their model in which, as assumed here, low-ability individuals do not acquire education when migration takes place, although high-ability individuals invest more in education when incentives improve. The model presented here assumes, as in most papers dealing with the brain gain, that individuals can only acquire a fixed amount of education.

9. The new data set on migration by education attainment put together by Docquier and Marfouk (chapter 5 in this volume), and which covers 174 countries for 1990 and 195 countries for 2000, indicates that, for 1990, the average migration share—that is, the migration probability—of the middle- and high-education groups put together is about twice as large as in the low-education group. The recent immigration policy change favoring skilled migrants is reflected in the 2000 figures, with the share of the middle- and high-education groups about 2.5 times larger than in the low-education group. Although the share of the middle- and high-education groups is larger than that of the low-education one, 2 to 2.5 times larger is less than infinitely larger, which is the assumption in the new brain-drain literature in which the share of migrants in the low-education group is set equal to zero.

10. How does the migration premium for skilled labor compare with that for unskilled labor? If the skills obtained in the source country differ substantially from the skills used in the destination country, the migration premium for skilled labor is likely to be small. This might occur, for instance, in the case of lawyers if the legal systems differ between source and destination countries, or in the case of managers if source country firms are small, use outdated management methods, and operate in a protected market, or simply because the skills are perceived to be inferior because of lack of information. Some of these issues are examined in the following section on "Brain Waste." If the skills are similar

and highly mobile, as in the case of scientists and engineers (especially if they studied in a destination country), one might expect the skill premium not to be very large either (unless a corner solution is reached in which all the highly skilled leave). Thus, the migration premium for unskilled labor might be larger than that for skilled labor.

11. A more detailed analysis is provided in McKenzie and Rapoport (2005).

12. Thus, migration not only lowers the level of education but also education inequality, with the latter caused by a reduction in the rural education level of those at the upper end of the distribution rather than an increase at the bottom of the distribution.

13. The results hold under privately provided education as well.

14. Note that if fiscal considerations were unimportant, because the impact on education is small, the weak education response to a brain drain would likely imply a net brain loss. Thus, general equilibrium effects are especially important when the brain gain is large enough to matter.

15. Of course, a smaller brain gain implies a smaller tax increase, which simply means that the equilibrium tax rate and brain gain must be solved simultaneously.

16. Interestingly, Beine, Docquier, and Rapoport's (2003) model includes a variable representing physical capital, research and development expenditures, and infrastructures in their growth regression, so that a reduction in that variable, associated with an increase in the investment in education, might impact welfare and growth.

17. Costa (2003) examines the long-run relationship between health and economic activity. Alderman, Hoddinet, and Kinsey (2003), Martorell (1999), and Strauss and Thomas (1998) examine the link between nutrition and productivity.

18. In the face of high food income elasticity, estimates at low incomes, and the implication that the poor suffered from malnutrition, the nutrition literature argued that what mattered is not food but nutrient intake. The literature showed a low-income elasticity for a variety of nutrients (calories, proteins, and so on) because, starting at low incomes, food expenditures shift from nutrient to nonnutrient attributes. This shift occurs as income increases (because of greater demand for variety, ease of preparation, and taste), with the implication that the poor do not suffer from malnutrition. Schiff and Valdés (1990a, 1990b) contributed to that literature by arguing that what matters is not nutrient intake but nutritional status, which depends on various household and community variables as well as on nutrients. Because investments in the former clearly depend on income (for example, refrigerators and clean water), nutritional status is likely to be quite elastic with respect to income (and thus be worse for poor people), even if nutrient intake is not.

19. This might occur because, although a benign (and knowledgeable) government would be expected to take these negative externalities into account, individual households would not.

20. The model for which such expectations are used is known as the cobweb model. The assumption of such expectations is certainly more plausible for the brain gain than in the case of crop prices, the case for which the cobweb model was originally developed. One reason is that the assessment of the probability of migration is made by different individuals every period, while the same farmers and traders operate over many periods and, therefore, have a better understanding of the markets in which they operate. A second reason is the availability of information. Information on (spot and futures) commodity prices is available in real time on a continuous basis through various electronic media outlets, which is certainly not the case for the future migration probability. Consequently, learning about the latter is much harder than for agricultural prices and is thus less likely, making the assumed expectations formation rule quite plausible in the migration case. Note that the same expectations rule obtains in the case of uncertainty (for example, if there is a random disturbance term in equation 6.1) in various rational expectations equilibrium models, resulting in a "random walk" where $p_t = p_{t-1} + e_{t-1}$ and e_{t-1} is a "white noise" error term, so that $E_{t-1}(p_t) = p_{t-1}$. Note that in this case, the expectations solution is the result of individuals exploiting all the available information, rather than the result of ignorance about how the market operates. Such a model may provide a good description of homogeneous commodities traded on a centralized commodities exchange but not for the case of migration.

21. Convergence to the steady state is faster under perfect foresight and rational expectations, and is slower under adaptive expectations.

22. The 2×2 model is assumed for simplicity. The same outcome obtains in an m x m model ($m > 2$) with labor classified according to m skill categories.

References

Adams, R. 2003. "International Migration, Remittances and the Brain Drain: A Study of 24 Labor-Exporting Countries." Policy Research Working Paper, no. 3069. World Bank, Washington, DC.

Alderman, H., J. Hoddinet, and B. Kinsey. 2003. "Long Term Consequences of Early Childhood Malnutrition." Mimeo. Department of Economics. Dalhousie University, Halifax.

Beine, M., F. Docquier, and H. Rapoport. 2001. "Brain Drain and Economic Growth: Theory and Evidence." *Journal of Development Economics* 64(1): 275–89.

———. 2003. "Brain Drain and LDC's Growth: Winners and Losers." IZA Discussion Paper, no. 819, July. Institute for the Study of Labor, Bonn.

Bhagwati, J. 1976. "The International Brain Drain and Taxation. A Survey of the Issues." In *The Brain Drain and Taxation. Theory and Empirical Analysis*, ed. J. Bhagwati. Amsterdam: North Holland.

Bhagwati, J., and J.D. Wilson. 1989. *Income Taxation and International Mobility*. Cambridge, MA: MIT Press.

Carrington, W.J., and E. Detragiache. 1998. "How Big is the Brain Drain?" IMF Working Paper, no. 98. Institute for the Study of Labor, Washington, DC.

———. 1999. "How Extensive is the Brain Drain?" *Finance & Development* 36(2): 46–49.

Commander, S., M. Kangasniemi, and L. A. Winters. 2004. "The Brain Drain: Curse or Boon? A Survey of the Literature." In *Challenges to Globalization. Analyzing the Economics*, ed. R.E. Baldwin and L. A. Winters. Chicago and London: University of Chicago Press.

Costa, D.L., ed. 2003. *Health and Labor Force Participation Over the Life Cycle: Evidence from the Past*. Chicago and London: University of Chicago Press.

Docquier F., O. Lohest, and A. Marfouk. 2005. "Brain Drain in Developing Regions (1990–2000)." Mimeo. CADRE. University of Lille, and Research Program on International Migration and Development. International Trade Unit. Development Economics Research Group (DECRG). World Bank, Washington, DC.

Docquier, F., and A. Marfouk. 2004. ""Measuring the International Mobility of Skilled Workers—Release 1.0." Policy Research Working Paper, no. 3381. World Bank, Washington, DC.

Docquier, F., and H. Rapoport. 2004. "Skilled Migration: The Perspective of Developing Countries." Policy Research Working Paper, no. 3382, August. World Bank, Washington, DC.

Dumont, J.-C., and G. Lemaitre. 2005. "Counting Immigrants and Expatriates in OECD Countries: A New Perspective." Directorate for Employment, Labour and Social Affairs. Paris: OECD.

Faini, R. 2005. "Does the Brain Drain Boost Growth?" Mimeo. University of Rome, and Research Program on International Migration and Development. International Trade Unit. Development Economics Research Group (DECRG). World Bank, Washington, DC.

Fan, C.S., and O. Stark. 2005. "Addition through Depletion: The Brain Drain as Catalyst of Human Capital Formation and Economic Betterment." Mimeo. University of Klagenfurt, Klagenfurt.

Hamada, K., and J. Bhagwati. 1976. "Domestic Distortions, Imperfect Information and the Brain Drain." Chapter 7 in *The Brain Drain and Taxation. Vol. II: Theory and Empirical Analysis*, eds. J. Bhagwati and M. Partington, 139–53. Amsterdam: North Holland.

Haque, N.U. 2005. "'Winner-Take-All' Distribution of Talent: A New Approach to the Brain Drain." Research Program on International Migration and Development. International Trade Unit. Development Economics Research Group (DECRG). World Bank, Washington, DC.

Javorcik, B.S., C. Özden, and M. Spatareanu. 2004. "Does South-North Brain Drain Contribute to North-South FDI?" Mimeo. Research Program on International Migration and Development. International Trade Unit. Development Economics Research Group (DECRG), December. World Bank, Washington, DC.

Johnson, G.H. 1968. "An 'Internationalist' Model." In *Brain Drain*, ed. Walter Adams, 69–91. New York: The Macmillan Company.

Lucas, R.E., Jr. 1988. "On the Mechanics of Economic Development." *Journal of Monetary Economics* 22(1): 3–42.

Lucas, R.E.B. 2004. "International Migration Regimes and Economic Development." Report prepared for the Expert Group on Development Issues (EGDI) in the Swedish Ministry of Foreign Affairs.

————. 2005. "International Migration: Lessons from Recent Data." Presentation in the Migration Seminar Series. World Bank, Washington, DC, March 8.

Martorell, R. 1999. "The Nature of Child Malnutrition and its Long-Term Implications." *Food and Nutrition Bulletin* 20: 288–92.

Mattoo, A., I. C. Neagu, and C. Özden. 2005. "Brain Waste? Educated Immigrants in the US Labor Market." Mimeo. Research Program on International Migration and Development. International Trade Unit. Development Economics Research Group (DECRG), March. World Bank, Washington, DC.

McKenzie, D., and H. Rapoport. 2005. "Migration Incentives, Migration Networks and the Dynamics of Education Inequality in Rural Mexico." Paper presented at the IDB "Economic Integration, Remittances, and Development" Conference. Inter-American Development Bank, Washington, DC.

Mountford, A. 1997. "Can a Brain Drain be Good for Growth in the Source Economy?" *Journal of Development Economics* 53(2): 287–303.

Organisation for Economic Co-operation and Development (OECD). 2003. "Trends in International Migration: SOPEMI – 2003 Edition." OECD, Paris.

Patinkin, D. 1968. "A 'Nationalist' Model." In *The Brain Drain*, ed. W. Adams. New York: Macmillan.

Romer, P. 1986. "Increasing Returns and Long Run Growth." *Journal of Political Economy* 94 (October): 1002–37.

Schiff, M., and A. Valdés. 1990a. "Nutrition: Alternative Definitions and Policy Implications." *Economic Development and Cultural Change* 38(2): 281–92.

————. 1990b. "Poverty, Food Intake and Malnutrition: Implications for Food Security in Developing Countries." *American Journal of Agricultural Economics* 72(5): 1318–1322.

Schultz, T.W. 1961. "Investment in Human Capital." American Economic Association Presidential Address. *American Economic Review* 51(1): 1–17.

Solimano, A. 2001. "International Migration and the Global Economic Order: An Overview." Policy Research Working Paper, no. 2720. World Bank, Washington, DC.

Stalker, P. 1994. *The Work of Strangers. A Survey of International Labour Migration.* International Labour Office, Geneva.

Stark, O. 2004. "Rethinking the Brain Drain." *World Development* 32(1): 15–22.

Stark, O., A. Casarico, C. Devillanova, and S. Uebelmesser. 2004. "The New Economics of the Brain Gain: Mapping the Gains." Paper presented at the Conference on Advanced Perspectives on Migration and Mobility. University of Bonn, September 30–October 1.

Stark, O., C. Helmenstein, and A. Prskawetz. 1997. "A Brain Drain with a Brain Gain." *Economics Letters* 55(2): 227–34.

————. 1998. "Human Capital Depletion, Human Capital Formation, and Migration: A Blessing or a 'Curse'?" *Economics Letters* 60(3): 363–67.

Stark, O., and Y. Wang. 2002. "Inducing Human Capital formation: Migration as a Substitute for Subsidies." *Journal of Public Economics* 86(1): 29–46.

Strauss, J., and D. Thomas. 1998. "Health, Nutrition and Economic Development." *Journal of Economic Literature* 36(2): 766–817.

Vidal, J.-P. 1998. "The Effect of Emigration on Human Capital Formation." *Journal of Population Economics* 11(4): 589–600.

World Bank. 2000. "Higher Education in Developing Countries: Peril and Promise." Report of the Task Force on Higher Education and Society. World Bank, Washington, DC.

7

EDUCATED MIGRANTS: IS THERE BRAIN WASTE?

Çağlar Özden

Introduction

The welfare of migrants is one of the key issues that need to be considered when migration policies are evaluated. The literature to date has mostly focused on the assimilation of the migrants in the labor market, mainly through their earnings and wage growth (Chiswick 1978; Borjas 1985, 1994; Jasso, Rosenzweig, and Smith 1998). However, the type of jobs that the migrants obtain is a crucial issue that influences their performance in the destination country. This is especially important for the highly educated migrants. The U.S. Census data indicate that there are striking differences in the occupational attainment of immigrants who have similar education backgrounds but are from different countries. Highly educated immigrants from certain countries are less likely to obtain skilled jobs. Among the lowest likelihood of obtaining skilled jobs are migrants from several Latin American, Eastern European, and Middle Eastern countries.

In this chapter, we first present an analytical model that identifies the main determinants that lead to these differences. The key differences are the probabilities of successfully entering a destination country for migrants from different countries and different education backgrounds. Then we present a simple empirical analysis that tests the predictions of the theoretical model. Among these predictions are attributes that affect the quality of human capital accumulated at home. Examples are expenditure on tertiary education and the use of English as a medium of education. Other attributes lead to a selection effect—these variables have differing effects on migrants with different skill levels. These include the gross domestic product (GDP) per capita, the distance to the United States, and the openness of U.S. immigration policies to residents of a given country. Finally, among the most important variables is the ease with which people with different education backgrounds can migrate to other countries. Our empirical analysis

227

shows that all of these variables have significant effects on the professional place-ment of educated migrants in the United States.

How immigrants perform in host country labor markets is one of the funda-mental questions in the migration literature (Borjas 1994). The existing literature focuses primarily on earnings as a measure of performance. We examine, instead, occupational outcomes, particularly of the highly educated and those with profes-sional qualifications. Earnings do not reveal what immigrants actually do, although they are likely to be correlated with occupational choices. If the global creation and allocation of human capital are a concern, then it is of interest what kind of jobs the highly educated immigrants obtain. For example, if most univer-sity graduates or professionals from a country obtain unskilled jobs when they migrate, then obtaining a better sense of their eventual destiny may help them and their countries improve their allocation of expenditures on education and train-ing (see Mountford 1997 for an analysis of the impact of brain drain on sending countries).

Model

Suppose the college graduates in country j are uniformly distributed over the range $[a_j-1, a_j]$ in terms of the value of their human capital in the country into which they emigrate. Thus, the measure of population is normalized to 1 and the average human capital level in country j is given by $a_j-1/2$. Without loss of any generality, we assume $a_j<1$ and only the people with human capital level above 0 are able to obtain skilled jobs in the destination country. The workers in the range $[a_j-1,0]$ would be placed in unskilled jobs and the ones in $[0,a_j]$ would obtain skilled jobs if they were to emigrate. We can interpret a_j as the country-specific human capital index, because higher a_j implies that a higher portion of the work-ers obtain skilled jobs. Figure 7.1 below represents the distribution of a_j over the relevant range.

We assume that the labor market in the destination country is efficient. The human capital level of each migrant worker is correctly identified in the market,

FIGURE 7.1   Distribution of a_j

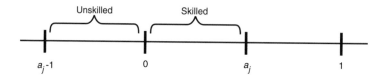

and he or she is placed in an appropriate job. However, we can only observe their diploma in the census data, not their individual human capital.

The probability of migrating to the north is influenced by various factors. Some of these depend on the individual migrant—such as the ability to finance the trip or the willingness to be away from home. Other factors are specific to the home country or the community to which the migrant belongs—such as the support provided to migrants or the presence of official or informal social networks in the destination country, which would help with problems of settling and adjustment. Finally, there are the migration policies of the destination country— whether there are specific policies and programs targeting certain source countries, professions, and skills or allowing family reunification. To simplify the model, all of these factors can be represented by a single probability for each individual. More specifically we assume that the probability of entering the destination country is denoted by p_j, if the human capital of the migrant is in $[a_j - 1, 0]$, and is given by q_j, if the human capital level is in $[1, a_j]$. All of the Organisation for Economic Co-operation and Development (OECD) countries, which accept significant number of migrants, have policies in place that discriminate in favor of skilled and educated migrants. So, we assume that $q_j > p_j$. We should emphasize two points. First, these probabilities reflect all types of migration, legal or illegal, based on family preferences or job qualifications. Second, these are also source-country-specific variables. It is possible that lower-skilled migrants from country j might be able to emigrate more easily compared with highly skilled people from another country. This possibility might be the result of geographic proximity, language, cultural compatibility, or the presence of established migrant communities, which lowers migration costs. For example, it is probably easier for a lower-skilled Mexican to migrate to the United States compared with a more highly skilled Ethiopian.

In this simple model, the total number of migrants from country j is given by $[1 - a_j]p_j + a_j q_j$ when we normalize the population of the country to 1, as we assumed at the beginning of this section. The ratio of migrants who obtain skilled jobs is given by $\dfrac{a_j q_j}{[1 - a_j]p_j + a_j q_j}$. This is the main variable we presented in figure 7.1 in the previous section, which we can obtain from the U.S. Census data. This ratio is increasing in a_j; as the average level of human capital in country j is increased, a higher portion of the migrants are placed in skilled jobs. It is also increasing in q_j and decreasing in p_j. If the probability of migrating successfully increases for people who have higher (lower) human capital, then the ratio of migrants in skilled jobs increases (decreases) for country j. The key issue is to determine the kind of factors influencing these three variables. We mentioned some of these factors above; identifying their relative importance forms the basis of our empirical analysis in the following section. Before proceeding to the empirical analysis, however, we extend the model in one more direction.

The most difficult decision for a migrant is probably the decision whether to migrate itself. However, as equally important is the decision on where to migrate. Most OECD countries provide attractive opportunities, particularly for highly skilled or educated migrants. Less-skilled migrants (or even illegal migrants) have many different options when the migration decision is made. When we observe the migration levels and compositions, say, for the United States, we need to take into account the migration opportunities in Europe, Canada, and Australia. For example, if Japan were to significantly relax its migration policies overnight, this policy shift could have a large effect on the migration flows from other Asian countries into the United States, Canada, and Australia.

We now modify our model slightly to incorporate the option to migrate to a second country. To keep the model simple, we assume that the wage levels and the labor market placement (skilled versus unskilled jobs) are identical in both destination countries for a given level of human capital. The only difference is the probability of successful migration from country j to either destination country. Assume the two destination countries are labeled as x and y. The probability of migration from country j to country x is given by p_j^x and q_j^x for people with low and high levels of human capital, respectively. We again assume that $p_j^x < q_j^x$, but it is possible to have $q_j^x < p_j^y$. In other words, it is possible that it is easier for people with lower levels of human capital to migrate to country y compared with people who have higher levels of human capital migrating to country x. For example, it is probably the case that it is easier for unskilled Mexicans to migrate to the United States than it is for skilled Mexicans to migrate to Japan.

Under this new scenario with multiple destinations, the portion of migrants with low human capital (in the range $[a_j-1, 0]$) who migrate to country x is given by $\dfrac{p_j^x}{p_j^x + p_j^y}$. There is a similar ratio for migrants with high human capital. Then, the number of migrants in country x is given by $[1 - a_j]\dfrac{p_j^x}{p_j^x + p_j^y} + a_j\dfrac{q_j^x}{q_j^x + q_j^y}$ and the ratio of immigrants in country x from country j who obtain skilled jobs is given by the following:

$$r_j^x = \left[a_j\frac{q_j^x}{q_j^x + q_j^y} \right] \Big/ \left[[1 - a_j]\frac{p_j^x}{p_j^x + p_j^y} + a_j\frac{q_j^x}{q_j^x + q_j^y} \right] \qquad (7.1)$$

The effect of the overall level of human capital in country j, a_j, and the probabilities of migration, p_j^x and q_j^x, on this expression are the same as before. The interesting issue is the effects of migration probabilities to country y on the labor market placement of migrants in country x. When p_j^y increases—that is, when it becomes easier for people with low levels of human capital to migrate to country y—the average human capital level of migrants from country j to country x increases. This, in turn, increases the portion of migrants placed in skilled jobs. An increase in q_j^y has the exact opposite effect for the same rationale. For example, if it becomes easier for unskilled Tunisians to migrate to France, then the average human capital level of Tunisians migrating to the United States will increase along with their average job market performance.

This simple analytical model identified the main forces that shape the "average placement" of migrants in the labor market of a destination country. The following forces increase the portion of migrants placed in skilled jobs: (a) the overall human capital level of the sending country, a_j; (b) the ease of migration to that country for people with high human capital levels, q_j^x; and (c) the ease of migration to other destination countries for people with low human capital levels, p_j^y. Conversely, the following decreases the overall placement level of migrants from a given country: (a) the ease of migration to that country for people with low human capital levels, p_j^x; and (b) the ease of migration to other destination countries for people with high human capital levels, q_j^y. All of these forces are quite intuitive. Before proceeding to the empirical analysis that aims to identify the variables that capture these effects, we need to mention an implicit assumption in the model and the following empirical analysis. The model assumes that the migrants are randomly selected among their respective populations (low skill or high skill). This is a rather strong assumption that might limit the analysis. However, without explicit knowledge about the labor market performance of the migrant in his or her home country, it is rather difficult to overcome it. Unfortunately, the U.S. Census does not provide such data.

Data

Although there is a substantial body of theoretical literature on the brain drain (see Bhagwati and Hamada 1974; Bhagwati and Partington 1976; Stark, Helmenstein, and Prskawetz 1997), the scarcity of data imposes significant restraints on empirical analysis. Chapter 5 by Docquier and Marfouk in this volume is an important contribution in this respect, and we use some of the data described there. Additionally, U.S. Census data provides detailed social and economic information on foreign-born people in the United States. The data relating to the immigrants in the United States are from the 1 percent sample of the 2000 U.S. Census.[1] The U.S. Census data are restricted to foreign-educated males who are between 25 and 65 years old and employed at the time of the census.[2] Each individual observation in the census has a population weight attached to it, which is that representative observation's proportion in the overall U.S. population.

We end up with more than 200,000 observations in our data set, which corresponds to around 4.5 million people in the United States. Each individual in the census declares an education level and a profession. For simplicity and to have concordance with other data sources, we divide the migrants into two groups—people with at least a bachelor's degree and people without a bachelor's degree. There are more than 500 separate occupations in the census and we group them into two main categories, which are based on the job description and the average educational attainment.[3] The categories are as follows:

- High Skilled—The average education for all workers in these categories is a minimum of 16 years and includes professionals, scientists, managers, accountants, engineers, social workers, and teachers.
- Less Skilled—The average education for workers in these categories is less than 16 years and includes technicians, police, secretaries and administrative assistants, waiters, salespersons, cashiers, construction laborers, automotive mechanics, and drivers.

The following graphs present basic migration patterns from the Docquier and Marfouk (chapter 5 in this volume) data and the U.S. Census data (2000). Figure 7.2 is the total migration from a group of select source countries to the United States and the rest of the world. The largest migrant-sending country in the world is Mexico, and almost all of these migrants go to the United States. A large portion of the population of several Western European countries also emigrates in large numbers. We should note that this reflects intra-European migration, which is rather different from migration from developing countries. We see that migrants from Latin America mostly come to the United States, whereas migrants from Eastern Europe, the Middle East, and Africa prefer Western Europe. The portion of migrants from Asia to the United States is slightly above 50 percent.

In terms of the education composition of the migrants, in figure 7.3, we see that a large portion of Latin American migrants have very low levels of education, whereas the European migrants are highly educated. The portion of the migrants with tertiary education from other regions exhibits wide variation. For the Middle East and many African countries, it is actually above 50 percent, whereas it is slightly below 50 percent for Eastern Europe and around 40 percent for Asia. There are two factors that influence the education composition of migrants. The first factor is the prevalence of tertiary education in the native population, and the second factor is the incentives to migrate among different education levels. There

FIGURE 7.2   Migration Patterns from Select Countries

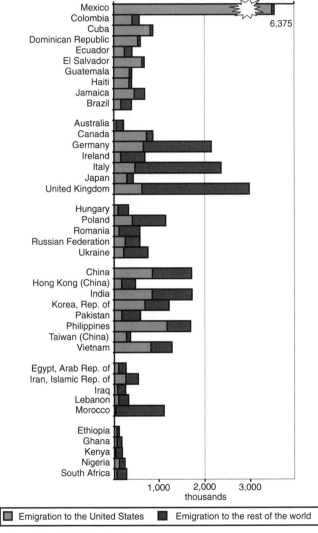

Emigration to the United States versus the Rest of the World, aggregate, 2000

☐ Emigration to the United States	■ Emigration to the rest of the world

Source: Docquier and Marfouk (this volume).

FIGURE 7.3 Migration Patterns from Select Countries for People with Tertiary Education

Share of emigrants to EU-15 and the United States, from selected countries, 2000

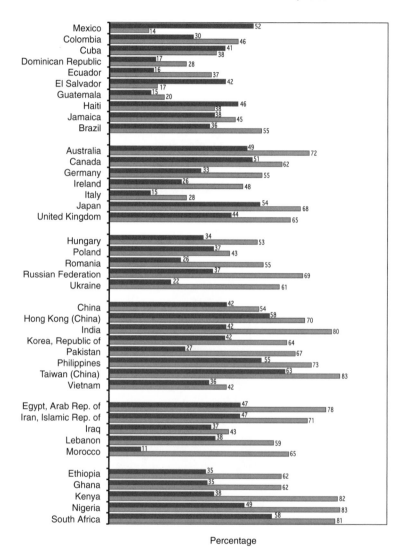

Percentage

United States ■ EU-15

Source: Docquier and Marfouk (this volume

are many studies indicating that it is generally easier for middle-class and relatively educated people to migrate (figure 7.3 confirms this).

Another important pattern emerging from figure 7.3 is how the educated migrants from a given source country are divided among different destination countries. As mentioned above, we see that the majority of migrants from Latin America come to the United States, whereas African and Middle Eastern migrants predominantly prefer Europe. However, migrants from Africa and the Middle East to the United States are more educated compared with migrants from the same regions to Europe, as seen in figure 7.3. The same pattern holds for migrants from Asia and Eastern Europe, but this is not the case for Latin American migrants. These patterns are likely to be caused by the ease of migration for potential migrants with different education levels to different destinations.

Figure 7.4 compares the education composition of migrants to the United States with the native population in a select group of countries. The vertical axis represents the portion of the migrants who arrived in the United States in the 1990s and who hold a tertiary degree. The horizontal axis is the portion of the population who is enrolled in tertiary education for the appropriate age group. We are comparing the education levels of migrants to the tertiary education enrollment

FIGURE 7.4 Tertiary Education at Home and among Immigrants to the United States, 1990s

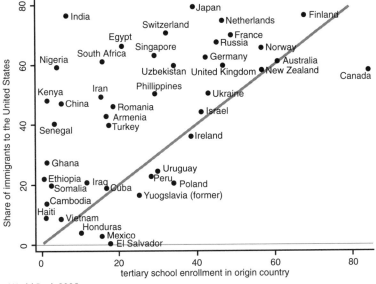

Source: World Bank 2005.

rate, rather than overall tertiary education level, because the migrants tend to be younger and emigrate during or following the completion of their education. Figure 7.4 tells us that the education level among Latin American immigrants is even lower than the average levels in their home countries. Conversely, immigrants from Africa, the Middle East, and Asia to the United States are more educated than the Latin American immigrants and their fellow citizens. This confirms that immigrants do not constitute a random sample from the population of their home countries.

Finally, we present the education composition of all migrants in the United States and Europe in 1990 and 2000. It is interesting to note that the migrant stocks are quite similar in total. However, the European numbers include intra-European flows as well, which implies that migration from developing countries to the United States is much higher than the migration to the European Union countries. However, despite the relatively large share of migrants from developing countries, migrants to the United States are relatively more educated. This selection effect might be the result of the relative ease with which highly educated people can migrate to the United States. The labor market and migration policies

FIGURE 7.5 Composition of Migrants to Europe and the United States by Education

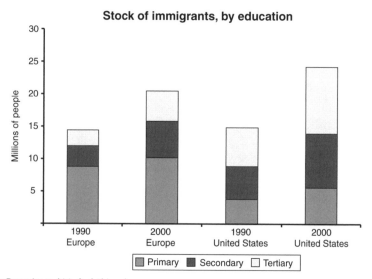

Source: Docquier and Marfouk this volume.

seem to favor the more educated in the United States, especially when compared with Europe.

Empirical Framework

Our empirical framework is designed to test the implications of the analytical model presented earlier. We first calculate the portion of the migrants with tertiary education who obtained skilled jobs. To isolate cohort effects, we focus only on migrants who arrived in 1990s. We also perform the empirical tests separately for the people who are employed so that we can exclude students. We calculate this ratio for each country and present some of them in figure 7.6. It is evident that these ratios vary significantly across countries. The likelihood of obtaining skilled jobs is lowest for Latin American countries and highest for European and Asian migrants. There are large variations across countries of origin even when individuals have identical age, experience, and nominal education. Again, some of the lowest probabilities are for Latin American and Eastern European countries. In other words, ostensibly identical education degrees are not treated equally in the U.S. labor market.

Figure 7.6 shows that there is significant variation in the labor market placement of immigrants from different countries, even if they have the same level of education on paper. If the labor market in the United States is efficient and there is no discrimination, then the numbers in figure 7.6 reflect the "average quality" of the immigrants from a particular country. In this section, we aim to identify the determinants of these quality differences by country of origin based on empirical analysis motivated by the earlier theoretical model.

The previous literature (Chiswick 1978; Borjas 1987; Jasso and Rosenzweig 1986) focused on the differences in the earnings of individual immigrants and attempted to provide explanations on the basis of differences in their levels of education and other explanatory variables that typically include source-country attributes. Conversely, we attempt to explain differences in the labor market placement of individuals who have nominally identical levels of education. Furthermore, we introduce factors that influence the migration decision to a specific country—especially the ease of migration to other countries—which contribute to the source-country-specific selection effect.

Quality variables explain why identical education qualifications obtained in different source countries are valued differently in the U.S. labor market. *Selection* variables explain the differences in the abilities of migrants from different source countries, because they are drawn from different segments of the ability distribution. In our theoretical model, this refers to the unskilled versus skilled immigrants.

FIGURE 7.6   Portion of Migrants with Tertiary Education Who Obtain Skilled Jobs, 1990s Arrivals

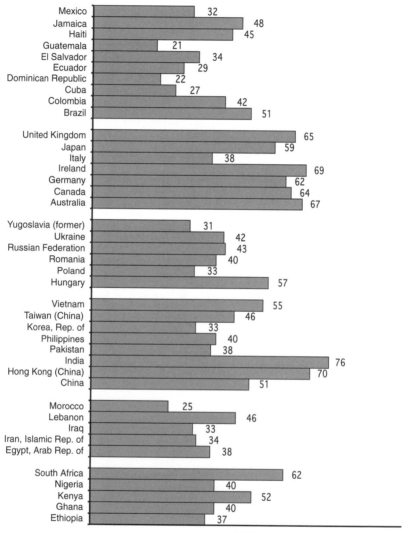

Foreign-born males with bachelor's degrees from
their home countries who have skilled jobs

Source: U.S. Census Bureau 2000.

As our dependent variable, we use the portion of migrants with tertiary education who are placed in skilled jobs in the United States. This is the variable in equation 7.1 and it is presented in figure 7.5 for a group of countries. It is defined as r_{kt}, where k is for country and t is for cohort (1990s arrivals in this case):

$$r_{kt} = \alpha + \beta_1 DIST_k + \beta_2 CONFLICT_{kt} + \beta_3 ENGLISH_k + \\ \beta_4 EDUC\_exp_{kt} + \beta_5 GDP_{kt} + \beta_6 ROW\_MIG_{kt} + \varepsilon_{kt} \qquad (7.2)$$

Note that equation 7.2 is estimated only for the 1990s cohort. The explanatory variables are as follows: natural log of the distance to United States (DIST); the presence of military conflict (CONFLICT); English language dummy (ENGLISH); natural log of tertiary education expenditure per student (EDUC_exp); natural log of the home-country GDP per capita (GDP); and ratio of immigrants that have migrated to the rest of the world (ROW_MIG).

Among the quality variables, we have the natural log of tertiary education expenditure (EDUC_exp) per student during the relevant period adjusted for purchasing power parity and a dummy variable (ENGLISH), which takes the value of 1 if English is among the commonly spoken languages in the home country. Both of these variables should have a positive effect on human capital and lead to more favorable placement in the U.S. labor market.

Among the selection variables, we have a set of source-country variables: natural log of the home-country GDP per capita adjusted for purchasing power parity, distance from the United States (DIST), and a dummy variable (CONFLICT), which reflects the presence of military conflict in the home country during the decade the migrant arrived in the United States.

Instead of just home-country GDP, it would have been preferable to have data on the average earnings of graduates or professionals, and the distribution of such earnings, but such data are available only for a small number of countries. For higher GDP countries, the opportunity cost of migrating is high, and so only individuals with high income potential would emigrate to and remain in the United States. Furthermore, as Borjas (1987) has argued, because the distribution of income in many of the other industrial countries is more equal than that in the United States, we would again expect those at the upper end of home-country distributions to migrate to the United States. For countries with per capita GDP substantially lower than that of the United States, the relative distribution of income is irrelevant, and it can be assumed that both low- and high-ability people would wish to migrate. Conversely, financial constraints in poorer countries might allow only the relatively wealthier people to migrate. Thus, the effect of source-country GDP per capita is likely to matter but the net effect might be ambiguous.

Distance has conventionally been regarded as an important determinant of the cost of migration, which would have a positive selection effect. Furthermore, people from distant countries (such as in Africa or the Middle East) may have closer migration options (such as Europe and the Persian Gulf). If the U.S. labor market rewards human capital relatively more than these other destination countries, then immigrants will again self-select and the United States will attract the higher-quality migrants from distant countries.

The presence of conflict in the home country should lower the threshold of those who would want to migrate because it reduces the opportunity cost of staying. In low-GDP countries, where everybody might have the desire to migrate, military conflict may act as a powerful push factor. Furthermore, political instability might also have a quality effect, causing a decline in education and human capital accumulation of the citizens. So we expect a negative effect of conflict on labor market placement.

The final variable we introduce (ROW_MIG) reflects the other destinations available to potential migrants. These are captured by the probabilities of entering other countries in the theoretical model. In the regression, we use the ratio of immigrants with tertiary education (who went to countries other than the United States) to all citizens with tertiary education—immigrants to the United States, immigrants to the rest of the world, and the ones who did not emigrate. This variable captures the ease of migration to the rest of the world.

The following estimation strategy could be an alternative. A multinomial-logit estimation is performed in the first stage for all migrants with their professional placement as the dependent variable and their individual characteristics as the explanatory variables. In addition, country dummies are included to capture all other effects. The probability of obtaining a specific job is calculated for a representative individual from each country based on the logit estimation results. Then, these probabilities are used as the dependent variables and regressed on country-specific explanatory variables to assess their relative importance. Furthermore, one can obtain other variables of interest and perform similar analysis for different combinations of education levels and job categories. We hope to pursue this approach in a future study.

Empirical Results

In table 7.1, we present the results from an ordinary least squares (OLS) regression with robust standard errors and weighted by the number of immigrants from each country within that education level. We estimate different specifications and do not include the ease of migration variable (ROW_MIGR) initially. In the first column, the dependent variable is the country-specific ratio of immigrants with

TABLE 7.1   Country-Level Determinants of Probability of Obtaining A Skilled Job, 1990s

Dependent variable	Educated migrants in skilled profession	Educated migrants employed in skilled profession
Log of distance to the	0.050**	0.051**
United States	(2.53)	(2.59)
Military conflict	−0.129**	−0.128**
	(−2.56)	(−2.48)
English	0.101**	0.109***
	(2.38)	(2.73)
Log of tertiary education	0.070**	0.067**
expenditure per student	(2.59)	(2.33)
(PPP adjusted)		
Log of per capita GDP	−0.016	−0.024
(PPP adjusted)	(−0.52)	(−0.74)
Number of observations	101	101
F-statistic	26.45***	24.92***
R-square	0.562	0.556

Sources: U.S. Census Bureau 2000 and World Bank 2005.

Note: Weighted OLS regression with White robust standard errors. t-statistics in parentheses. *** denotes significance at the 1 percent level; ** denotes significance at the 5 percent level; * denotes significance at the 10 percent level. GDP = gross domestic product; PPP = purchasing power parity; OLS = ordinary least squares.

college degrees who obtain a skilled job whereas, in the second column, the dependent variable is the ratio of employed immigrants. We define an individual to be employed if the annual wage income is above $8,000. The purpose of focusing on employed migrants is to isolate the impact of students, but this does not seem to change any of the results. In both cases, distance (DIST), English (ENGLISH), and tertiary education expenditure (EDUC_*exp*) have positive and significant coefficients, while military conflict (CONFLICT) is negative and significant. GDP per capita (GDP) is not significant.

The results imply that immigrants from countries where English is a common language and expenditure on tertiary education is high perform better in the U.S. labor market. This is not surprising as both variables increase the relevant human capital of the immigrants for the U.S. labor market. For example, coming from an English-speaking country increases the likelihood of obtaining a skilled job in the United States by 10 percent for a hypothetical college graduate. Similarly, a 10 percent increase in tertiary education increases the same probability by 7 percent.

TABLE 7.2   Country-Level Determinants of Probability of Obtaining A Skilled Job, 1990s, with European Migration Policy Indicators

Dependent variable	Educated migrants in skilled profession	Educated migrants employed in skilled profession
Log of distance to the United States	0.054*** (3.25)	0.055*** (3.44)
Military conflict	−0.125*** (−2.68)	−0.122*** (−2.63)
English	0.108*** (2.68)	0.118*** (3.16)
Log of tertiary education expenditure per student (PPP adjusted)	0.079*** (2.84)	0.077*** (2.66)
Log of per capita GDP (PPP adjusted)	−0.016 (−0.55)	−0.023 (−0.81)
Share of educated immigrants in ROW as portion of total	−0.409** (2.16)	−0.488** (−2.37)
Number of observations	101	101
F-statistic	26.56***	21.31***
R-square	0.589	0.595

Sources: U.S. Census Bureau 2000 and World Bank 2005.

Note: Weighted OLS regression with White robust standard errors. t-statistics in parentheses. *** denotes significance at the 1 percent level; ** denotes significance at the 5 percent level; * denotes significance at the 10 percent level. GDP = gross domestic product; PPP = purchasing power parity; ROW = rest of world.

Distance has a positive effect on average immigrant quality, suggesting that the effects of migration costs are rather strong. And the negative sign on the coefficient of the military conflict variable (CONFLICT) implies that the average quality of immigrants seem to increase with political stability.

The final issue is the introduction of variables that represent the ease of migration into Europe for a given country. For this, we use the stock of migrants (with tertiary education) in the rest of the world (all countries except the United States) from a given country in 1990 as a percentage of the total population. The presence of a large migrant community from a given country is indicative of relaxed policies as well as support for migration. As the analytical model predicted, the ease of migration to Europe for low-skilled people improves the overall professional performance of migrants to the United States. The reason for this is that Europe attracts more people from the low end of the human capital spectrum. Similarly, if the skilled migrants can more easily migrate to Europe, then the average quality of placement in the U.S. labor market deteriorates.

Conclusion

This chapter develops a theoretical model to investigate the labor market performance of educated immigrants and then uses U.S. Census data for empirical analysis, continued in Mattoo, Neagu, and Özden (2005). We find striking differences among immigrants from different countries of origin. With some exceptions, educated immigrants from Latin America and Eastern Europe perform poorly, especially when compared with immigrants from developing countries in Asia and developed countries. A large part of the variation across countries can be explained by attributes of the country of origin that influence the quality of relevant human capital, such as expenditure on tertiary education and the use of English as a medium of instruction. Performance is also adversely affected by conflict at home, which could have a quality impact (by weakening the institutions that create human capital) and a selection effect (by lowering the threshold quality of immigrants). U.S. immigration policies play a critical role in explaining cross-country variation because a large proportion of immigrants from some countries (such as Mexico) are admitted through family preferences. Among the most important findings of this chapter is that the migration policies and environment of the rest of the world also have a significant impact on cross-country variation. If other countries attract a relatively large portion of the educated population of a source country, then the average quality of migrants to the United States declines along with likelihood of skilled job placement.

Endnotes

1. Extracts from the U.S. Census samples were made through IPUMS (Integrated Public Use Microdata Series), which is a database maintained by Minnesota Population Center at University of Minnesota (http://beta.ipums.org/usa/index.html).

2. The census asks the respondents their level of education, but not where they obtained it. However, we know the age at which the immigrant entered the United States. So based on this information, we designate a person "U.S. educated" if that person arrived in the United States before he or she would have normally finished his or her declared education level. For example, if a university graduate arrived at the age of 23 or older, then he or she is considered "foreign educated."

3. Education attainments were obtained by computing the average years of education in each profession, with all U.S.-born and foreign-born people (males and females) included.

References

Bhagwati, J., and K. Hamada. 1974. "The Brain Drain, International Integration of Markets for Professionals and Unemployment: A Theoretical Analysis." *Journal of Development Economics* 1(1): 19–42.

Bhagwati, J., and M. Partington, ed. 1976. *The Brain Drain and Taxation. Vol. II: Theory and Empirical Analysis.* Amsterdam: North Holland.

Borjas, G. 1985. "Assimilation, Changes in Cohort Quality, and the Earnings of Immigrants."*Journal of Labor Economics* 3(4): 463–89.

———. 1987. "Self-Selection and Earnings of Immigrants." *American Economic Review* 77(4): 531-53.

———. 1994. "The Economics of Immigration." *Journal of Economic Literature* 32(4): 1667–717.

Chiswick, B. 1978. "The Effect of Americanization on the Earnings of Foreign-born Men." *Journal of Political Economy.* 86(5): 897-921.

Jasso, G., and M. Rosenzweig. 1986. "What's in a Name? Country-of-Origin Influences on the Earnings of Immigrants in the United States." In *Research in Human Capital and Development*, vol. 4, ed. Oded Stark. Greenwich, CT: JAI Press.

Jasso, G., M. Rosenzweig, and J.P. Smith. 1998. "The Changing Skill of New Immigrants to the United States: Recent Trends and Their Determinants." NBER Working Paper, no. 6764. National Bureau of Economic Research, Washington, DC.

Mattoo, A., C. Neagu, and C. Özden. 2005. "Brain Waste? Educated Migrants in the US Labor Market." World Bank Policy Research Working Paper, no. 3581. World Bank, Washington, DC.

Mountford, A. 1997. "Can a Brain Drain Be Good for Growth in the Source Economy?" *Journal of Development Economics* 53(2): 287–303.

Stark, O., C. Helmenstein, and A. Prskawetz. 1997. "A Brain Gain with a Brain Drain." *Economics Letters* 55(2): 227–34.

U.S. Census Bureau. 2000. "United States Census 2000." U.S. Department of Commerce, Washington, DC.

World Bank. 2005. *World Development Indicators.* World Bank, Washington, DC.

8

SKILLED IMMIGRANTS, HIGHER EDUCATION, AND U.S. INNOVATION

Gnanaraj Chellaraj, Keith E. Maskus, and Aaditya Mattoo

Introduction

Policies governing the entry of foreign citizens with education and skills have been under considerable debate in the United States in recent years. During the dotcom boom of the late 1990s, American information technology companies pushed strongly for increases in H1B visas, which permit temporary entry of skilled programmers and other professionals. The issuance of these visas has since been scaled back, which may be both a cause and consequence of the much-discussed offshoring of U.S. programming jobs to India and other nations. In the wake of the terrorist attacks of September 11, 2001, U.S. immigration authorities also have clamped down on the number of visas issued to foreign students wishing to gain a graduate education in the United States. While these restrictions have been relaxed somewhat more recently, they may have precipitated a worldwide decline in the number of foreign students who study science and engineering in the United States, as discussed in the next section. In general, there are increasing calls among some American policymakers to restrain the volume of immigration, including skilled workers.

While the motivations for such concerns are varied, opponents of further restrictions focus on one potential negative outcome of limiting skilled immigration. Specifically, the view is widely held that bringing in foreign-trained doctors, engineers, managers, and scientists helps relieve domestic shortages of such skills, thereby promoting continued U.S. leadership in innovation and technology.

245

Similarly, education officials express concerns that if American universities train a declining share of international graduate students, their ability to perform both basic and applied research will suffer, which is an issue of particular importance as those institutions rely more heavily on licensing incomes.

These are important concerns, which we will discuss in the following section. In this chapter, however, our concern essentially is to investigate in a straightforward way the veracity of such claims. We do this by summarizing the results of a recent study of ours that sheds light on the role of skilled foreigners and students in U.S. science and technology (Chellaraj, Maskus, and Mattoo 2005). In particular, this study investigated the contributions of foreign graduate students and skilled immigrants to patenting activity, finding powerful and positive effects. In this chapter, we also consider briefly the implications of the source distribution of skilled immigrants. Together, these findings suggest strongly that a general decline in the interest of foreign students and professionals in migrating, even temporarily, to the United States will have sharply negative implications for innovation capacity and competitiveness.

The chapter proceeds as follows. In the next section we review recent trends in immigration of skilled workers and discuss the policy environment. In the third section we summarize the central results of the innovation study, while in the fourth section we discuss the implications of relative changes in source countries as originators of immigrants. We offer brief concluding remarks in the final section.

Skilled Immigration Trends and Policy

In this section we review basic data on trends in the arrival of skilled immigrants and foreign students in the United States. Then we consider relevant policy questions.

Trends in Skilled Immigration and Education

The data in figure 8.1 demonstrate the significant increase since 1990 in skilled immigration into the United States. For this purpose, skilled immigration is defined to include employment-based immigrant categories, covering priority workers, professionals with advanced degrees or aliens with exceptional ability, skilled workers, professional workers, and a few other categories. These are people (and their families) who intend to migrate permanently to the United States, rather than on the temporary H1B visas. As shown in figure 8.1, the number of skilled immigrants was just below 60,000 in 1990, rose sharply by 1993, and fell to its original level by 1999. There was a surge in such immigration in 2001 and 2002, however, before falling sharply in 2003 in the wake of tighter restrictions. It is evi-

FIGURE 8.1   Skilled Immigrants

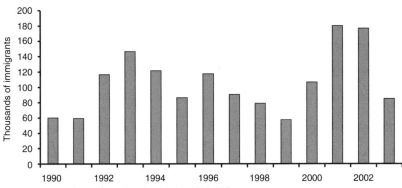

Source: U.S. Citizenship and Immigration Service 1990–2004.

dent that there is considerable volatility in these figures, associated with both cyclical and policy factors.

Another measure of the availability of foreign skills resident in the United States is the number of H1B visas issued for people with "specialty occupations," those that are almost entirely based in advanced technologies. This number peaked in 2001, at 331,206 visas. The number of visas issued after that was much lower, at 197,537 visas in 2002 and 217,340 in 2003, generally reflecting a tightening of the number of such visas issued.

Finally, it is important for our discussion to note trends in foreign graduate students in the United States. One simple measure is provided in figure 8.3, which shows the number of foreign students enrolled in U.S. universities each year from 1990 to 2003. While this includes both graduate and undergraduate enrollments, it captures broadly what has happened in terms of the presence of skilled foreign students in the United States. Later in this chapter, we focus specifically on graduate enrollments. At this point, we simply note the dramatic increase in the number of foreign students enrolled in U.S. universities and colleges in the 14-year period, rising from 326,264 in 1990 to a peak of 698,595 in 2001.

However, visas issued fell by 10.5 percent between 2001 and 2003, indicating a sharp decline in enrollments for the present cohort of foreign students. Visa applications for students fell by 74,000 between 2001 and 2003 (Florida 2005). Applications from Chinese, Indian, and Korean students dropped 45 percent, 28 percent, and 14 percent, respectively, over the same period.

FIGURE 8.2   H1B Beneficiaries, 1992–2003

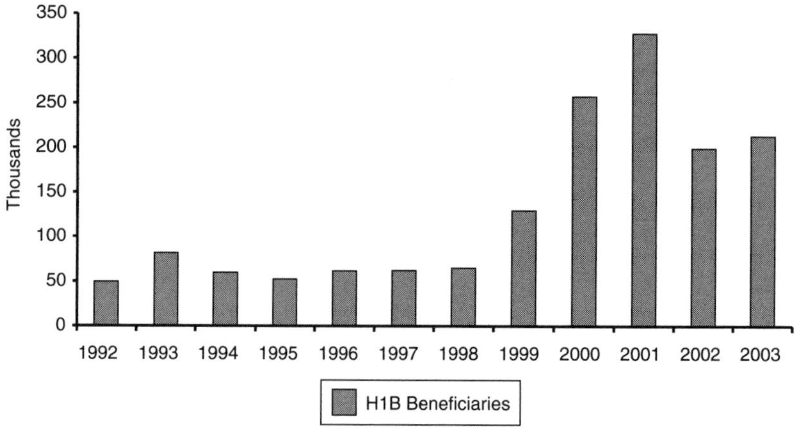

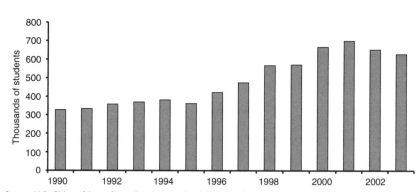

Source: U.S. Citizenship and Immigration Service 1990–2004.

FIGURE 8.3   Foreign Students

Source: U.S. Citizenship and Immigration Service 1990–2004.

Additional perspective on this last decline is available from other sources. For example, an industry association reports that universities have seen large declines in foreign student applications since 2002 (Institute for International Education 2004). Moreover, foreign graduate enrollments slipped by perhaps 6 percent between 2003/04 and 2004/05. It is likely that some portion of these reductions is associated with tighter visa restrictions after the September 11 attacks, which have made it more difficult to obtain a visa on a timely basis.

However, in addition to this supply-side effect, there has been a reduction in demand for foreign-student visas, as universities in Australia, the United Kingdom, Singapore, and elsewhere have become more competitive at attracting and training advanced students (Chellaraj, Maskus, and Mattoo 2005). Indeed, many countries now actively subsidize foreign graduate students in technical and managerial fields, in the hope that the skills those students possess will translate into higher domestic productivity (Hira 2003). This benefit could emerge as students frequently choose to remain and work in the locations in which they are trained, and they are increasingly encouraged to do so by receiving countries (such as Singapore).[1]

Policy Concerns

Since the onset of far-tighter restrictions on the issuance of U.S. education visas in the wake of the 2001 terrorist attacks, immigration policy for foreign graduate students has become the subject of intense debate. Those who are concerned about the policy shift claim that it will harm the nation's innovation capacity. For example, U.S. university officials are increasingly concerned that these restrictions could cause a crisis in research and scholarship.[2] The same point has been made in a number of editorials.[3] Lawrence Summers, president of Harvard, warned that the decline in foreign students threatens the quality of research coming from U.S. universities.[4]

If limits and delays in the number of visas issued to foreign graduate students in science and engineering and, more generally, to foreign skilled workers have the long-term impact of limiting innovation, productivity would suffer. Technological improvements largely have been driven by the rate of innovation, which has been increasing in recent years as measured by the rapidly growing number of patents awarded to U.S. industries and universities (Kortum 1997; Hall 2004).

The United States remains at the cutting edge of technology despite frequent complaints about quality deficiencies in its secondary education system.[5] Among the major developed countries and the newly industrial countries, the United States ranks near the bottom in mathematics and science achievement among eighth graders.[6] What may reconcile these facts is that the United States attracts large numbers of skilled immigrants that enter directly into technical fields (Gordon 2004). Moreover, the education gap is filled by capable international graduate students and skilled immigrants from such countries as India, China, and the Republic of Korea. For its part, the United States sustains a significant net export position in the graduate training of scientists, engineers, and other technical personnel.

It is worth noting that foreign graduate students traditionally have demonstrated a high propensity to remain within the United States, at least for the early portion of their careers (Finn 2001; Bratsberg and Ragan 2002). Aslanbeigui and Montecinos (1998) found that 45 percent of international students from developing countries planned to enter the U.S. labor market for a time and 15 percent planned to stay permanently. Despite attempts since the early 1980s by the U.S. Congress to forbid the employment of international students after graduation,[7] and in some cases to restrict the flow of international students to domestic universities,[8] the United States still allows a significant proportion of these students to stay and work after graduation and often grants permanent residence. Thus, graduate training of foreign students may have long-lasting impacts on innovation capacities.

There are a variety of channels through which the presence of foreign graduate students could affect innovation and productivity. These students serve first as direct inputs into knowledge creation by working within university laboratories and coauthoring scientific papers. Second, because they may stay in the United States and become faculty or, more likely, technical personnel in private industry, their knowledge base supports additional inventiveness. Moreover, scientific papers and patent applications developed with their inputs directly support further innovative activities, both within universities and in the broader economy. For example, the Bayh-Dole Act of 1980 permits U.S. universities to claim intellectual property rights on inventions developed within their laboratories, even if the research was supported by public grants. Those patents may, in turn, be licensed to commercial enterprises, which is a growing phenomenon.

Moving beyond graduate students, the presence of technical workers, such as software engineers and technical designers, under temporary H1B visas, may have a significantly positive impact on innovation in a variety of industries. Furthermore, and perhaps most significantly, permanent immigration of workers in skilled occupations, including both faculty and private practitioners in engineering, medicine, and information technologies, should have a direct effect on innovation and patenting. For example, the proportion of foreign-born faculty with U.S. doctoral degrees at U.S. universities has increased sharply during the past three decades, from 11.7 percent in 1973 to 20.4 percent in 1999. For engineering, it rose from 18.6 percent to 34.7 percent in the same period.[9] These relative changes in the sources of scientific talent have coincided with large increases in innovation capacity, as measured by patent applications and scientific papers.

A Study of Innovation Impacts

While the claim that foreign graduate students and skilled personnel should enhance innovation seems self-evident, it had not been tested statistically before the study we now summarize (Chellaraj, Maskus, and Mattoo 2005). In that study, we estimated a number of versions of the so-called "ideas production function," which may be listed as follows:[10]

$$\dot{A}_t = \delta H_{A,t}^{\lambda} A_t^{\phi} \tag{8.1}$$

This specification indicates that the number of new ideas $\dot{A}$, typically measured by patent applications or patent grants in a particular year, depends on the stock of knowledge A (measured by cumulative patents issued in the past) and the use of human capital and other scientific inputs H. The parameter ϕ governs the returns to past knowledge in terms of generating new ideas. If the value of ϕ exceeds 0, there is a "standing on shoulders" effect and past knowledge is productive. If the value of ϕ is less than 0, there are diminishing returns to past knowledge and new invention becomes more difficult. The parameter λ is the elasticity of new ideas with respect to technical inputs. Finally, the coefficient δ reflects the overall productivity with which the economy (or specific institutions) converts inputs and past knowledge into new ideas.

We broke down the technical inputs into several key variables, some of which had not been examined in this context. These variables included foreign graduate students as a percentage of total graduate students, the cumulative number of skilled immigrants as a share of the labor force, the cumulative number of doctoral scientists and engineers as a percentage of the labor force, and scaled real expenditures on research and development (R&D). In addition, we included the accumulated stock of patent grants scaled by the labor force, a dummy variable capturing the influence of the Bayh-Dole Act of 1980, the unemployment rate to capture cyclical impacts on innovation, and a time trend to control for overall technology movements. The dependent variables were patent applications or patent grants, with the latter also broken down into grants issued to universities and other institutions.[11]

The data were aggregate time series of these variables for the United States during the time period from 1965 to 2001. Explanatory variables were lagged either five years (in the case of patent applications) or seven years (in the case of patent grants) to reflect the time period required to convert inputs into patentable ideas. Basic econometric tests suggested that the scaling procedures chosen, along with the time and unemployment controls, were sufficient to ensure the absence of serial correlation in the residuals.[12]

We summarize the results here (detailed results are presented in annex 8.A) by listing estimated elasticities for the variables capturing foreign graduate students and skilled immigration.[13] The coefficients in table 8.1 demonstrate clearly that the relative presence of foreign graduate students has a strongly positive impact on future patent applications and grants. That is, a 10 percent increase in the share of foreign graduate students in the total number of graduate students tends to increase total U.S. patent applications by 4.8 percent, patent grants earned by universities by 6.0 percent, and patent grants earned by nonuniversities (largely commercial firms) by 6.8 percent. The last of these findings is particularly interesting, because it suggests strongly that the presence of foreign graduate students spills over into wider gains in U.S. innovation through the channels described above.

The results in table 8.1 and detailed results presented in annex 8.A also demonstrate that an increase in the ratio of cumulative skilled immigrants,[14] as a proportion of the U.S. labor force, has a positive, although smaller, effect on the development of new ideas.[15] A 10 percent rise in this ratio over the same time period tended to increase future applications by 0.8 percent and university patent grants by 1.3 percent.

The impacts listed in table 8.1 are large in the context of contributions to the patenting of new ideas. These elasticities may be put in perspective by computing the implied impacts on patenting from a change in enrollments or skilled immigration. Computed at sample means, a 10 percent rise in the ratio of foreign graduate students to total graduate students would imply an increase in later applications of 6,636 (or around 4.7 percent of the mean total applications of 141,092). Thus, we compute a marginal impact of another foreign graduate student to be around 0.6 patent applications in the economy as a whole.[16] Regarding university and nonuniversity grants, the calculations imply that a 10 percent rise in the ratio of foreign graduate students would generate another 56 university grants and an additional 5,979 nonuniversity grants.[17] Accordingly, the enrollment of foreign graduate students ultimately generates more nonuniversity patent awards.

The results may be used for similar computations of the effects of skilled immigration. A ten percent rise in the cumulative number of skilled immigrants

TABLE 8.1   The Impacts of Foreign Graduate Students and Skilled Immigrants on Patent Applications and Grants, 1965–2001

	Applications	University grants	Other grants
Foreign graduates	0.48 (7.46)***	0.60 (3.64)***	0.68 (5.95)***
Skilled immigrants	0.08 (2.40)**	0.13 (2.78)***	0.09 (2.63)***

Source: Chellaraj, Maskus, and Mattoo 2005.

Note: ** denotes significance at the 5 percent level; *** denotes significance at the 1 percent level.

would increase later patent applications by 1,037, university grants by 12, and nonuniversity grants by 814. Again, skilled immigration has considerably smaller impacts on patenting activity than do enrollment of foreign graduate students. In summary, it seems that skilled immigrants have a positive impact on total patent applications and patents awarded to universities, industries, and other enterprises. This result highlights the contributions made by skilled immigrants to innovation in the U.S. economy. Overall, it seems that foreign students and skilled immigrants play a major role in driving scientific innovation in the United States.

Relatively open access to international students has allowed U.S. universities to accept the most capable graduate students in science and engineering. In turn, international graduate students contribute to innovation. This conclusion stems from the fact that international graduate students are relatively concentrated in such fields as science and engineering. In a number of highly ranked engineering schools, international students account for nearly 80 percent of doctoral students.[18] Overall, the presence of international students along with skilled immigrants is a significant factor behind sharp increases in innovation and patenting at U.S. universities and the ultimate beneficial spillovers to broader innovation.

The Sources of Skilled Immigration[19]

Recent research suggests that an innovation-friendly immigration policy needs to look beyond the aggregate number of educated immigrants entering the United States. Engagement of the educated in skilled (and potentially innovative) activities depends on where the immigrants come from and how they enter the United States. U.S. Census data reveal striking differences in the occupational performance of highly educated immigrants from different countries, even after controlling for individuals' age, experience, and level of education. With some exceptions, educated immigrants from Latin American and Eastern European countries are more likely to obtain unskilled jobs than immigrants from Asian and industrial countries. For example, a hypothetical 34-year-old Indian college graduate who arrived in 1994 has a 69 percent probability of obtaining a skilled job, while the probability is only 24 percent for a Mexican immigrant of identical age, experience, and education.

A large part of the variation can be explained by attributes of the country of origin that influence the quality of human capital, such as expenditure on tertiary education and the use of English as a medium of instruction. For example, coming from an English-speaking country increases the likelihood of obtaining a skilled job in the United States by 11 percent for a hypothetical college graduate. Similarly, a 10 percent increase in tertiary education increases the same probability by 7.5 percent.

In addition to the attributes of the home country, the selection effects of U.S. immigration policy also play an important role in explaining variations in occupational performance. There are three main ways to legally enter the United States: (a) family preferences, (b) lotteries for underrepresented nationalities and as refugees, and (c) skills-based programs such as the H1B visas where a prior offer of employment commensurate with skills is a requirement for entry. The first two routes do not discriminate among immigrants based on their education or skill levels, but the third route has strict skill requirements. If there are already many immigrants from a given country, then family preferences make it easier for potential immigrants from that country to enter the United States. Conversely, if the family preferences, lottery, and asylum policies are restricted, we see an improvement in the average human capital of immigrants because H1B visas become the primary route for entry. Immigrants from such countries as India and China have been the largest beneficiaries of H1B visas in recent years (figure 8.4) and also have performed best in terms of occupational placement (Mattoo, Neagu, and Özden 2005).

To be sure, immigration policy cannot be driven by innovation concerns alone. But it is useful to recognize that the impact on innovation depends not only on the overall number of educated immigrants, but also on where these immigrants come from and how they enter the United States. From a U.S. perspective, the negative impact of innovative activity would be greater if immigration restrictions

FIGURE 8.4   HIB Beneficiaries by Country, 2003

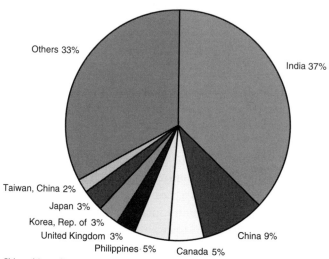

Source: U.S. Citizenship and Immigration Service 1990–2004.

altered the composition away from source countries that create higher quality (or more U.S.-compatible) human capital or away from allowing entry that is conditional on an offer of skilled employment.

Conclusion

We have argued that there is empirical evidence to support the view that foreign graduate students and skilled immigrants are significant inputs into developing new technologies in the U.S. economy. The impacts are particularly pronounced within universities but also affect nonuniversity patenting. There is evidence to suggest that educated immigrants from particular source countries, such as China and India, and those who enter the United States contingent on offers of employment are mostly likely to engage in skilled activities.

The significant contributions of international graduate students and skilled immigrants to patenting and innovation in the United States may have international and domestic policy implications. At the international level, it is evident that the United States has a significant direct comparative advantage in exporting the services of higher education, especially in training scientists, engineers, and related personnel. This advantage generates additional benefits, both directly as foreign students contribute to innovation in the United States and indirectly as exploitation of the fruits of this innovation generates domestic economic rents.

However, continued dominance of the United States in this regard cannot be taken for granted. As other countries such as Singapore (Furman and Hayes 2004; Koh and Wong 2005) improve their offerings of scientific graduate education and encourage these students to stay on after graduation, visa restrictions in the United States could have adverse implications for competitiveness. The United States is likely to face increasing global competition for talent from countries such as China.[20] Moreover, global liberalization of higher education services would permit U.S. universities to get around visa problems by locating research campuses in other countries,[21] such as Singapore, that welcome international talent (Amsden and Tschang 2003). It is also noteworthy that U.S. corporations have significantly increased patenting activity and innovation abroad (Maskus 2000). In response to this increase, legislation has been introduced in the U.S. Congress in 2005 to facilitate the movement of skilled immigrants into the United States.[22]

Hence, a central implication of this chapter is that reducing foreign students and skilled immigrants, particularly from certain source countries, through tighter enforcement of visa restraints could reduce innovative activity significantly. Indeed, with the rapid economic development of countries in such regions as Southeast Asia, and with global job mobility increasing, such restrictions are likely to be self-defeating, at least in economic terms.

Endnotes

1. http://www.hindu.com/thehindu/features/singedu/stories/2004080800140200.htm
2. Recently, a letter to this effect was published by a broad coalition of U.S. academics representing 25 organizations and 95 individuals. See Grimes and Alden 2004.
3. Brumfiel 2004; *The Economist* 2004.
4. Grimes 2004.
5. See, for example, National Governors Association, "The High School Crisis and America's Economic Competitiveness to be Discussed," September 29, 2003, at http://www.nga.org/nga/newsRoom/1,1169,C_PRESS_RELEASE%5ED_5948,00.html.
6. For comparison with other countries, see the results of the Trends in International Mathematics and Science Study (TIMMS) at http://timss.bc.edu/timss2003.html.
7. In 1982 and again in 1984, legislation sponsored by Senator Simpson and Representative Mazzoli, and supported by anti-immigrant groups such as the Federation of American Immigration Reform (FAIR), forbidding the employment in the United States of international graduates of U.S. universities, passed both chambers of Congress before dying in the Conference Committee. In 1995, Senator Simpson and Representative Lamar Smith unsuccessfully resurrected the proposal.
8. Senator Feinstein tried to put a moratorium on all international students soon after the September 11, 2001, attack. The proposal was shelved after protests from U.S. universities. Representative Rohrabacher has proposed that U.S. universities replace international students with domestic students although the latter may be less qualified.
9. http://www.nsf.gov/sbe/srs/seind02/append/c5/at05-24.xls.
10. Stern, Porter, and Furman 2000; Porter and Stern 2000.
11. One of the issues in the specification of the model is the direction of causality. While skilled immigration and the presence of international students are argued to positively impact patenting, patenting and scientific progress could also attract skilled immigration and foreign students, and the two could be simultaneously determined. The use of lagged values of immigrant and student presence addresses the problem to a certain extent.
12. For further details, refer to the manuscript available at http://spot.colorado.edu/~maskus/papers/patentpaper_March%2016_2005.pdf.
13. Other variables had the anticipated coefficients, with most highly significant.
14. Cumulative skilled immigrants are defined as the number of skilled immigrants accumulated over the preceding six-year period, divided by the labor force. Skilled immigrants include those entering the country on H1B visas. They do not include L visa holders, because these are essentially temporary postings, generally granted to foreign corporations such as Toyota and BMW with plants in the United States.
15. For this purpose, "skilled immigration" was measured as inflows of immigrants in employment-based categories.
16. These figures are calculated at means across the entire sample. If these elasticities were applied to the far-higher average patent numbers in the late 1990s, the corresponding predicted increases in innovative activity would be larger.
17. The mean number of nonuniversity awards is far larger than that of university grants, so these volume impacts are sensible.
18. Institute for International Education 1990–2004.
19. This section is based on Mattoo, Neagu, and Özden (2005).
20. Of immediate concern for the United States is global competition for the skilled workforce from China. According to the British government's Department of Trade and Industry (DTI), China engages in significant recruitment of U.S. and other scientists, luring them with promises of greater freedom and well-funded centers, particularly for stem cell research (Morrison 2005).
21. http://smh.com.au/articles/2004/04/21/1082530235581.html. http://dukemednews.duke.edu/news/article.php?id=6687.

22. The Jackson legislation, Kennedy-McCain Legislation, and the Cornyn-Kyl legislation would allow unused employment-based immigration visas in the previous years to be used in the current and future years. However, the Tancredo legislation, which is not given much chance of debate, let alone enacted into law, proposes to sharply curtail skilled immigrants and restrict them to two years of employment in the United States. However, the Jackson, Kennedy-McCain, and Cornyn-Kyl legislations are not going to be of much help if the U.S. State Department regulations such as Section 214(b) continue to be bottlenecks.

References

Amsden, A.H., and F.T. Tschang. 2003. "A New Approach to Assessing the Technological Complexity of Different Categories of R&D (With Examples from Singapore)." *Research Policy* 32(4): 553–72.

Aslanbeigui, N., and V. Montecinos. 1998. "Foreign Students in U.S. Doctoral Programs." *Journal of Economic Perspectives* 12(3): 171–82.

Bratsberg, B., and J.F. Ragan. 2002. "The Impact of Host Country Schooling on Earnings—A Study of Male Immigrants in the United States." *Journal of Human Resources* 37(1): 63–105.

Brumfiel, G. 2004. "Security Restrictions Lead Foreign Students to Snub US Universities." *Nature*, September 15.

Chellaraj, G., K.E. Maskus, and A. Mattoo. 2005. "The Contribution of Skilled Immigration and International Graduate Students to U.S. Innovation." World Bank Manuscript, Washington, DC.

The Economist. 2004. "Visas and Science: Short-Sighted." May 8.

Finn, M.J. 2001. "Stay Rates of Foreign Doctorate Recipients from US Universities in 1999." Oak Ridge Institute for Science and Education, Oak Ridge, TN.

Florida, R. 2005. *The Flight of the Creative Class: The New Global Competition for Talent.* New York: HarperCollins Publishers Inc.

Furman, J.L., and R. Hayes. 2004. "Catching Up or Standing Still? National Innovative Productivity among 'Follower' Countries, 1978–1999." *Research Policy* 33(9): 1329–354.

Gordon, Robert J. 2004. "Two Centuries of Economic Growth: Europe Chasing the American Frontier." NBER Working Paper, no. 10662. National Bureau of Economic Research, Washington, DC.

Grimes, C. 2004. "Colleges Get a Hard Lesson in Making the US Secure." *Financial Times*, April 28.

Grimes, Christopher, and Edward Alden. 2004. "Academics Warn of Crisis over Visa Curbs." *Financial Times*, May 12.

Hall, Bronwyn H. 2004. "Exploring the Patent Explosion." NBER Working Paper, no. 10605. National Bureau of Economic Research, Washington, DC.

Hira, A. 2003. "The Brave New World of International Education." *The World Economy* 26(6): 911–31.

Institute for International Education. 1990–2004. "Open Doors." New York.

Koh, W.T.H., and P.K. Wong. 2005. "Competing at the Frontier: The Changing Role of Technology Policy in Singapore's Economic Strategy." *Technological Forecasting and Social Change* 72(3): 255–85.

Kortum, Samuel. 1997. "Research, Patenting, and Technological Change." *Econometrica* 65(6): 1389–420.

Maskus, K.E. 2000. *Intellectual Property Rights in the Global Economy.* Washington, DC: Institute for International Economics.

Mattoo, Aaditya, Ileana Cristina Neagu, and Çaglar Özden. 2005. "Brain Waste? Educated Immigrants in the US Labor Market." World Bank Policy Research Paper, no. 3581. World Bank, Washington, DC.

Morrison, M. 2005. "Who's Leading the Way?" *Parade Magazine, Washington Post.* July 10.

Porter, Michael E., and Scott Stern. 2000. "Measuring the 'Ideas' Production Function: Evidence from International Patent Output." NBER Working Paper, no. 7891. National Bureau of Economic Research, Washington, DC.

Stern, Scott, Michael E. Porter, and J.L. Furman. 2000. "The Determinants of National Innovative Capacity." NBER Working Paper, no. 7876. National Bureau of Economic Research, Washington, DC.

U.S. Citizenship and Immigration Service. 1990–2004. *Yearbook of Immigration Statistics.* Department of Homeland Security, Washington, DC.

ANNEX 8.A International Students, Skilled Immigration, and Patenting Activity in the United States, 1965–2001

	IPA (8)	UIPG (9)	OIPG (10)
CONSTANT	5.068 (3.09)***	2.705 (1.29)	3.589 (2.31)***
FORTGR	0.480 (7.46)***	0.604 (3.64)***	0.676 (5.95)***
SEDDOCCUM	0.200 (2.03)**	0.445 (2.82)***	0.564 (5.09)***
IMCUM	0.075 (2.40)**	0.128 (2.78)***	0.092 (2.63)***
SK	0.762 (3.00)***	0.732 (1.71)*	0.940 (3.25)***
RD	−0.177 (−1.19)	n.a.	n.a.
URD	n.a.	0.021 (0.10)	n.a.
ORD	n.a.	n.a.	0.383 (2.46)**
TOTPATSTOCK	0.526 (3.96)***	n.a.	n.a.
UPATSTOCK	n.a.	0.439 (1.83)*	0.183 (1.10)

ANNEX 8.A *(continued)*

	IPA (8)	UIPG (9)	OIPG (10)
OPATSTOCK	n.a.	0.211 (0.56)	−0.158 (−0.51)
BD	0.140 (2.55)***	0.288 (3.13)***	0.257 (4.22)***
TIME	−0.007 (−1.29)	0.014 (0.57)	0.014 (−3.67)***
UNEMPLOY	0.006 (0.13)	0.141 (1.60)	0.037 (0.72)
R-Squared	0.94	0.99	0.94
DW	1.60	1.82	2.52

Source: Chellaraj, Maskus, and Mattoo 2005.

Note: IPA is patent applications and IPG is patents granted, both as a percentage of labor force. UIPG is patents granted to universities as a proportion of labor force, OIPG is patents granted to nonuniversity institutions as a proportion of labor force. FORTGR is foreign graduate students as a proportion of total graduate students. SEDDOCCUM is the cumulative number of doctorates earned in engineering and science in U.S. universities over a period of five years as a percentage of labor force for IPA and over a period of seven years for UIPG and OIPG. IMCUM is the cumulative number of skilled immigrants over a period of six years after which it is lagged seven years as a proportion of the labor force. SK is total doctoral scientists and engineers as a proportion of labor force. RD is total real research and development (R&D) expenditures as a proportion of labor force. URD is real university R&D expenditures as a proportion of labor force, and ORD is real nonuniversity R&D expenditures as a proportion of labor force. TOTPATSTOCK is cumulative patents awarded over a period of five years as a proportion of labor force. UPATSTOCK is cumulative patents awarded to universities over a period of seven years as a proportion of labor force. OPATSTOCK is cumulative patents awarded to nonuniversity institutions over a period of seven years as a proportion of labor force. BD is the dummy variable for the Bayh-Dole Act with a value of "0" before 1980 and "1" after 1980. TIME variable is a time trend. UNEMPLOY is the unemployment rate. DW is the Durbin-Watson test for autocorrelation. Variables in the IPA equations are lagged five years, while those in the IPG equations are lagged seven years. Figures in parentheses are t-ratios and marked as significantly different from zero at the 1 percent (***), 5 percent (**), and 10 percent (*) levels. n.a. = not applicable.

INDEX

A

Africa, 152, 167, 173
age
  Filipino characteristics, 85
  household heads, 59
  Mexican migrants, 39, 40
  Philippines
    migrant households, 94t–95t
    nonmigrant households, 96t–97t
    premigration income effects, 79n
    probability of migration, 37
age of entry, 156–157
American Competitiveness and Work
    Force Improvement Act of 1998, 152
Annual Poverty Indicators Survey (APIS),
    90, 116
Asian financial crisis (1997), 82, 87
  Filipino migrants, 115–116
Asian migration rate, 11
asylum seekers, 3, 4

B

Bayh-Dole Act of 1980, 250
border crossings, 132
brain drain, 14
  absolute or relative measurements, 173
  African countries, 167
  benefits, 201
  data bias, 193

determinants, 215–216
education and growth studies, 219
education impact, 209, 220t
growth and welfare impacts, 203, 219f
intensity on source country, 166
Islamic and Arab countries, 172–173
lack of data, 153, 231
migration probability, 216
negative, 151, 220
OECD statistics, 193
positive externalities, 10
public expenditures, 221
regional differences, 9–12
risk aversion, 211–212
steady state, 221
studies, 192–194
brain gain, 11–12
  alternative curves, 205f
  benefiting countries, 186–187
  education return, 209
  general equilibrium, 214
  heterogeneity, 206–208
  in OECD countries by country, 178t–
    181t, 182t–185t
  long-term benefit, 217
  migration probability, 216
  negative, 210–211
  net brain loss, 205–206
  partial equilibrium analysis, 204

261